PAWNED
REDEEMING OUR GOD-GIVEN SEXUALITY

PAWNED

REDEEMING OUR GOD-GIVEN SEXUALITY

DR. GARY WARREN FOSHEE

Deep River
BOOKS

PAWNED: *Redeeming Our God-Given Sexuality*

Copyright © 2022 Gary Warren Foshee. All rights reserved. Except for brief quotations in critical publications or reviews, no part of this book may be reproduced in any manner without prior written permission from the publisher. Write: Permissions. Deep River Books, Sisters, Oregon.

Deep River Books
PO Box 310
Sisters, OR 97759

Cataloguing-in-Publication Data

Pawned: Redeeming Our God-Given Sexuality by Gary Warren Foshee

Includes bibliographical references.
ISBN 13: 9781632695758

1. Sex—Religious aspects—Christianity.
2. Marriage—Religious aspects—Christianity.
3. Sexual ethics.

I. Foshee, Gary. II. Pawned.

Library of Congress Control Number: 2022910599

Manufactured in the U.S.A.   2022

Unless otherwise indicated, Scripture quotations are from the *Holy Bible, English Standard Version*®. ESV®. Copyright © 2001 by Crossway, a publishing ministry of Good News Publishers. All rights reserved.

Scripture quotations marked KJV are taken from the *King James Version* Public domain.

Scripture quotations marked NKJV are taken from the *New King James Version*®. Copyright © 1982 by Thomas Nelson. Used by permission. All rights reserved.

Scripture quotations marked NIV are taken from the *New International Version*®, NIV® Copyright ©1973, 1978, 1984, 2011 by Biblica, Inc.® Used by permission. All rights reserved worldwide.

Scripture quotations marked CEV are from the Contemporary English Version® Copyright © 1995 American Bible Society. All rights reserved..

Cover Design by Jason Enterline

DEDICATION

This book is dedicated to the courageous men and women
who triumphantly redeem their sexuality and
restore the sanctity of sex in
their lives and marriages.

CONTENTS

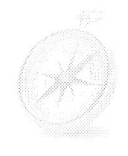

Introduction: A Fog of Sexual Confusion. 11
1. Pawned Sexuality 17
2. The Gift of Sex 29
3. Sexual Compass 37
   A Sexual Compass for Christians 37
      Masturbation 40
      Sodomy 45
      Homosexuality 48
      Frequency 55
      Pornography 62
      Oral Sex 64
      Positions, Dressing Up, Role Playing, and Pole Dancing 69
      Fornication 71
      Adultery 74
      Cybersex 82

4. Sexual Desire: Women 85
   Concupiscence 85
   Dominion 89
   The Mystery of the Fall of Adam and Eve ... 90
      Conception Sorrow 91
      The Serpent's Thorn 92
      Obedience 96
   Thriving under the Fall of Adam and Eve ... 98
5. Sexual Desire: Men 101
   SEAL Team FOUR 101
   Captain Jack Sparrow 104
   Ouch 105
   Crosshairs 106
   Body Trust 109
   Mick 111
   Little Foxes 113
   Golden Nugget 117
6. The Heart of Sex 121
   Six Excuses Obstructing the Healing Process of Sexual Trauma 126
      But It's My Fault 128
      But It Felt Good 129
      But I Can't Find the Key 131
      But I Can't Trust God 133
      But I Thought It Would Just Go Away 139
      But I Can't Forgive 145

7. The Heart of Sex in the Old Testament. 151
    Sex at Creation 152
        The Gift of Procreation 152
        Becoming One Flesh 154
    Sex Before the Law 157
        Sodom and Gomorrah 157
    Sex in the Pentateuch 158
        God Establishes Healthy Sexual Boundaries 159
        God Confronts Sexual Immorality 160
    Sex Throughout the Old Testament 162
        David and Bathsheba 163
        Shulamite and Solomon 165
        The Nation of Israel 168
8. The Heart of Sex in the New Testament 173
    The Gospels 174
    The Writings of Paul 176
    Revelation and New Creation 179
9. Sexual Idolatry. 185
    Sexual Addiction 186
    Cycles of Sexual Addiction 195
    Treatment 199
    Recognizing Childhood Sexual Abuse 205

Conclusion 207
Appendix A: Patterns and Examples of Sex Addiction. 211
Bibliography. 213
About the Author 225
Endnotes 227

INTRODUCTION

A FOG OF SEXUAL CONFUSION

"Do you not know that your body is the temple of the Holy Spirit who is in you, whom you have from God and you are not your own? For you were bought at a price; therefore glorify God in your body and in your spirit, which are God's" (1 Cor. 6:19-20, NKJV).[1]

A relentless and calculated war on sexuality rages around the world and in spiritual realms. Immoral sexual ideologies and practices have breached biblical battle lines, clouding the hearts and minds of humanity in a fog of sexual confusion. The royal compass of holiness and self-control, established by God to protect the gift of sex, has been replaced by a hedonistic compass of infatuated lusts and self-idolatry detouring people into a cesspool of sexual immorality. Make no mistake about it. The target of this war is Christian singles and married couples of all ages, and every day an alarming number of Christians are wounded and destroyed by engaging in immoral sexual practices.

One of the most priceless and treasured gifts God entrusted to humanity is the gift of sex. No other gift simultaneously connects the physical, emotional, mental, and spiritual dimensions of humanity into a shared experience between two individuals. Godly sex is passionate, loving, affectionate, holy, and, might I say, absolutely amazing!

Singles who honor God with their bodies, and married couples who honor marriage and keep their marriage bed pure, experience sustained sexual fulfillment at levels unachievable by the carnal sexual practices taught and accepted throughout the world. Why is sustained sexual fulfillment out of reach for those who indulge in sexual practices that do not honor marriage or keep the marriage bed pure? It's because people pawn their sexuality to a polished and cunning pawnbroker, who prowls around like a lion devouring the weak, willing, and wounded. His lie is, "Pawn your sexuality and, in return, you will get the most intimate and exhilarating experience without having to go through the extensive process required for love and intimacy to grow, blossom, and mature."

Christians and non-Christians alike pawn their sexuality and receive in themselves the due penalty of their mistake—a cheap thrill, laced with shame and guilt, that fails miserably to satisfy the deep wellsprings of emotional and physical intimacy godly sex provides. As Romans 6:21 highlights, "But what fruit were you getting at that time from the things of which you are now ashamed? For the end of those things is death." The pawned experience has no resemblance to the priceless original design intended for humanity—two pure and innocent virgins whose fountains and gardens have been locked,[2] reserved for the one-flesh union established only by the covenant of holy matrimony.

A godly sexual compass is needed to redeem sexuality and restore the sanctity of sex. Without a true north (sound biblical teaching on sex and sexuality), people will, undoubtedly, turn to social and cultural norms or rely on their own carnal judgments to determine what sexual practices are and are not acceptable.[3] This book is that compass!

For anyone desiring to redeem their sexuality and restore the sanctity of sex, it is important to remember God's promise—you are not your own. Jesus paid an exorbitant price to redeem you (1 Cor 6:19)! The humiliation, pain, and horrific death Jesus endured on the cross of Calvary breaks the power of sexual sins and safeguards the natural sexual passions God intricately wove into every single person. God can and will make you pure and innocent again. He will restore your garden and open up your fountain, so you can experience a holy sexuality like never before.

This study reveals preeminent and compulsory truths that God envisioned for sex and his transcendental plans to protect and purify the marriage bed all the way to the time of the new creation. This book teaches singles and married couples how to redeem the gift of sex and honor God with their bodies. It provides Christian insight and a healthy sexual compass for a variety of sexual issues and practices. A powerful section on healing and restoration will enable all who have been sexually abused, molested, or raped to triumphantly redeem their sexuality. It also looks briefly at sexual addiction (SA), spiritual injury, and how to recognize signs of sexual abuse.

The overarching goal and purpose of the material and research presented throughout this book is to: (1) teach God's wonderful and beautiful design for sex; (2) teach Christians and non-Christians how to redeem their sexuality and restore the sanctity of sex in their lives and marriages; (3) present research, conclusions, and truths found throughout Scripture, in the most gentle and nonjudgmental way possible, while still boldly proclaiming scriptural truths; (4) correct false doctrines and religious views about God's design for sex while exposing the myths and destructive teachings of immoral sexual ethics widely taught and promoted in liberal schools, universities, institutions, and churches around the world; (5) bring healing and restoration to everyone who has been raped, molested, or sexually abused; (6) help people bring their sexual acts and sexuality back into harmony with God's Holy Word; and (7) provide a healthy and godly sexual compass that allows singles to honor God with their bodies and married couples to honor marriage while keeping their marriage beds pure.

Baskin-Robbins, an international ice cream franchise known for its famous "31 flavors," offers everything from Burgundy Cherry to Peppermint Fudge Ribbon, Rocky Road, and numerous other flavors. While watching TV one hot and sunny day, a commercial narrated by their CEO came on. The CEO talked about several new flavors recently added to the menu and then said, "Remarkable—out of all the flavors we serve, the top three best sellers every year are: number one—Vanilla; number two—Chocolate; and number three—Strawberry." Isn't that funny? The company spends millions of dollars a year researching and developing new flavors with multiple combinations of ingredients, only to discover their customers overwhelmingly prefer the traditional favorites.

The same principal applies to sex. Christians and non-Christians believe they can enhance their sexual satisfaction by adding lots of "toppings and ingredients," (i.e., immoral sexual practices) to their lives and marriage beds. However, in reality nothing beats good old "Vanilla, Chocolate, and Strawberry," (i.e., God's design for sex). God's design fulfills the deep wellsprings of emotional, physical, psychological, and spiritual intimacy. Sex doesn't need other "toppings and ingredients" when it follows God's design.

The simple fact about sex and redeemed sexuality is this: sex is holy and deeply satisfying when it follows God's design. If any sexual act or practice Christians or non-Christians engage in leaves them feeling shameful, guilty, dirty, or empty, then this book will help convey clarity, direction, and renewal. This book helps singles and married couples bring their sexual activities back into harmony with God's design. The sexual compass found throughout this book leads people out of the crippling feelings of shame, guilt, and disgust that pawned sexuality inflicts and, by the healing power of the Holy Spirit, restores individual bodies and marriage beds back to a state of innocence—the place where holiness and purity reign supreme.

Sexuality, however, is much more than physical and mental; it is profoundly spiritual. So I must advise you, if you continue reading this book, you will enter a spiritual battlefield unlike any you have ever known. The material in this book covers extremely sensitive subjects and practices about sex and sexuality. You will need to pray for strength and courage to finish reading it. I hope you find the research intriguing, freeing, and challenging.[4]

The miracle of redemption eagerly awaits you. May God's blessings be upon you as you honor him with your body.

1

PAWNED SEXUALITY

"Therefore God gave them up in the lusts of their hearts to impurity, to the dishonoring of their bodies among themselves, because **they exchanged the truth about God for a lie** and worshiped and served the creature rather than the Creator, who is blessed forever! Amen" (Rom. 1:24-25).

The dictionary defines the word *pawned* as, "To give or deposit as security for the payment of money borrowed. To risk; hazard: *pawn one's honor.*"[5] Wow! Did you notice the last three words, "Pawn one's honor"? So sad. So devastating, but this is exactly what Scripture tells us happened. Because of the lusts of their hearts, "People exchanged the truth about God for a lie." They willingly pawned their sexuality for a lie, so they could dishonor their bodies among themselves. Christians and non-Christians do the same things today.

Secular practices and views on sexuality influence people of all ages, both Christian and non-Christian, to engage in sexual practices forbidden in Scripture. Numerous Christian denominations and leaders accept and openly teach sexual practices prohibited by God, confusing people who self-identify as Christians, thus distorting God's design for sex.[6] Other denominations and leaders remain relatively silent on these issues, unintentionally leaving their parishioners ill-prepared to address one of the most sacred fundamentals of being human—their sexuality.

The need for sound biblical teaching on sexuality remains critical. The digital age has revolutionized the way humans view, think, and act on issues pertaining to sexuality. Smart phones, social media, online dating sites, and easy access to instantly viewable and downloadable pornography all influence risky and unhealthy (both physically and spiritually) sexual behaviors. The need for a cogent Christian education calling Christian men and women to faithful obedience with regard to their sexuality remains paramount in the hypersexualized culture of the United States and around the world.

The prophet Hosea's words, "My people are destroyed from lack of knowledge" (Hos. 4:6), continue to highlight the importance of sound biblical instruction in every generation and society. The decline of morals in the United States and the accompanying rates of divorce, sexual promiscuity, pornography addiction, and sexual addictions inside the church provide stark reminders that American Christians are no exception to the problem. Sound biblical education on this topic gives Christians the knowledge and power to honor marriage and keep their marriage beds pure.

Leaders need biblical teaching on sex if they desire to help Christians overcome natural sexual desires and temptations, especially in a culture filled with sexual innuendos and a "sex sells" mindset. Believers also need biblical teaching to help them fully embrace the sexuality God intrinsically gave them as they discover and identify the healthy parameters meant to protect and nurture their sexuality.

Sex is big business. The sex industry makes billions of dollars a year. Sex sells, and it is available and accessible like never before. I was talking with a young Navy SEAL one day, and he stated, "Chaps, my generation grew up looking at porn. The Internet made it easy to view, and it was captivating." Once a child, tween, or teen gets a phone, iPad, computer, or tablet, he or she has access to information and entertainment that, if proper boundaries or measures are not implemented, could end up exposing them to information and images they shouldn't see.

Technology has radically changed access to inappropriate images and downloadable pornography. Even regular cable TV is no longer safe to watch. It is difficult to watch a movie, commercial, sitcom, drama, comedy, and even some cartoons, without seeing a sex scene. This is not just kissing and touching, or a topless scene, but a full blown or what could be categorized as a soft porn scene that leaves individuals highly stimulated and sexually charged. This is very different from shows I grew up watching like *Leave it to Beaver*, *The Andy Griffith Show*, or even *The Twilight Zone*—as crazy as that was.

God has a better way. His design for sex and sexuality transcends cultural norms and keeps individuals pure and holy. Unfortunately, every day, all around the world, teenagers, adults, and even the elderly willingly pawn their sexuality by engaging in sexual sins. Every time people engage in sexual immorality, i.e., premarital sex, adultery, porn, masturbation, and numerous other sexual sins, they pawn their sexuality and, in turn, "receive in themselves the due penalty of their sin."[7] This leads to sexual frustration and deep feelings of guilt, shame, and loneliness. It also distorts the meaning of sex, leaving Christians and non-Christians with misconceptions about sex and its purpose that are contrary to God's design. People who pawn their bodies to sexual sins inevitably view themselves as tainted, defiled, and degraded, which causes them to fall further into depravity and malicious acts that harm the body.

Pawned sexuality resembles the brokenness of society. It unites the holy with the unholy, the sacred with the profane, and the hallowed, sanctified, and consecrated, with the vile, accursed, and desecrated. Pawned sexuality treats the priceless gift of sex as a common, low-cost commodity, thus devaluing its meaning and purpose to the point that sex becomes nothing more than a mere product to barter, manipulate, and pander for personal and societal gratifications. In 1 Corinthians 6:13, 15-16, God says, "The body is not meant for sexual immorality but for the Lord. . . . Shall I then take the members of Christ and make them members of a prostitute? Never! Or do you not know that he who is joined to a prostitute becomes one body with her?" Uniting the holy with the unholy, and the righteous with the unrighteous pawns sexuality, devalues the purpose and meaning of sex, and has numerous consequences.

First, people who pawn their sexuality by engaging in sexual immorality subconsciously[8] begin to view their body as a common vessel instead of a holy vessel created by God and set apart as an instrument of holiness. Holy and priceless vessels are treated with honor and dignity and used strictly for sacred purposes. Thus, a Christian man or woman who views his or her body as a holy vessel will honor marriage[9] by waiting to have sex until marriage. Once married, the individual will joyfully fulfill and receive the conjugal[10] blessings of a pure marriage bed free from the shame, guilt, and little foxes[11] of pawned sexuality. Men or women who honor marriage and keep their sexuality in harmony with God's Holy Word, will cherish the precious gift of sex and their virginity will be a sacred treasure reserved and unlocked only on their wedding night.

Conversely, people who believe their body is a common vessel meant for general use see no reason to wait until marriage—and why would they? A common vessel is mass-produced and found in every marketplace and shop. A common vessel is used by all patrons for any vile occasion. A common vessel is not loved, cherished, and protected like a priceless vessel. Jacob worked fourteen years for Rachel.[12] He worked seven years for her without having any sexual relations with her and, after being deceived by her father, worked another seven years. He had fourteen years invested in his love, and he would do anything to protect that investment. Rachel was priceless to him, and what he went through to win her love and affection was a priceless act worthy of eternal recognition.

This is quite different from the "hookup," "committed," or "one-night-stand" relationships of today that require little, if any, investment. They leave individuals heartbroken, sexually and spiritually distraught, mentally unstable, and with major trust and identity issues. The aftermath of sexual immorality is costly and has, unfortunately, become a lesson more and more teenagers, young adults, and adults end up learning the hard way.

Second, people who pawn their sexuality by engaging in sexual immorality before marriage enter marriage with multiple one-flesh unions, and come to view themselves, their spouse, other men or women, and even God in unhealthy and unbiblical ways which have devastating effects on the marriage bed and the individual. The consummation of marriage is sex. When a man willfully has sex with a woman or a woman willfully has sex with a man, biblically,[13] they enter into marriage. Now, if they did not honor marriage[14] by first getting the blessing of the church and getting "officially" married, they commit fornication and the union is an unholy/unblessed union. As Dennis Hollinger asserts, "God designed that sex consummate the marriage, not initiate it."[15] Hollinger also suggests people who wait until marriage to have sex "Have better sex and enjoy it more."[16]

I counsel men and women all the time who have had so many sexual partners before marriage they no longer trust themselves or their spouse and find it extremely difficult to stay sexually satisfied by only having sex with their spouse. Often these men and women view sex as a weapon used for domination, control, and abusive acts of submission and degradation. Without even realizing it, Christian and non-Christians "classically condition"[17] themselves to the sexual hunt, the next sexual experience, and to sexual variety—fornication, adultery, orgies, homosexuality, bestiality, pedophilia, or sadistic and masochistic acts, etc. The idea of having sex with only one person for the rest of their life becomes a constant battle a lot of Christians and non-Christians end up losing and is another direct consequence of pawned sexuality. This is completely different from couples who remain virgins until marriage and can't imagine having sex with anyone other than their spouse.

Third, pawned sexuality fails to protect a person's "wells, springs, and gardens" and allows "little foxes" to run rampant, eating and polluting gardens God intended for marriage alone. In Song of Songs, God refers to a person's body parts as "wells, springs, shoots, fruits, and gardens." A private garden must be protected, tilled, fertilized, watered, and harvested at the right time. People who pawn their sexuality to sexual immorality allow strangers and trespassers[18] to trample and pollute their bodies without realizing the lingering consequences to their own sexuality and marriage bed.

Unfortunately, this is happening more frequently to children and adolescents than ever before. Sex education in public schools and universities teach inclusivity and acceptance on issues like homosexuality, gender identity, transgenderism, and even what constitutes a family. Education, peer pressure, and social acceptance have a significant impact on everyone, especially young and impressionable children. Cultural ideologies and immoral societal practices also manipulate adolescents and are highly influential during puberty where Satan (the ultimate pawnbroker) waits to plunder the young and naive child before he or she learns the truth about God's design for sex and before the child can build a healthy boundary denying access to trespassers.

Fourth, pawned sexuality can also come through sexual abuse, rape, and molestation. Although the victim is completely innocent of any sin, victims often blame themselves and fail to redeem their sexuality. This allows the trespasser/abuser to hold captive the victim's sexuality, because the sexual trauma experienced by victims leaves them feeling damaged, broken, and unworthy. Victims who fail to redeem their sexuality come to view sex as dirty, sinful, fearful, or painful and, with time, come to hate themselves, the gender of their abuser, and, sadly, even come to distrust and turn away from God. (I will speak more to this in chapter 6.) The list of consequences of pawned sexuality goes on and on and will be discussed in-depth in later sections. However, the most important point this book covers is that pawned sexuality can be redeemed and the sanctity of sex restored.

Before I say more about pawned sexuality, I want to be transparent about my life so you can understand the power of redemption and know my background and qualifications for speaking and writing on this subject. First of all, I am "The Most Sexually Satisfied Man on Earth." I can make such an audacious claim because God redeemed my life, and my wife and I honor God with our bodies and keep our marriage bed pure.[19] Second, I keep and maintain healthy boundaries that keep the "little foxes" out of our gardens. And I live by the biblically based "One-Flesh Covenants"[20] I created.

Life started out very difficult for me. I grew up on an eighty-acre farm in Jasmine, Arkansas. My mother and father were both alcoholics, and my father moved on to hard liquor and drugs, which ended up taking his life in February 2018. Growing up in a home governed by alcohol and drugs was difficult and abusive. At the time, I was unaware of the trauma happening around me, and I did not realize the lasting impact it would have.

The abusive, trauma-filled home I grew up in was my normal. It was all I knew, and like millions of others who grow up in these types of environments, trauma and abuse became a distorted normal that, unknowingly, had deep physical, mental, psychological, and spiritual consequences. These consequences leave people with a distorted view of themselves, men, women, relationships, God, love, sex, and the list goes on and on. This is the consequence of people not following God's original design for sex and life in general. So what effect did this have on me?

The effects trauma had on me played out in a variety of ways. First, I hated school and didn't do well academically. There was so much going on in my brain that I could not concentrate on school and the rigors of academics. I rarely made a grade above a "C," and

I missed the maximum days of school allowed to still pass. Second, I had a difficult time with relationships. Now don't get me wrong, I eagerly wanted a girlfriend and to have sex, but a long-term relationship was difficult because I had major trust and insecurity issues. The trauma I experienced kept me from feeling loved, accepted, and safe, and left me lonely, confused, and emotionally bankrupt. I felt unimportant, worthless, scared, vulnerable, and ultimately, I felt pawned by my parents, family members, friends, peers, and most of all, society.

Fortunately for me and my future wife and kids, everything was about to change. On July 1, 1990, in the mist of sexual sins, drunkenness, and selfishness, the miraculous happened—I was redeemed! Jesus, the Creator of the universe and everything in it, found me and said to me, "LIVE!" Fast asleep in my bed that Sunday morning, the Holy Spirit startled me with a gentle whisper, "Go to church. Gary, get up and go to church." I hadn't been to church in a while and had not planned to go that Sunday either. However, after several proddings from the Holy Spirit, I got up and went to my mother's church. I arrived late, and when I stepped out of the car, my body started to shake. I walked up to the door and, when I opened it, it was as if Jesus was standing there as the greeter. I slipped in during worship, sat in the back row, and immediately felt the power of God moving throughout the congregation. After several minutes of resisting the obvious moving of the Holy Spirit, I started to cry. And, after a few minutes of crying, I stood up, and walked down to the altar.

At that moment, the deep carnal lusts of the flesh controlling my life were broken and made subject to the power of the Holy Spirit now living and flowing powerfully throughout my body. For the first time in my life, I realized that my "normal" was not normal. Washed and cleansed by the blood of the cross, and with my eyes and ears finally opened to the truth, I made the most important decision of my life: I fell on my knees, repented of my sins, cried out to God, and prayed, "Father, not my will, but your will be done." The redeemed Gary stood up and walked boldly into the new life God prepared for him before time began.[21] The miracle of redemption awaits you as well.

With a new hope and realization that I was fearfully and wonderfully made and created to do great things, I enlisted in the United States Marine Corps in 1990. I served four years as a light armored reconnaissance (LAR) crewman at Camp Lejeune, North Carolina. In 1992, I deployed onboard the *USS Gunston Hall* and visited five countries: Spain, Israel, Greece, Morocco, and Italy. I became the lay reader for the ship and held nightly Bible studies on the mess decks. I got permission from the ship's chaplain to hold my own Divine Protestant services on Friday nights in one of the recreation rooms. It was during this time that I felt God reaffirm a call to ministry that I had received at age eleven. This deployment provided my first experiences with different cultures, religions, lifestyles, and sexual issues. I was honorably discharged from the Marines in 1994.

After the Corps, I attended several colleges before transferring to Bible college in 1997. I graduated from college in August 2000 and pastored my first church in Colorado. During my two-year pastorate in Colorado, I felt God calling me back to the military to serve as a chaplain. So, in 2002, I moved back to Springfield, MO to work on my Master of Divinity degree. I graduated from seminary in August of 2005 and was commissioned in the Navy to serve as a chaplain.

My ministry as a Navy chaplain has been rewarding. I have traveled the world and witnessed the struggle of humanity; my exposure to such widespread diversity has proven both humbling and eye-opening. The United States military exemplifies one of the most diverse institutions on earth. Represented within its ranks are people of every religion, ethnic group, social class, and gender. Serving in this environment and navigating issues of political correctness, inclusivity, sexual orientation, and several diametrically opposed opinions without others viewing me as discriminating has remained a challenge.

My first duty assignment in the Navy was to Naval Air Station (NAS) Whiting Field in Pensacola, Florida. NAS Whiting Field serves as the home to Training Air Wing FIVE, which trains over 1,200 pilots a year. My responsibilities included a chapel service every other week and weekly Bible studies. I also taught ethics to all incoming and outgoing personnel and served six squadrons with support, counseling, and visitations.

During this tour, I grew aware of the enormous and debilitating struggles people face regarding sexual issues. Over the course of three years, I primarily counseled men but also women who struggled with sexual addiction and other issues such as fornication, adultery, rape, masturbation, and questions related to gender identity. Because sexual issues and addiction became so prevalent in my counseling, I felt prompted to research the topic and provide awareness training to the command.

In the fall of 2008, I moved to San Diego, California, and reported onboard the *USS Green Bay* (LPD 20). As command chaplain, my responsibilities included counseling, ethics and leadership training, and advising the captain on all matters pertaining to ethical, moral, and religious/spiritual issues. Once again, I had numerous people in counseling reveal how sexual lust, passions, and immorality were destroying their lives, marriages, and careers. Because of my previous awareness of the challenges in the subject, I continued my education by attending a seminar about sexual addiction and started to frequently preach and teach on the topic.

I moved to Hawaii in the fall of 2010 and reported as command chaplain to Combat Logistic Battalion 3. My duties remained similar to previous commands except that I found myself working more with Marines suffering from combat trauma, post-traumatic stress disorder (PTSD), and traumatic brain injury (TBI). Service members who do not seek proper treatment or who neglect to follow prescribed treatment plans for these injuries often turn to self-medication to help ease or numb the pain. Their self-medication preferences often include alcohol, opiates, and illicit sex, which, when left unaddressed, inevitably lead to addiction.

After three years in Hawaii, I attended the clinical pastoral education (CPE) program at the Naval Medical Center San Diego. The center's clinical pastoral education consists of a one-year residence program with 1,200 hours of supervised clinical practice, four units of CPE, and four hundred hours of group and individual instruction. Graduation from the program required a final research project, so I focused my research on sexual addiction and spiritual injury.

In 2014, the men's ministry director from City View Assembly of God asked me to speak at the Men's Impact Conference in San Diego. I spoke on becoming a godly husband and focused most of my session on sexuality and keeping the marriage bed pure. Several pastors and ministry leaders attended the conference. After my session, they approached me with a desire to know more about sexuality. Many thanked me for the courage to go in-depth on the topic, and some wished more Christian leaders would teach and preach about sexuality from the pulpit. After the conference, the Teen Challenge director in San Diego invited me to speak at the local Teen Challenge center. I ended up speaking there once a month for fourteen months. I spoke on a variety of topics, but I focused predominantly on sexuality. In October 2014 I began my Doctor of Ministry degree, and after meeting with my doctoral adviser, it was quite clear God had been preparing me all those years to speak and teach on sex. So I decided to focus my studies and research on God's design for sex and sexuality.

I have spent years studying and researching God's design for sex. During countless hours of research, reading, and writing, I discovered the Golden Compass to sustained sexual satisfaction, which will be revealed throughout this book.

2

THE GIFT OF SEX

> "Then God blessed them, and God said to them,
> 'Be fruitful and multiply; fill the earth
> and subdue it'" (Gen. 1:28, NKJV).

At the heart of God's creation lies humanity, and at the heart of humanity lies sexuality. The biblical narrative reviewed in chapters 7 and 8 of this book records God's design for sex and sexuality from creation to new creation. The Bible reveals the successes and failures of individual people and nations in these areas and provides the framework to protect sex and individual sexuality from sexual acts and practices that lead to sexual immorality, fornication, and adultery, and ultimately away from the holy life God desires for his people.

The Bible also defines the meaning of sex. As Dennis Hollinger notes, "Above all, it [the Bible] implicitly provides us with an overarching meaning of sex, which in turn forms the theological bedrock for any commands and principles about physical intimacy."[22] The Bible remains the only authoritative source when it comes to the heart of sex and God's design for sexuality.

When God created Adam and Eve, he gave them a providential charge: "Be fruitful and multiply and fill the earth" (Gen. 1:28). With this charge, God gave humanity the holy gift of sex. The attempts to accurately interpret the gift of sex by theologians, scholars, and Christian leaders, both past and present, have often focused more on the consequences of unholy sexual behavior rather than the holy aspects God intended. As Bill and Pam Farrel affirm, "We have definitely lost our way as a society when it comes to trivializing and devaluing sexuality as a gift, intended by God for marriage."[23] Christians deserve a healthy interpretation that allows them to embrace the sensual passions God intricately wove into human sexuality.

Christians look to church leaders for guidance on all types of issues. A study conducted by the United Church of Christ found that more than eight out of ten members reported they look to their church as a resource on sexuality-related decisions and concerns.[24] Ever since the sexual revolution of the sixties and seventies, some Christians have fundamentally abandoned biblical instructions regarding sexual activity. As Norman Geisler points out,

> The secular views of sexual license have penetrated the Christian church. . . . One of the difficulties in the Christian context is that Christians often take their guidance from what other Christians 'do,' rather than what they 'ought' to do.[25]

If this statement is true, the need for sound biblical teaching on sex and sexuality is of utmost importance.

Christians need a definitive scriptural compass, commanded by wisdom,[26] to help them establish healthy sexual parameters and perimeters in their lives and marriages—a compass keeping them holy and their marriage beds pure. Yolanda Turner and William Stayton state, "Religious leaders are in a unique position to transform, inform, and influence society's understanding of sexuality and religion—through the pulpit, pastoral care of individuals and families and involvement in local communities, the media and politics."[27] They conclude that a seminary education does not prepare most students to adequately speak and teach in-depth on the topic of sexuality and sex education.

The Bible has much to say about sex, sexual practices, and sexual sins.[28] Although people disagree about what constitutes sex or sexual activity, Joe McIlhaney Jr. and Freda Bush provide some clarity: "The most reasonable definition suggested by recent brain studies indicates that sexual activity is any intimate contact between two individuals that involves arousal, stimulation, and/or a response by at least one of the two partners."[29] The Song of Solomon is a beautiful and romantic melody between two love-struck lovers who shower each other with natural sexual desires and intentions. While the Song of Solomon and numerous other passages from the Bible speak about healthy sexual desire and pleasures, these topics are rarely taught from the pulpit, in Sunday school, youth group, or even men's and women's groups. I believe the reason stretches back to early teachings and views on sex and sexuality that misrepresent the heart of sex God designed.

The Early Church fathers significantly contributed to negative views on sex, women, and married priests. Originally, Catholic priests could own land, marry, have children, and live a normal life. However, extreme asceticism and views on virginity, procreation, and celibacy slowly pressured priests to divorce their wives, abandon their children, and sell their land with all profits going to the church. The one aspect about sex prevalent throughout the Catholic Church was that sex is for procreation.[30] Pope Paul VI writes, "It is necessary that each and every marriage act remain ordered to the procreation of human life."[31] In a recent series on the sacraments, Pope Francis concludes,

> A sacrament that leads us to the heart of God's plan, which is a plan of alliance with his People, with all of us, a plan of communion. . . . The image of God is a married couple, man and

woman, not only man, not only woman, but rather both. This is the image of God: love, God's alliance with us is represented in the alliance between man and woman. . . . We were created to love, as a reflection of God and his love. And in matrimonial union the man and woman realize this vocation, as a sign of reciprocity and the full and definitive communion of life.[32]

A relationship originating from any foundational principle other than uniting a man and a woman into a "One-Flesh Covenant" is outside of God's design and meaning for sex. God created sex, and sex is holy when kept within the boundaries he established. Erroneous ideologies and teachings regarding sex and sexuality confuse Christians, who already have trouble navigating sexual issues, making their sexual journey tempestuous and difficult. Laurie Jungling describes how Augustine's views on sex considerably influenced church leaders and much of Western ideology on this topic:

> Augustine's concepts of order and sexuality are deeply interrelated in his theology and are still embedded in contemporary Christian theology and human society. This comes not without a price, however. Despite Augustine's recognition that sexuality was an intended part of God's good creation, the order he arranged condemned sexuality to a place of degradation and disgust by making it the primary window through which Christians and consequently much of the Western world view the 'sin-sick' soul. And although he rescued the *created* body from the evils of the Manichean and Platonic flesh, the order he arranged returned a *sinful* body to a place of suspicion and renunciation. Augustine may not have intended the negative results of his theology, but we must hold him, and those who followed him, accountable lest we fail to learn what damage our ideas can do to those who do not fit our vision of the order of things.[33]

Throughout *Confessions*, Augustine uses negative connotations when referring to sex and sexual desire. For Augustine, sexual desire was "muddy concupiscence of the flesh," "carnal corruptions," "thorns," and "chains."[34] Stanley Grenz believes that Augustine's emphasis on original sin spilled over to his view of human sexuality. With regard to Augustine, Grenz says,

> The effects of the Fall are present in sexual activity in two ways: First, sexual intercourse is the transmitter not only of life from one generation to the next, but also of original sin. Second, because of its unavoidable link to passion and thus to compulsiveness, every act of coitus is tainted by evil.[35]

David Hunter thinks Augustine's views on sex were confused by his sexual desires from his adolescence:

> In Augustine's description of his adolescent adventures, he observed that his youthful sex drive led him to confuse the search for love and friendship with the satisfaction of his sexual desires: 'The bubbling impulses of puberty befogged and obscured my heart so that it could not see the difference between love's serenity and lust's darkness.'[36]

Augustine's deep desire for holiness and personal convictions obviously obscured his ideas on sexuality and sexual desire. Although his views on sexual desire may have been genuine, they weren't biblical. One read of the Song of Solomon refutes Augustine's views and teachings on sexual desire.

Augustine's teachings on sexual desire repressed and tarnished the God-given gift of sexuality. His ultra-pious views and ascetic ways served his own personal convictions and internal issues with which he struggled. His negative views concerning sex and sexuality continue to influence Christians from various traditions. However, views on what constitutes healthy and holy sex and sexuality have changed.

Tim Gardner believes the Christian understanding of the gift of sex has gone through several shifts over the last 1,500 years. Gardner suggests the first era viewed sexuality as the means and method for procreation. The second era, which came centuries later, affirmed that God really did want married couples to enjoy sex. The third era, which surfaced most recently, thought people should take full advantage of all research and medical data on the topic. Gardner believes Christians should not tolerate any sexual dysfunction and should take full advantage of the technology that enhances its pleasure. He also thinks the latest developments in Christian perspectives regarding sex cause people to view it in the context of all life, including one's spiritual life and what he calls the "Meta-Sex" age.[37] Meta means "beyond" and denotes "something of a higher or second-order" and goes beyond pleasure and techniques.[38] It understands how everything surrounding sex affects it in unexpected ways.

Christian leaders owe it to their members, and parents to their children, to teach, not just on the passages of Scripture that deal directly and indirectly with sexual sins, but on the Scriptures that speak about the healthy benefits of recognizing sex and sexuality as a gift from God and all the passions, desires, and emotions God intended. Kathlyn Breazeale explains: "For Christian couples, sexual desire for each other provides a means of experiencing the power and intensity of God's love for creation, a creation that God declared is 'good' (Gen. 1:31)."[39] When people view their natural sexual desires as thorns and chains, they feel ashamed when they should feel normal, genuine, and loved.

Gardner believes shame causes people to hide God-given sexual desires and thus keeps couples separate:

> Shame fosters the belief that certain things about me must be kept hidden. We engage in sex, we may even in some ways be 'making love,' but we don't experience sex in a way that touches our souls. A brick wall of shame and self-condemnation keeps us separate.[40]

Godly sex unites and reaffirms the "One-Flesh Covenant" of holy matrimony. It never causes shame; nor does it cause couples to hide and cover themselves the way Adam and Eve covered their bodies and hid from God. Furthermore, Gardner says, "Shame erects a barrier to enjoying godly intimacy."[41] The gift of sex, when used according to God's design, allows married couples to enjoy godly intimacy and keep their marriage beds pure.

Modern culture is changing fast, especially on the issue of sex, sexual identity, gender roles, and sexual orientation, as Jonathan Grant describes:

> Modern culture has this sort of influence on our way of seeing life. If Christian vision involves seeing with two eyes—one divine and the other human—modern culture covers one eye so that we begin to see only from the human perspective. In essence, it compromises our spiritual depth perception and tempts us to become the center of brevity of our own lives. One of the critical roles of Christian leaders, including parents, is to be guardians of the lens. We need to attend to the lens because Scripture calls us to see with new eyes, from the perspective of eternity.[42]

Grant suggests that the church can refocus its vision through the lens of the gospel of Christ. God, through his Word, provides the only sexual compass for Christian singles and couples to keep their sexuality pure and the marriage bed undefiled by the immoral sexual acts taught and practiced throughout the world. Life is risky, and surrendering your will to follow God's will, your sexuality to follow God's assigned sexuality, may seem like a risk too daunting to take.

Clovis Chappell describes from the nature of Jewish life that they understood how a person had to face risks to bring about gain:

> The Jews as a rule were not a seafaring people. They dreaded the sea. It was to them a thing of menace and of mystery. To

venture upon the sea was to make a most dangerous adventure. . . . But while the Jew realized that the man who ventured upon the sea ran a great risk, he also was honest enough to face the further fact that such a risk might bring vast gain. . . . If he faced dangers that others did not face, he had the thrill of great experiences in which these others could not share. He had a breadth of view that was impossible to the man that remained in the security of his native village.[43]

The psalmist also concludes, "They that go down to the sea in ships, that do business in great waters; these see the works of the Lord, and His wonders in the deep" (Ps. 107:23-24, KJV). The Golden Compass of Sustained Sexual Satisfaction, which God gives throughout the Scriptures and that I discuss next, provides sound, biblical navigation on challenging and complicated sexual issues and activities Christian singles and married couples face daily. Some may find it risky to read as they may have to make a few navigational adjustments and plot a new course in the sexual waters they currently sail. However, as Chappell and the psalmist observed, the man or woman who remains in the security of their native village will never have the breadth of view as the ones who risk everything to learn the truth and "See the works of the Lord, and his wonders in the deep" (v. 24).

As you read the next chapter, I challenge you to read with an open mind and try not to agree or disagree with anything I present at first. Read it. Study it. Meditate on it. Most importantly, pray on it before making any decisions or plotting a new course. Take the risk, and get a new breadth of view. What do you have to lose? The gains far exceed whatever loss you may incur. In fact, they're incomparable.

3

SEXUAL COMPASS

"Marriage should be honored by all, and the marriage bed kept pure, for God will judge the adulterer and all the sexually immoral" (Heb. 13:4, NIV).

A Sexual Compass for Christians

The temptations of sexual immorality do not bypass Christians. As the Apostle Paul notes, in speaking to the Corinthian church, "It is good for a man not to have sexual relations with a woman. But because of the temptation to sexual immorality, each man should have his own wife and each woman her own husband. The husband should give to his wife her conjugal rights, and likewise the wife to her husband" (1 Cor. 7:1-2). Unfortunately, without sound biblical teaching on sex and sexuality, numerous Christians, both single and married, rely on their own carnal judgments to determine what sexual practices are acceptable and non-acceptable.[44] They need a sexual compass to help navigate these realities.

Dale Kuehne uses the term "iWorld" to describe people who use internal instincts as their moral and sexual compass. "iWorld" people believe freedom of the individual reigns supreme. This type of thought and behavior, Kuehne notes, has caused significant damage to the relational structure of Western society:

> The iWorld's most significant impact has been on the relational structure of Western society. The driving force in the development of the iWorld was the desire to champion the ideal of individual choice. While the focus was not on sexual freedom per se, this has become one of its most cherished freedoms. By challenging and changing our understanding of what it means to be human, the iWorld fundamentally altered our perception of human nature, the self, and the purpose of family, relationships, and sexuality.[45]

In contrast to using one's internal instinct as a moral and sexual compass, however, believers can look to the Scriptures. The Bible mentions various acceptable and non-acceptable sexual practices, but it also remains silent on others. God created sex, and sex is holy when kept within the boundaries he established. As Gardner emphasizes,

> The full truth about sex is this: It is both sacred and polluted, holy and desecrated. The sacredness of sex is not based on how we treat it or mistreat it. Its sacredness is based on its essence, which comes from God. Sex is holy because God created it to be holy.[46]

Sex provides the spice that keeps marriages from becoming a boring pursuit of chores, as Bill and Pam Farrel note:

> None of us got married so we could load up on chores. We got married out of hope. We got married because we believed there was some kind of magic between us. We got married

because we believed we could have great sex together. A satisfying sex life can add dignity to all the other pursuits of life. It is the thing to look forward to after a dull or miserable day at work. Sex is the moment of connection that creates a deep bond, even when sprinkled weeks or months apart. Sexual union adds an underlying deposit of strength that can help hold couples together when life threatens to pull them apart.[47]

If God didn't want people to enjoy sex, he most certainly had the creative authority to utilize the "stork." Steve Gallagher reiterates that as long as sex happens between husband and wife, and as long as they don't deviate from God's sexual design, sex is good: "God wants married couples, who he has enjoined, to enjoy each other—thus, he made it [sex] a pleasurable experience. However, confusion and perversion emerge when people deviate from the purpose for which God ordained."[48] Godly sex brings about clarity, feelings of purity and acceptance, and passionate desires of joy.

The boundaries God gave in Scripture protect sex and keep it holy; they don't hinder it. Hollinger notes, "The biblical commands against adultery and fornication are intended to protect the beauty and meaning of God's good gift."[49] Sex between a man and a woman who are married to one another is a gift from God and not a sinful act implemented after the fall. Daniel Heimbach reflects this perspective and writes, "According to God, good sex is holy sex, and for sex to be holy it must be consistent with God plus nothing."[50] God implemented healthy parameters to protect sex and sexuality and to keep Satan from turning the act itself into a depraved, self-gratifying, isolated event. Carrie Miles declares,

> He [God] meant for us to want romance, committed love, and even sex. The biblically ideal marriage includes harmony and compatibility, passion and compassion, self-fulfillment as well as self-sacrifice, and equality as a necessary stepping-stone to unity.[51]

Immoral sexual behavior desecrates the one-flesh unity and supplants God's rightful place within the marriage covenant. The following discussion will help provide a compass on several sexual practices with which Christians struggle.

Masturbation[52]

Some Americans (among them even many preachers) accept and encourage the practice of masturbation. One study found "among Americans aged eighteen to fifty-nine, about 60 percent of the men and 40 percent of the women said they masturbated in the past year."[53] Some say sexual tension needs sexual release. The idea is that masturbation will help release the natural sexual tension inside and keep the person from engaging in sexual immorality, fornication, or adultery. Unfortunately, people who masturbate never experience the built-up libido and the advantages it adds to the sexual encounter. Masturbation does not release sexual tension, nor does it keep people from sexual sins. It is like feeding a starving lion a prime rib steak extra rare. The only thing accomplished is an intensified hunger.

Jewish rabbinic oral law prohibits masturbation. In fact, the prohibition is so strict, one passage in the Talmud states, "In the case of a man, the hand that reaches below the navel should be chopped off" (Niddah 13a). Rabbi Shmuley Boteach, who has authored several books on sex, writes, "Every act of masturbation serves as a powerful sexual release that in turn lessens our vital need for sex with someone else. In the context of marriage, this is disastrous."[54] Boteach suggests when couples make each other their primary sexual outlet, they tend to treat each other better.

The danger of masturbation can be found in Ivan Pavlov's experiment with dogs and the term "classical conditioning."[55] Pavlov was a Russian physiologist who studied salivation in dogs. He suggested dogs did not need training on how to salivate because they already had an unconditioned response. All they needed was an unconditioned stimulus to trigger them (i.e., food). As his research and experiments progressed, Pavlov noticed the dogs started salivating when anyone simply walked in the room, regardless if they had food or not. Similarly, sexual drive is an unconditioned response for everyone post-puberty.[56] Attraction to beautiful things, especially the human body, is natural, and seeing a beautiful man or woman can induce an unconditioned stimulus. For men, this could be a beautiful woman wearing a bathing suit or tight and revealing clothing. The unconditioned response is a desire for sexual gratification. Now enter the conditioned stimulus—masturbation.

When a person uses masturbation as the conditioned stimulus instead of sex with their spouse, they condition their body and mind to believe sex is nothing more than an isolated event for mere personal gratification and what some call "monosexuality." People often masturbate in isolation, which itself is narcissistic and leads to bondage. Ted Roberts believes "solo" sex leads to sexual bondage and is a sign of immaturity and woundedness that's void of intimacy. He says, "Our sexuality is a revelation of God's very nature. But the revelation is destroyed when sex is 'solo'—when it isn't characterized by a responsible and caring relationship between a husband and wife. Sexual bondage is always a solo experience."[57] Masturbation does not lead to the one-flesh union God designed.

Furthermore, the hand, dildos, and vibrators put more pressure on the genitals than they were designed for, and in the process the genitals become desensitized and/or need more stimulation to become aroused.[58] The end result corrupts and distorts the actual experience of sex, which opens the door for lust and masochistic and sadomasochistic behaviors. Hollinger shifts the focus from the act of masturbation and focuses on the deeper moral issues often involved: "The crucial moral issue is not so much the act itself with its intense physical excitement and pleasure. Rather, the two primary ethical issues related to masturbation are lust and the solitary nature of this act in contrast to the nature of sex, which is companionship oriented."[59] Masturbation stirs up the natural unconditioned stimulus and response in humans for sexual satisfaction and leads away from the heart of sex God designed for covenantal marriages.

A single person should refrain from sexual release until he or she marries and then find release only through intercourse with his or her spouse.[60] For the married, they too should make their spouse their only sexual outlet, and this should only occur through intercourse. Mark Driscoll says,

> If a single man wants to have an orgasm, he needs to first become a man and undergo the hard work of courting and marrying a woman. If a married man wants to have an orgasm, he needs to first undergo the hard work of loving, leading, and romancing his wife. But, lazy men are prone to rub one out in the shower each morning rather than undergo the labors usually associated with responsible masculine married life.[61]

The heart of sex never shortcuts romance; nor does it bypass reality. The heart of sex works to keep a pure marriage bed where sexual intercourse is the only sexual outlet a Christian married couple experiences.

Another argument against masturbation involves the issue of lust. Jesus said, "Anyone who looks at a woman lustfully has already committed adultery with her in his heart" (Matt. 5:27). Whether single or married, anyone who has ever masturbated knows most people do not masturbate to a blank mind—in their mind, they are having sex with someone. Thus, they have committed adultery, fornication, and/or sexual immorality. "Self-idolatry" lies at the root of masturbation, and according to the Book of Wisdom, "The idea of making idols was the beginning of fornication and the invention of them was the corruption of life."[62] Masturbation plunders intimacy, replacing it with self-idolatry that corrupts the individual and the true sexual intimacy God designed. Some people ask, "What if your spouse is the image in your mind?" Thus, the need for a sexual compass.

First Thessalonians 4:3-5 says, "This is the will of God, your sanctification: that you abstain from sexual immorality; that each one of you know how to control his own body in holiness and honor, not in the passion of lust like the Gentiles who do not know God." Throughout the Bible, God speaks about self-control. Proverbs says, "A man without self-control is like a city broken into and left without walls" (Prov 25:28). Self-control is defined as "the ability to control oneself, in particular one's emotions and desires or the expression of them in one's behavior, especially in difficult situations."[63] The heart of sex is a heart of control and reality. It does not portray an image, even if it is of a person's spouse, and then masturbate to it. The heart of sex keeps a pure marriage bed where sexual intercourse with one's spouse is the only sexual outlet.

God designed sex to happen in the context of marriage alone. Sex should never be an isolated event with the end goal of personal satisfaction and orgasm. Sex is about unity, consummation, procreation, love, mutual pleasuring, giving and receiving, and honoring the one-flesh union of the marriage covenant.[64] Masturbation starts people down a slippery slope. Once a person becomes conditioned to other objects and more pressure, they have to turn to other things that lead away from holiness in order to find satisfaction. A person who has self-control to the point that he or she does not masturbate will have much less chance of ever committing adultery, becoming a sex addict, or engaging in sexual immorality. As Sirach 20:3 says, "Like a eunuch lusting for intimacy with a maiden is he who does right under compulsion."[65] The person who does right under sexual compulsion will enjoy the heart of sex without feelings of shame, guilt, or dirtiness.

When I rededicated my life to Christ in 1990, I stopped masturbating, and now I have not masturbated for over thirty years. This one act alone transformed my life and future and has contributed to me being a faithful husband who is in control of, and confident in, my sexuality. After God created Adam and Eve, he told them to "Be fruitful and multiply, and fill the earth" (Gen 1:28, NASB). God did not stop there, though. He continued and said six very important words: "And bring it under your control" (v. 28, CEV).

Masturbation is the prelude to porn, fornication, adultery, lust, and sexual immorality, and it is a roadblock keeping God's children from the fruit of the Spirit of self-control. Some ministers actually teach their parishioners to use masturbation when they are separated from their spouse as a deterrent to adultery rather than teaching them about the power of the fruit of the Spirit of self-control, which will pay huge dividends in the long run.

A Navy chaplain referred a young married man to me one day who struggled with several sexual issues, one of them being compulsive masturbation (he was masturbating four-five times a day). During our first session, Josh[66] stated that a fifteen-year-old female babysitter molested him at the age of ten. The abuse left Josh conflicted because he liked what she did to him and what he did to her. However, the sexual encounter sparked an insatiable sexual appetite which led Josh to porn, masturbation, orgies, and several other sexually abusive acts.

I only had one counseling session with Josh, due to a deployment that took him out of the area; however, I received the following email from him about a month after our session:

> Hello Sir,
>
> On the day we spoke I've yet to masturbate. The thoughts are relentless and every aspect of the female form stirs the thoughts, but I quickly change my thoughts. I've been woken up once by an extremely strong impulse to do so, but tossed and turned and returned to sleep.
>
> While I'm not knowledgeable in the subject of addiction, I did suspect the mind is trying to revert to normalcy. I very strongly hope the pain I'm experiencing daily is the process of mental purging and that this is a necessary struggle to reset my sexual attractions.

Josh is exactly right. His body and mind are trying to reset to normal, the normal God created and desires for all humanity. The struggle Josh experienced was necessary to purge the distorted practices of the world that held him captive for so long and kept him from the true sexuality and sexual experiences God designed. If Josh embraces the struggle and redeems his sexuality, he will not only, "Reset his sexual attractions," he will also experience a brand-new sexuality he never dreamed was possible.

Masturbation has nothing to do with the heart of sex God intended for humanity. Christians must bring their sexual desires and temptations under control. They must master their bodies, and there is no better time to learn how to do that than when you are single.

Sodomy

The topic of anal sex/sodomy among Christians continues to highlight the need for an authoritative sexual compass pointing to God's ultimate design for sex. The Bible records that there was a time when "everyone did what was right in his own eyes" (Judg. 21:25). Paul reiterates the same message to the Corinthians: "'I have the right to do anything,' you say—but not everything is beneficial. 'I have the right to do anything'—but not everything is constructive" (1 Cor. 10:23, NIV). A disturbing number of Christian couples use the same principle today (which is nothing more than hedonism) as their sexual compass.[67]

God forbade the practice of anal sex, also known as sodomy, in Mosaic Law and considered the practice an abomination (Deut. 23:17; Lev. 18:22; 18:29; 20:13). The word "sodomite" (Heb, *Qadesh*) refers to an unclean temple prostitute. Throughout Scripture, "sodomite" has a negative connotation regarding anyone, male or female, who engaged in or participated in immoral sexual acts, including anal intercourse. God instructed the Israelites to remove from the land and have no interactions with "shrine prostitutes, prostitutes, sodomites, whoremongers, and those who lusted after strange flesh" (both male and female) throughout the Bible.[68] In the book of Job, Elihu says, with regard to the wicked, "They die in their youth and perish like sodomites" (36:14). This parallelism could imply that people who practiced anal sex/sodomy lived proverbially short lives, due possibly because they contracted venereal diseases.[69]

Consummation, unification, and procreation are fundamental foundations of sex. The penis and vagina live in symbiosis, serving as procreative vessels and reciprocatory portals of life, transmitting and receiving sperm, thus fulfilling God's ultimate plan to "be fruitful and multiply, and fill the earth" (Gen. 1:28). The rectum is a portal of death and serves no function in the procreative and unifying design of sex. God wants the marriage bed pure and undefiled. He did not design the rectum for external penetration.

The rectum consists of tight muscles used to expel feces from the body and has no natural lubrication. Its lining rips easily and bleeds when external objects are plunged into it, allowing semen and blood, infected with HIV and other venereal diseases, to enter the bloodstream. Furthermore, men who sodomize women and then engage in vaginal sex distribute blood and feces into the vagina, which can cause vaginitis and other infections, ultimately upsetting the natural bacterial balance of the vagina. God designed the rectum for one purpose and one purpose only, to remove fecal matter from the body. Christians currently practicing or considering sodomy should reconsider this abominable act.

People orgasm to all kinds of distorted, unnatural sexual practices. Furthermore, people can naturally orgasm during dreams, what the Bible refers to as "nocturnal emissions."[70] Because the rectum is located in close proximity to the genitals and other erogenous zones, it coincidentally or by other means, becomes stimulated during sexual intercourse, and some men and women report they have actually orgasmed while being sodomized; this, however, is in conjunction with stimulation of the clitoris and prostate.[71] Unfortunately, this has led some Christians to believe that the rectum is an erogenous zone and thus an area for sexual exploration and enjoyment. I disagree. Sex is deeply physical and psychological, and the ability to orgasm, or because it feels good, does not constitute the right to trespass in an area God deemed off limits. The story of the garden of Eden serves as an example to illustrate this point.

The garden of Eden was a tropical paradise possessing everything needed to live a healthy and productive life: water, food, shelter, community, and safety. Humans, animals, birds, reptiles, and insects lived in perfect harmony in the garden and did not fear one another. God gave them every herb-bearing seed and every tree with seed in its fruit for food. In its midst, God placed the tree of life and the tree of the knowledge of good and evil. It is a profound mystery why Adam and Eve never ate from the tree of life. It is probably synonymous with the choices people make today—to never choose the free gift of salvation afforded to them by Jesus' sacrifice on the cross. Instead, Adam and Eve chose to disobey God and ended up making the most detrimental mistake in recorded history.

In Genesis 2, God spoke directly to Adam and Eve, saying, "You may surely eat of every tree of the garden, but of the tree of the knowledge of good and evil you shall not eat, for in the day that you eat of it you shall surely die" (Gen. 2:16-17). Eve, deceived by the ultimate pawnbroker—Satan—and convinced she would "be like God" (3:5), believed that the fruit on the tree of the knowledge of good and evil was pleasing to the eye, good for food, and desirable to make one wise. Even though she acknowledged God's command to not eat or even touch it, she partook of the forbidden fruit.

Adam, likewise, in full knowledge of God's command, followed the lead of his wife and, remarkably, they both realized the serpent was right. The forbidden fruit was pleasing to the eye, good for physical nourishment, and for gaining knowledge, but there was one problem—the fruit was forbidden and off limits. The impending consequence (spiritual death) would be unimaginable for Adam and Eve, humanity, and ultimately, the Son of God himself.

With eyes wide open, innocence lost, and the knowledge of evil imprinted on their minds, Adam and Eve realized they were naked and in need of covering; for the first time, they were afraid and hid from God's presence.

Sodomy is a forbidden fruit God deemed off limits. The tree of the knowledge of good and evil was in the midst of paradise just like the rectum is in the midst of the portals of life (the vagina and penis) and numerous other erogenous zones. Don't make the same deadly mistake Adam and Eve made and find yourself guilty of an abomination that, on judgment day, could have an eternal consequence. The Bible says, "There is a way that seems right to a man, but its end is the way to death" (Prov. 14:12). For all who practice the act of sodomy, their end will be death and eternal separation from God's presence. If you are guilty of this trespass, stop trespassing, ask for forgiveness, and allow God to redeem your sexuality and restore your marriage bed and garden/fountain back to purity.

Homosexuality

One of the best counseling sessions I've ever had happened with a homosexual woman. We befriended one another through coaching basketball and, to tell the truth, she could coach circles around me. Susan[72] and I lived on the same base, and she knew I was a chaplain who viewed homosexuality as a sin. I knew she was a homosexual, but we didn't let that get in the way of our friendship and mutual respect of each other and of basketball. A couple of years went by, when, one day, I received an email from Susan. She wanted to speak with me, so we set a date and time to meet. A few days later, Susan walked into my office, and after some small talk and a basketball discussion, she said, "Chaps, I feel I can trust you, and I didn't know where else to turn." (It took two years to earn her trust). After a long silence, she continued: "Chaps, a few years ago I miscarried, and I just don't know what to do. It eats at me every day, and I can't stop thinking about it; it's tearing me apart."

Now, let me confess, I had no idea what she wanted to talk about. Thinking quickly, I simply asked, "Was the baby a boy or a girl?"

"A boy."

"What is his name?" I asked.

Her eyes opened wide as she said, "Mark."

Without hesitating, I said, "Susan, I am so sorry for the loss of your son, Mark." Well, let me tell you, when I said, "Mark," she sobbed immensely for quite a long time.

Finally, she looked straight into my eyes and said, "Thank you. You are the first person who has ever acknowledged Mark's existence."

As simple as my reply may sound, it was exactly the thing she needed to hear to finally heal a wound deep within. We talked for a long time that day, and God truly performed miracles. After we prayed together, she left, and a few days later she sent me an email thanking me for seeing her and helping her close an open wound. I wish I had saved that letter, but, unfortunately, I didn't. We met a few more times and talked about other issues going on in her life, and we continued to see each other at games and the playoffs. (Her team destroyed mine, by the way, and knocked us out of the tournament. So much for having mercy on the chaplain!)

This story highlights the importance of sharing the love of Christ to all, regardless of sexual orientation, religion, race, or gender. Susan felt disregarded by her partner and the LGBTQ community and turned to a religious leader for support. In this instance, our religious beliefs about homosexuality did not obstruct or forestall the care and support needed. All that mattered to Susan was speaking to someone she could trust, someone who would address the deep wound she carried within.

No matter what your belief is regarding this topic, treating people with love, respect, and dignity remains paramount when establishing friendships, offering care and support, or simply being a beacon of hope. I've discovered most people really don't care what someone believes or doesn't believe about a particular topic. The hurt, sick, or disregarded are drawn to people who are gentle and kind. People who work hard, can agree to disagree, and who share without expecting anything in return. People who meet them where they are at and journey with them regardless of beliefs, passions, or sexual orientation.

The topic of homosexuality, though, is an important and extremely sensitive issue throughout the world. Numerous people won't even entertain a discussion on the topic if their lifestyle or identity aren't accepted, supported, and promoted. As a matter of fact, as soon as a different opinion about homosexuality or the LGBTQ community is mentioned, other than the one they have, they label the other person as homophobic, intolerant, or a bigot, and believe they are experiencing sexual discrimination, etc. This is not a surprise coming from non-Christians; however, for those who identify as a Christian, this is unacceptable behavior. Christians should never shy away from any discussion, on any topic. If and when areas of disagreement arise the Bible says Christians should "gently instruct."[73]

So what does the Bible say about homosexuality and all the other sexual identities and terms used today?[74] God lays out several regulations and boundaries regarding sex in the book of Leviticus—boundaries people are not to cross, regardless of what they believe, how they feel, what they are taught by people and institutions, or how they sexually label and identify themselves. The first comes from Leviticus 18:22—"You shall not lie with a male as with a woman; it is an abomination," and the second, 20:13—"If a man lies with a male as with a woman, both of them have committed an abomination; they shall surely be put to death; their blood is upon them."

In the New Testament, Paul confronts the Romans about their ungodliness and unrighteousness, which he attributes to their "foolish hearts" becoming "darkened," leading them to exchange the glory of God for idolatry (Rom. 1:21-23). The people of Rome were so engrossed in idolatrous practices that they ended up corrupting their own sexuality.[75] Men lusted after other men, and women lusted after other women. In the process, they exchanged natural sexual relations for unnatural sexual relations (vv. 26-27). These sexual practices came from "the lusts of their hearts" (v. 24) and caused the people to become unclean and guilty of idolatry.

John Stott explains:

> The history of the world confirms that idolatry leads to immorality. A false image of God leads to a false understanding of sex. Paul does not tell us what kind of immorality he has in mind, except that it involved *the degrading of their bodies with one another* (24). He is right. Illicit sex degrades people's humanness; sex in marriage, as God intended, ennobles it.[76]

Paul goes on to say, God "gave them up" or "turned them over" to their own lust, which led to the "degrading of their bodies."[77] Men and women turned from the natural sexual desire for heterosexual sex and were inflamed with shameful lust for homosexual/lesbian relationships and sexual practices (vv. 26-27).

Stott says homosexuals try to get around the truths about homosexuality that God lays out in Scripture by teaching that passages like Romans 1:26-27 don't apply to them. The premise homosexuals use assures them they were born a homosexual; thus, God is not speaking to them but to people who engage in homosexuality and were born a heterosexual. So the practice of homosexuality by a heterosexual is "unnatural/strange flesh." Stott concludes:

> Verses 26-27 are a crucial text in the contemporary debate about homosexuality. The traditional interpretation, that they describe and condemn all homosexual behavior, is being challenged by the gay lobby. Three arguments are advanced. First, it is claimed that the passage is irrelevant, on the ground that its purpose is neither to teach sexual ethics, nor to expose vice, but rather to portray the outworking of God's wrath. This is

true. But if a certain sexual conduct is to be seen as the consequence of God's wrath, it must be displeasing to him. Second, 'the likelihood is that Paul is thinking only about pederasty' since 'there was no other form of male homosexuality in the Greco-Roman world,' and that he is opposing it because of the humiliation and exploitation experienced by the youths involved. All one can say in response to this suggestion is that the text itself contains no hint of it. Third, there is the question what Paul meant by 'nature.' Some homosexual people are urging that their relationships cannot be described as 'unnatural,' since they are perfectly natural to them. John Boswell has written, for example, that 'the persons Paul condemns are manifestly not homosexual: what he derogates are homosexual acts committed by apparently heterosexual people.' Hence Paul's statement that they 'abandoned' natural relations, and 'exchanged' them for unnatural. Richard Hays has written a thorough exegetical rebuttal of this interpretation of Romans 1, however. He provides ample contemporary evidence that the opposition of 'natural' (*kata physin*) and 'unnatural' (*para physin*) was 'very frequently used . . . as a way of distinguishing between heterosexual and homosexual behavior.' Besides, differentiating between sexual orientation and sexual practice is a modern concept; 'to suggest that Paul intends to condemn homosexual acts only when they are committed by persons who are constitutionally heterosexual is to introduce a distinction entirely foreign to Paul's thought-world,' in fact a complete anachronism.[78]

What started out as sexual in nature ended with an efflux of sins and evil behavior, e.g., wickedness, covetousness, maliciousness, envy, murder, strife, deceit, gossip, slander, hatred of God, insolence, boastfulness, disobedience to parents, faithlessness, ruthlessness, and heartlessness (vv. 28-31). People think they can get around

God's Word with excuses like, "I was born this way" or "But I am a woman"—even though they were born with the anatomy of a male, or "But I am a man"—even though they were born with the anatomy of a female. Or they believe a doctor can override God's creation and change their sex by having an operation and hormone therapy. This is a lie, a delusion, and the result of pawned sexuality. Stop believing the lie and seek the truths found throughout God's Holy Word. Don't be like Israel who refused to hear the truth and asked Isaiah to prophecy lies and illusions:

> Go now, write it on a tablet for them, inscribe it on a scroll, that for the days to come it may be an everlasting witness. For these are rebellious people, deceitful children, children unwilling to listen to the Lord's instruction. They say to the seers, 'See no more visions!' and to the prophets, 'Give us no more visions of what is right! Tell us pleasant things, prophesy illusions. Leave this way, get off this path, and stop confronting us with the Holy One of Israel!' (Isa 30:8-11).

Don't be like the Romans who exchanged the truth for a lie and received in themselves the penalty for the error:

> Therefore, God gave them up in the lusts of their hearts to impurity, to the dishonoring of their bodies among themselves, because they exchanged the truth about God for a lie and worshiped and served the creature rather than the Creator, who is blessed forever! Amen. For this reason, God gave them up to dishonorable passions. For their women exchanged natural relations for those that are contrary to nature; and the men likewise gave up natural relations with women and were consumed with passion for one another, men committing shameless acts with men and receiving in themselves the due penalty for their error (Rom. 1:24-27).

People don't get to choose their sex or gender identity. They did not create themselves. That's why there is a day of judgment, where God will hold everyone responsible for what they did with the body he created. I don't own Gary. I didn't create Gary. But I can assure you, God will hold me responsible for what I did with Gary.

Paul, in 1 Timothy, warns of false teachings contrary to sound doctrine and God's design:

> As I urged you when I was going to Macedonia, remain at Ephesus so that you may charge certain persons not to teach any different doctrine, nor to devote themselves to myths and endless genealogies, which promote speculations rather than the stewardship from God that is by faith. The aim of our charge is love that issues from a pure heart and a good conscience and a sincere faith. Certain persons, by swerving from these, have wandered away into vain discussion, desiring to be teachers of the law, without understanding either what they are saying or the things about which they make confident assertions. Now we know that the law is good, if one uses it lawfully, understanding this, that the law is not laid down for the just but for the lawless and disobedient, for the ungodly and sinners, for the unholy and profane, for those who strike their fathers and mothers, for murderers, the sexually immoral, men who practice homosexuality, enslavers, liars, perjurers, and whatever else is contrary to sound doctrine, in accordance with the gospel of the glory of the blessed God with which I have been entrusted (1 Tim. 1:3-11).

The penalty for homosexuality is death and separation from God for all eternity and is not what God designed for humanity. Several Scriptures make this crystal clear:

> Do you not know that the unrighteous will not inherit the kingdom of God? Do not be deceived. Neither fornicators, nor

idolaters, nor adulterers, nor homosexuals, nor sodomites, nor thieves, nor covetous, nor drunkards, nor revilers, nor extortioners will inherit the kingdom of God. And such were some of you. But you were washed, but you were sanctified, but you were justified in the name of the Lord Jesus and by the Spirit of our God (1 Cor. 6:9-11).

But the cowardly, unbelieving, abominable, murderers, sexually immoral, sorcerers, idolaters, and all liars shall have their part in the lake which burns with fire and brimstone, which is the second death (Rev. 21:8).

Now the works of the flesh are evident: sexual immorality, impurity, sensuality, idolatry, sorcery, enmity, strife, jealousy, fits of anger, rivalries, dissensions, divisions, envy, drunkenness, orgies, and things like these. I warn you, as I warned you before, that those who do such things will not inherit the kingdom of God (Gal. 5:19-21).

Paul, in writing to the saints in Ephesus about Gentiles, states, "You must no longer walk as the Gentiles do, in the futility of their minds. They are darkened in their understanding, alienated from the life of God because of the ignorance that is in them, due to their hardness of heart. They have become callous and have given themselves up to sensuality, greedy to practice every kind of impurity" (Eph. 4:17-19). The heart and the mind in this passage both play a role in the demise of God's original plan for human sexuality. Don't live one more moment in the lie of homosexuality. Pawn the lie and redeem the truth! Then you will live in the sexuality God designed and be satisfied with the gift of sex.

Frequency

One of the most heated sexual topics married couples argue about, both Christian and non-Christian, is frequency! When sex doesn't happen according to God's design, major issues arise, and frequency will be a topic couples fight about and struggle with until the marriage bed is brought back into alignment with Scripture. I address this topic quite frequently in counseling. Women usually say, "He wants sex all the time; it's all he ever thinks about." And men say, "She never wants sex. Every time I try, she pushes me away or ignores me altogether." A dormant marriage bed is unscriptural and toxic. Just as a vacant lot fills with weeds, trash, rats, and eventually becomes a dumping ground for all kinds of things, a marriage without sex wastes away and eventually fills with little foxes and immorality.

A married couple who hasn't had sex for weeks, months, and, tragically, even years, has pawned their marriage bed, surrendered their sexual desire, and is completely out of sync with God's design for sex. In 1 Corinthians 7, God reminds husbands and wives they should fulfill their marital duty and give each other their "conjugal rights,"[79] which are "The sexual rights or privileges implied by and involved in the marriage relationship: the right of sexual intercourse between husband and wife."[80] Husbands and wives should resolutely—with all their hearts, fulfill their conjugal rights by sexually sharing their bodies with one another as a divine act of love and obedience to God.

Before a person gets married, his or her garden and spring is to remain locked, reserved for the covenant of marriage alone. The unmarried individual has the responsibility of protecting, cultivating, and watering the garden. No other person should ever be allowed to visit, look upon, eat of, or drink from the private garden or spring. There should be signs posted all around the garden and spring like, "No Trespassing," "Private Property," "No Entry Allowed," or my favorite, "All Trespassers Will Be Shot!"

When a single person "burns with passion" and feels they no longer can control themselves, Scripture tells them it's time to get married: "To the unmarried and the widows I say that it is good for them to remain single, as I am. But if they cannot exercise self-control, they should marry. For it is better to marry than to burn with passion" (1

Cor. 7:8-9). Once a person marries, his or her body is no longer their own private possession/property. God expects that individual to hand over the garden key to their spouse.

Paul encourages married couples to share their bodies with each other by saying, "Do not deprive one another" (1 Cor. 7:5). However, this is a concession, not a command. Although sex isا God-given right, it should never be demanded or coerced. God designed sex to keep the marriage bed "verdant." Visiting it every few weeks, months, or years is not God's idea of verdant. Unless a medical condition exists, a married couple should strive to fulfill the conjugal rights of their spouse and not deprive that spouse of intimate sexual relations. Conjugal rights belong to the spouse, not the individual!

The frequency of sex varies from couple to couple, and there is no norm, mainly due to the numerous issues related to the health of the marriage bed, the physical health and age of the husband and wife, the emotional intimacy they share, and—the big one—how they view sex. The frequency of sex in marriage is first determined by the health of the marriage bed. If the marriage bed is overrun by "little foxes" (explained further in chapter 5), the couple will experience misplaced sexual desire. For some, a marriage bed overrun by little foxes, e.g., sexually immoral practices, abusive and depraved sexual acts, porn, adultery, and selfishness diminishes sexual desire due to feelings of betrayal, shame, distrust, anger, and outright disgust. A husband or wife hurt by little foxes eventually shuts down emotionally, psychologically, and sexually.

A pure marriage bed, however, enhances sexual desire, increasing frequency and sexual satisfaction. Couples who keep the little foxes at bay, use their spouse as their only sexual outlet, and who honor God with their bodies are much more willing to have sex even when they are tired, upset, or not in the mood. Couples who honor marriage and keep their marriage beds pure also experience holy sex, the sex God designed, which is sustainable, satisfying, and comforting. I say "comforting" because holy and pure sex unites and enhances the

"One-Flesh Covenant," which in turn causes both husband and wife to passionately long for the next sexual union and all the good feelings and euphoric sensations involved.

Second, the frequency of sex is determined by the health and age of the individual. A number of factors contribute to sexual performance and desire, which inevitably affect frequency. Libido[81] is influenced by an array of psychological, social, and biological factors, e.g., stress, relationship issues, work, family, lifestyle, medical conditions, medications, etc. Youth has its advantages. Libido replenishes faster when people are young and in people who work out regularly. Teenagers and young adults can have sex multiple times a day. Older adults, not so much. Although health and age factor into the equation of frequency, proper diet, regular exercise, emotional and psychological health, alcohol consumption, drug use, and low testosterone also enhance or diminish libido.

4 Tips for Improving Libido

1. Healthier lifestyle choices. Improve your diet, get regular exercise and enough sleep, cut down on the alcohol, and reduce stress.
2. Change to a new medication, if the one you're on is affecting your libido.
3. Testosterone replacement therapy.
4. Counseling.[82]

Third, the frequency of sex is determined by the emotional intimacy shared between the couple. Intimacy is not only physical but deeply emotional, and understanding the difference is important in building a verdant and active marriage bed. Just as sex can take place without any emotional intimacy involved (e.g., one-night stands, rape, orgies, etc.) sex can dry up and cease without it. Emotional intimacy, according to Kelli Hastings, "Encompasses the degree of comfort, passion, romance, a feeling of closeness to a partner, and often times focuses on communication or emotional conflicts with a partner or spouse."[83] Within marriage, emotional intimacy is measured by the amount of time a couple spends together laughing, traveling together, hanging out, sharing memories, working out, and even how they show mutual respect to each other when dealing with difficult situations and disagreements.

Regarding the relationship of emotional intimacy to frequency of sexual intercourse, marriage counselor, David Kantor, says,

> The raw sexuality and libido that come naturally with our biological inheritance are small and over time play a decreasing part in sexual intimacy. If that young desire is not replaced with deep sharing and receiving, then you really won't have an intimate life. But every time we connect on a deep level, we feel a need for sexual intimacy.[84]

Emotional intimacy and its effects on frequency should not be underestimated. Gary Rosberg and Barbara Rosberg believe the key to a wife's sexual excitement is a strong connection to her heart, which comes through emotional intimacy:

> One key to a wife's sexual excitement, responsiveness, and ability to initiate sex is a strong connection to her heart. These women feel that their sex lives are satisfying when both partners receive first an emotional and/or spiritual connection and then a physical connection. In other words, when a husband emotionally connects to his wife, he prepares her for sexual intimacy.[85]

The following are five ways to increase emotional intimacy and improve the frequency of sex in both men and women.

5 Ways to Increase Intimacy in Your Relationship

1. **Trust deeply**. Deep love requires deep trust. It is part of what love is to believe that your partner will protect and cherish your heart. In order to build emotional intimacy in your relationship, you must trust your partner wholeheartedly.
2. **Attune to your higher purpose**. Each of you have a particular aspiration that you feel deeply about. When you can combine your dreams together to work toward a mutual goal, you build something together as a couple.
3. **Release negative thinking**. Commit to release the need to be right, the need to control your partner, the need to point out wrongs, and the need to keep score. When you remove these barriers to emotional intimacy in your relationship, you leave only the positive, supportive, and kind emotions to give your partner.
4. **Be present**. The gift of your full attention is a way to increase emotional intimacy in your relationship. When your partner is speaking, give them your full attention. Listen as if they were the most important person in your life, because they are.
5. **Be your best self**. Be accountable for your own emotional health. You cannot give more of yourself to your partner until you have more to give. Focus your energy on becoming your best self and you will have even better emotional intimacy in your relationship.[86]

Fourth, the frequency of sex is determined by the way a husband or wife views sex. A large portion of my *Heart of Sex* seminar focuses on teaching singles and couples the truth about God's design for sex. Just like everything else in the universe, there are pros and cons to every action, including sex. When sex follows God's design, there are pros;

when it doesn't, there are cons. Part of my seminar focuses on tearing down false views, beliefs, ideologies, and assumptions about sex. People who grow up with traditions that teach sex is sinful, dirty, or for procreative purposes only develop mindsets and attitudes about sex contrary to God's design. Sexual assault survivors who never take back their sexuality or receive professional and spiritual help often develop negative views, beliefs, and practices as well, which ends up distorting their view of themselves, men, women, God, and sex.

Sex is a gift God gave humanity to enjoy frequently within the context of marriage and not for procreative purposes solely. After one of my seminars, I emailed a survey to the participants. One of the questions on the survey was, "What is the most significant impact this seminar had on your life and marriage?" One reply I received back was, "It really helped me [to] grasp [that] sex is holy and good within marriage and [that] I don't need to feel any shame." Another was, "Sex is an act of love to my spouse, and a gift to him and me, from God." One of my favorites, and the reason why I teach on sex, was, "It has brought into focus [that] God can clean me of my past sexual sins and make me pure for my spouse now." People who have negative views and false beliefs about sex will naturally avoid having sex, and having sex frequently won't even be up for discussion.

I will now address the elephant in the room and answer the million-dollar question: How often should married couples have sex? Let me pause here for a moment as I know everyone just inhaled deeply. Breathe out slowly; everything will be fine. As stated earlier, there is no norm. The frequency of sex varies and depends on the topics I just mentioned above. I have noticed in counseling though, if a person desires to have sex every day, and/or multiple times a day, or not at all, there are usually deep emotional, psychological, physical, spiritual, and sexual issues needing professional and spiritual help—which is why they are in my office.

I believe couples should have sex at least a couple times a week unless the wife is on her menstrual period.[87] Another important factor affecting frequency is duration. Men who want to "willy-nilly" every night, and drag it out for hours and hours, exhaust their wives and make them feel more like a sex object than a mutual lover, companion, and friend. Don't overindulge—in the long run, it will cost you.

Pornography

The English word *pornography* comes from two Greek words: *porne*, "a harlot," and *graphein*, "to write." Pornography literally means "the writing of a harlot."[88] New Testament authors regularly interpret *porneia* as "sexual immorality." Other versions include "idolatry," "whoredom," and "fornication." Pornography literally means "to surrender or willingly abandon sexual purity." In other words, you willingly pawn your sexuality. This word revolves around the concept of "selling off." Sexual immorality is the "selling off" of sexual purity and includes any type of sexual act forbidden in Scripture.

Other forms of pornographic behavior include visiting strip clubs, porn shops, erotic massage parlors, peep shows, sexual chat rooms, or participating in phone sex or cybersex. Nothing compares to the viewable porn sites easily accessible over the Internet, though. Pornographic magazines are the fifth most discarded item in hotels.[89] Numerous studies on pornography reveal a direct connection with violent crimes, especially rape. A study conducted in Oklahoma County, Oklahoma, reported that as the number of pornography shops closed, the number of rapes went down.[90] A chilling example of the destructive nature and distorted predominance pornography imposes on individuals comes from the firsthand account of a notorious serial killer, Ted Bundy, shortly before he was executed:

> This is the message I want to get across: As a young boy, and I mean a boy of 12 or 13, I encountered . . . in the local grocery store and in the local drug store, . . . pornography that people call 'soft core.' ... I tell you that I am not blaming pornography. I am not saying that it caused me to go out and do

certain things. And I take full responsibility for whatever I've done. . . . That's not the question here. The question and the issue is how this kind of literature contributed and helped mold and shape these kinds of violent behaviors in me. In the beginning it fuels this kind of thought process. Then, at a certain time it's instrumental—I would say crystallizing, making it into something which is almost like a separate entity inside. . . . Once you've become addicted to pornography—and this is a kind of addiction like other kinds of addiction—I would keep looking for more potent, more explicit, more graphic kinds of material . . . you begin to wonder if maybe actually doing it will give you that which is beyond just reading about it or looking at it. . . . I've lived in prison for a long time now and I've met a lot of men who are motivated to commit violence just like me. And without exception, every one of them was deeply involved in pornography—without question, without exception, deeply influenced and consumed by an addiction to pornography.[91]

This story is a chilling example of the power that pornography asserts over individuals. Unfortunately for Ted, it completely destroyed his life and the lives of his victims.

Pornography has no place in the lives of Christians. The Bible says, "Whatever is true, whatever is honorable, whatever is just, whatever is pure, whatever is lovely, whatever is commendable, if there is any excellence, if there is anything worthy of praise, think about these things" (Phil. 4:8). Sadly, reports show a small margin between the sexual behavior of Christians and non-Christians. Kuehne highlights the struggle that Christians continue to have with sexual issues:

George Barna and other social scientists provide abundant evidence concerning the degree to which the sexual revolution has affected the church in terms of the sheer quantity of adultery, fornication, and use of pornography by professing

Christians. Remarkably little difference can be found between the sexual behavior of Christians and that of non-Christians in the United States.[92]

The battle with pornography continues in the lives of Christian singles and married couples. Fortunately, the Bible offer hope. Proverbs 28:13 says, "Whoever conceals their sins does not prosper, but the one who confesses and renounces them finds mercy" (NIV). A vibrant relationship with Christ remains free of relational roadblocks. People addicted to pornography live in continuous cycles of shame and guilt that detour them from the deep wellsprings of love and sexual satisfaction God designed. Hosea warned the people of his time about the dangers of sexual immorality and the captivity it holds over people's hearts: "Harlotry, wine, and new wine enslave the heart" (4:11, NKJV). The same is true today; "enslavement" has just been renamed and labeled "addiction."

Christians must not allow their struggles with porn to define their relationship with Jesus, as Heath Lambert emphasizes:

> The truth that God wants you to know is that your relationship with Jesus is bigger than your struggle with porn. If the only time you're interested in walking with Jesus is when you want his help to get over porn, you're not walking in the fullness of the loving relationship that Jesus wants to have with you.[93]

The heart of sex lies grounded in reality. The airbrushed bodies of young men and women found in pornographic magazines and the degraded images portrayed in pornographic movies keep individuals entranced in a world of fantasy that slowly dilutes the image of God and the meaning of sex God designed for his children.

Oral Sex

The topic of oral sex among Christians continues to highlight the need for a healthy sexual compass. There are a few passages in the Song of Solomon that seem to suggest the lovers are performing oral sex on each other although theologians disagree widely on these passages. Regardless of how you interpret these Scriptures, a person should be sensitive to their spouse with regard to any sexual practices performed during coitus. If any sexual activity leads to feelings of shame, guilt, or dirtiness, then it probably isn't right for that individual, and the feelings of that individual should be respected. Douglas Rosenau declares,

> When the Bible does not directly deal with a behavior like oral sex or masturbation, we turn to other scriptural values to help govern our sexual behaviors. Whether oral sex, using a vibrator, or trying new positions, we are called to be lovingly considerate and wise; never should we do anything that violates our mate's sensibilities or offends our mate's sexually. Our bodies are God's temple and should be treated respectfully and not damaged. We are told to be self-disciplined and balanced, with oral sex or any erotic stimulation never becoming the focus of our whole lovemaking and intimate connecting. Making love is a celebration of our one-flesh companionship and should never be associated simply with orgasm, intercourse, or genital pleasuring.[94]

Ronald L. Conte Jr., a Catholic theologian, groups oral sex with other sexual sins and believes oral sex is evil and immoral. Conte believes oral sex is not unitive or procreative and thus not a part of God's plan for sex:

> Unnatural sexual acts (oral sex, anal sex, and manipulative sex, i.e. masturbation of self or of another) are intrinsically evil and always gravely immoral because these acts are not unitive and procreative. The deprivation of the marital or unitive or procreative meaning from any sexual act causes the moral object to be evil, and the act itself to be inherently immoral. In order to have a good moral object, each and every sexual act must be not only marital, but also unitive, and procreative. Any sexual

act that is non-marital, or non-unitive, or non-procreative is an intrinsically evil act.[95]

Although I agree that every sexual encounter between a wife and husband should be unitive and procreative, there is more to sex than simply having intercourse, which Conte seems to suggest in his statement. Foreplay should always precede intercourse. Kissing, caressing, and genital stimulation are essential in exciting the erogenous zones of both male and female and helps lubricate the vagina and increase blood flow into the penis.

I believed oral sex was a sin for the majority of my life, and it was not until my research for my doctoral project that I changed my view. Several passages in the Song of Solomon seem to allude to the practice of oral sex. One possible reference supporting oral sex comes from chapter 2, verse 3. It says, "With great delight I sat in his shadow, and his fruit was sweet to my taste." In this verse, Solomon stands over the Shulamite and, as she rests in the shadow cast by his stature, she tastes his sweet fruit. Apparently, the two lovers are outside enjoying a beautiful sunny day in the countryside and the Shulamite is performing oral sex on her lover.

Another passage of Scripture addressing oral sex comes a few chapters later:

> A garden locked is my sister, my bride, a spring locked, a fountain sealed. Your shoots are an orchard of pomegranates with all choicest fruits, henna with nard, nard and saffron, calamus and cinnamon, with all trees of frankincense, myrrh and aloes, with all choice spices—a garden fountain, a well of living water, and flowing streams from Lebanon. Awake, O north wind, and come, O south wind! Blow upon my garden, let its spices flow. Let my beloved come to his garden, and eat its choicest fruits. I came to my garden, my sister, my bride, I gathered my myrrh

with my spice, I ate my honeycomb with my honey, I drank my wine with my milk (Song 4:12-5:1).

Gardens, shoots, fountains, springs, and wells are used throughout the Song of Solomon and other parts of the Bible in reference to male and female genitals. Although there are different interpretations on the language used in this passage, statements such as "eat the choice fruits," "blow upon my garden," and "I ate my honeycomb with my honey, I drank my wine with my milk" appear to be colorful language used by the lovers in reference to performing oral sex on each other. The same colorful language is used again in chapter 6:2-3, "My beloved has gone down to his garden to the beds of spices, to graze in the gardens and to gather lilies. I am my beloved's and my beloved is mine; he grazes among the lilies." This passage seems to suggest Solomon is grazing in "his garden" which is the Shulamite's body and enjoying her "spices and lilies."

Even theologians who believe oral sex is permissive in marriage still view oral sex outside of marriage as a trespass of chastity that violates the marriage covenant. Lauren Winner notes that oral sex constitutes a sexual act and is considered a form of fornication:

> Christians recognize, at least intuitively, that oral sex constitutes sex—that if a husband had oral sex with someone other than his wife, he would have committed adultery; and that a single person's having oral sex would constitute a trespass of chastity.[96]

Perhaps one basis of this view is due to the fact that the mouth plays a significant role in sexual affection and intimacy. The Shulamite says, "Let him kiss me with the kisses of his mouth! For your love is better than wine" (Song 1:2). And in 5:16, she says, "His mouth is sweetness itself; he is altogether lovely." In Song of Solomon, "garden" (Heb., *gan*) is used by the lovers to refer to their genitals. *Gan* is figuratively used of a chaste woman or a bride. David Jeremiah encourages men to learn from Solomon's example in the Song:

> Solomon wants to be gentle with a loving but apprehensive bride. As a man with physical drives, he feels a sense of urgency. For her sake, he is soft and soothing with her using words rather than force . . . Speak to your wife in language she understands—loving, appreciative tones—and her own passion will kindle into flame. Approach her selfishly according to your own needs and impulses, and you will drive her away.[97]

Men who follow Solomon's example will earn the trust of—and enhance their sexual encounters with—their wives.

Rosenau believes the passages in the Song of Solomon describe the erotic passions inside the body that fuse "body, emotion, fantasy, and soul."[98] He says,

> Sex is the curious and excited exploration of each other's erogenous zones to create pleasure. We as lovers are to entrust our private parts to our mates, for indeed 'my own vineyard is mine to give,' and we should learn to have no shame or inhibitions with the genital area.[99]

However, a couple should carefully consider before they practice what some refer to as "outer-course." Oral sex is often done in conjunction with other dangerous sexual activity. There are some reported cases of people getting HIV and other viruses from oral sex.[100] If the mouth has any microscopic breaks along the gum line or the cheeks, a virus could theoretically enter.[101]

A married couple should never engage in anything that makes one or both feel shameful, guilty, or dirty. As stated earlier, my view on this topic changed after my research, but my practice of it hasn't. I, regardless of the reason, never felt comfortable performing or receiving oral sex, and I continue to not practice it. At my seminars, there is a lot of time spent on this topic. I encourage couples to discuss this practice, and, if both are comfortable with it, great. However, if one is uncomfortable performing or receiving oral sex, then I suggest the couple stop, as it would cause harm to the marriage bed and would be inconsiderate of the feelings of the one who does not want to engage in the practice.

Positions, Dressing Up, Role Playing, and Pole Dancing

Numerous Christian couples have engaged in some interesting but questionable sexual practices. Some couples dress in costumes, role-play, and try all kinds of positions as ways to spice up their sex life and keep things exciting.[102] But do these added behaviors and accoutrements add to the sexual experience, or do they detract from God's design and purpose for the heart of sex?

When it comes to discussion on positions, it doesn't matter what positions couples choose, as long as they are not degrading, abusive, or humiliating. There are four main positions couples frequently try during intercourse: missionary or face-to-face, spoons or rear entry, side by side or scissors, and standing positions. There are several more, but a trusted sexual compass concerning sexual positions keeps all coital practices from ever resembling any type or form of rape, torture, or masochistic behavior. Paul warns the Ephesians about engaging in any behavior resembling sexual immorality and impurity (Eph. 5:3), and Proverbs says, "The perverse person is an abomination to the LORD" (3:32). Those Scriptures would serve as part of the compass for Christians with respect to this question.

Dressing up, role playing, and pole dancing may seem harmless, and in fact they may be, but there is a difference between these practices and wearing normal lingerie while having fun stimulating each other and keeping sex holy and the marriage bed pure. Holiness and righteousness enhance sexuality. Anamorphic (intentionally distorted) practices of the world degrade the image of God and diminish sexuality and the sexual experience God intended. A Christian should never resemble a harlot or display any type of promiscuous, immoral conduct. The Bible portrays a different image of godly men and women.

In Pavlov's experiment, the dogs were conditioned to things that had nothing to do with food (i.e., bells, lights, and lab coats). The same goes for humans. Numerous husbands and wives dress up, role-play, and engage in a host of other stimulating sexual practices. But in the process, and often unknowingly, they condition their spouse to unholy sexual images that quickly become uncontrollable. Thus, classical conditioning takes over, and the conditioned stimulus (dressing up, role playing) fuels the unconditioned response (a desire to have sex) that God organically designed inside every human being, leaving the individual in a cesspool of erotic emotions they may not have the morals to control.

Therefore, when their spouse sees a nurse (male or female), someone in uniform (military, Catholic boy or girl, police officer, firefighter, etc.) or anyone dressed up like their spouse conditioned them to in their bedroom, they could be automatically triggered. Just like Pavlov's dogs, they may "salivate" with an intense sexual desire. When this happens in a person without a good sexual compass and self-control, they indulge the flesh, which has caused countless marital issues leading to divorce and defilement of the marriage bed.

Regarding the question of the suitability of these types of practices, Boteach recommends that there should be boundaries even when it comes to sexual practices between married couples:

> One might reject the need for any religious guidance or pronouncements on sex in favor of a totally liberal sexual ethic that has no rules or impediments. But a sexual life without rules leads to the debasement and depersonalization of sex, where long-term love and pleasure is replaced by short-term

sensual indulgence that ultimately deadens our sexuality and leads us to treat our own bodies with contempt.[103]

There are numerous sexual practices on which Christians need guidance. A good sexual compass for Christian couples should follow two principles. First, all sexual practices must begin with God's design for the heart of sex. Second, Christian couples must first establish what God allows as they determine what is permissible for them. Ultimately, godliness should be the definitive factor directing the compass needle on all sexual practices regardless of whether or not Scripture addresses the issue.

Fornication

> "Flee from sexual immorality. Every other sin a person commits is outside the body, but the sexually immoral person sins against his own body" (1 Cor. 6:18).

Fornication (sex and sexual practices outside of marriage) is the number one cause of pawned sexuality and greatly alters sexual desire, which will be discussed in chapters 4 and 5. Christian and non-Christian adolescents, teenagers, and adults by the millions sin against their own bodies and enter marriage with polluted sexuality. Satan's best offense has always been to destroy lives as early as possible; destroying a person's sexuality is his favorite deception of them all. The younger that Satan can get to a person, the better, and this is why sexual education is the focus of so many institutions around the world and especially here in America. It is a battle that Christians are losing and one they need to focus all efforts on to conquer and defeat.

Children as early as elementary school age are taught sexual practices, ideologies, and identities contrary to God's design. Pop culture, movies, songs, magazines, public schools, and universities continue to teach and promote false views and ideologies of love and sex. Children, youth, and adults alike are bombarded with mixed and polluted images of love and sex that have no resemblance to the healthy models laid out in Scripture. When teens and adults engage in sex outside of marriage, they pawn their sexuality to a cunning pawn broker who charges an exorbitant price to redeem it. Often, the individual will never again reclaim their pawned sexuality and will boondoggle through life wondering what is wrong with them; they will blame anyone and everyone except themselves and the sin they committed against their own body.

When singles with pawned sexuality enter marriage, they often bring numerous people with them, destroying the marriage bed before it is even established. How? First Corinthians 6:16 says, "Or do you not know that he who is joined to a prostitute becomes one body with her? For, as it is written, 'The two will become one flesh.'" When singles engage in fornication, they become one with that person, and that bond, if not broken, will wreak havoc on the marriage and the marriage bed. The unholy bond also affects sexual desire, which alone destroys marriages and compromises marriage beds—leading to a plethora of sexual frustrations, issues, and problems.

A middle-aged man approached me after one of my presentations at a men's group one night and said, "Dr. Foshee, you wouldn't buy a car without first test driving it, would you?" To stay with his analogy, I promptly replied, "The new car God has planned for you doesn't need a test drive. And besides, if you take the car out and put 20,000 miles on it, you're no longer buying a new car, but a used one." He smiled and said, "Good point." We both had a good chuckle, but, sadly, this analogy is the reality of many Christians and non-Christians alike.

Sexual desire is natural and healthy when experienced within the parameters of Scripture and a person of self-control. When a single person feels they no longer desire to hold back their sexual desire and are ready to explore and release their sexual passions, it is time for that person to marry. The covenant of marriage is the only context in which sexual desire should be explored and released as noted by the Apostle Paul, "Now to the unmarried and widows I say this: It is good for them to remain unmarried, as I am. But if they cannot control themselves, let them marry. For it is better to marry than to burn with passion" (1 Cor. 7:9).

In the story of the prodigal son (Luke 15:11-32), a young lad asks his father for his inheritance. The loving father gives the son his inheritance, and a few days later, the lad embarks on a journey where he squanders every last penny on wild and reckless passions. Broke, hungry, and desperate, the prodigal lands a job feeding swine and soon finds himself longing to feed on the same slop he feeds the pigs. While stuffing his belly with slop, the young man has an epiphany: "My father's hired servants eat better than this." Wisely, he decides to return home, beg for his father's forgiveness and ask for a job as a servant. While still at a distance though, the father sees his son and, in one of the greatest scenes of love, forgiveness, and restoration ever told, the father runs and embraces his son and kisses him. The loving father covers his son in a robe, places a ring on his finger, and shoes on his bare feet. He then orders a fattened calf to be killed and throws a huge feast to celebrate his son's return.

This same story plays out in the lives of millions of teenagers and young adults every day who embark on sexual explorations and engage in sexual acts before they are married. Like the prodigal son, they end up squandering (pawning) their sexuality and spend the rest of their lives "feeding on the slop of pigs." This is the reality of pawned sexuality, and its effects on sexual desire and the marriage bed are astronomical. The story of the prodigal son stands as a warning for everyone desiring to rush into sex unprepared to navigate the turbulent waters of sexual temptations and the immoral practices of society. The prodigal son squandered his inheritance on wild living; even though he finally came to his senses, returned home to his father, and found forgiveness, he still returned home broke with his inheritance plundered. The consequences of his actions would haunt him for years. His older brother who stayed at home with the father never endured the pain, regret, shame, guilt, and consequences of his brother—the prodigal.

The story of the prodigal is in the Bible so that God's children don't have to learn the hard way. The men and women who engage in fornication all end up paying an exorbitant price to redeem it. I did, and thankfully, I finally came to my senses and returned to a Heavenly Father who ran down the road and embraced me. He put a robe around me and a ring on my finger and forgave me of my sexual immorality. This is why I love him so much and is why I want you, the reader, to hear the grace and mercy in this section. Don't feed any longer on the slop of swine and pawned sexuality. Return to God the Father and begin the journey of redemption that so many others are on. Redeemed sexuality will allow you to drink from unpolluted streams and eat from a private garden prepared by God for you and your spouse alone. The God of miracles and redemption eagerly awaits your return.

Adultery

Medusa, according to Greek mythology, was a beautiful mortal woman who had an affair with Poseidon, god of the sea. Jealous of the affair, Athena, Olympian goddess of wisdom and war, cursed Medusa and transformed her into a lethal monster of war. From her feet to her neck, Medusa had a beautifully sculpted body, a body all men greatly desire. Unfortunately, from the head up, her face was hideous, and her hair was venomous snakes that, with one glance, turned people into stone. The adulteress virtually does the same to her victims, as the Bible says:

> Do not lust in your heart for her beauty or let her captivate you with her eyes. For the levy of the prostitute is poverty, and the adulteress preys upon your very life. Can a man embrace fire and his clothes not be burned? Can a man walk on hot coals without scorching his feet? So is he who sleeps with another man's wife; no one who touches her will go unpunished (Prov. 6:25-29).

Larry distinctly remembers the night his heart was ripped apart by adultery:

> I can't remember my exact age, maybe 13, 14 or 15, but I explicitly remember a night that scarred my innocence and broke my heart. My mother was at Mary's house, a close friend she often partied with. It was getting late, and everyone was drunk and in high spirits. Because these parties often lasted late into the night, we slept over a lot and/or vice versa. Her friend had a son and a daughter the same age as me and my sister, so we liked going over to their house and playing. But one night was different than all the rest. It was normal for them to get sloppy drunk and cuss, yell, and fight with each other. There were several times they actually hit each other and had to be pulled apart. It was late one night, and I was lying in bed, but not asleep, when I heard voices outside the window. I got out of bed and opened the curtain to see my mother and some other guy kissing and caressing each other, and—you can imagine what happened next. A child should never be exposed to such an atrocity, but, unfortunately, I was, and that imprinted image still haunts my mind today.

An atrocity indeed. My heart weeps for Larry and others like him who have endured the pain and misery that adultery heaps on individuals, families, children, churches, and society. The Bible describes the adulteress as a woman of great power able to dominate strong and powerful men. Proverbs says, "Do not let your heart turn aside to her ways, do not stray into her paths; For she has cast down many wounded, and all who were slain by her were strong men. Her house is the way to hell, descending to the chambers of death" (7:25-27). The cost of pawning your sexuality and marriage bed to the adulterer/adulteress is high; some will never recover from the catastrophic financial, personal, and sexual consequences left in the aftermath.

In the book of Revelation, John writes a letter to the church in Thyatira. He starts out by commending them for their good deeds, love, and faith but then rebukes them for their tolerance of Jezebel. He says,

> But I have this against you, that you tolerate that woman Jezebel, who calls herself a prophetess and is teaching and seducing my servants to practice sexual immorality and to eat food sacrificed to idols. I gave her time to repent, but she refuses to repent of her sexual immorality. Behold, I will throw her onto a sickbed, and those who commit adultery with her I will throw into great tribulation, unless they repent of her works, and I will strike her children dead. And all the churches will know that I am he who searches mind and heart, and I will give to each of you according to your works (Rev. 2:20-23).

Churches all over the world have welcomed the teachings of Jezebel onto holy ground, allowing lifestyles and sexual practices contrary to God's eternal Word. Unfortunately, men and women by the droves, in an attempt to justify their sexual practices and identities, are flocking to these teachings and pawning their sexuality in record numbers. This should not come as a surprise to Christians, as God, in his omniscience, foretold that sexual sins would continue to increase in the last days.

In the spring of 2019, I visited the city of Constance, Germany. The beauty and grandeur of Constance and its harbor is absolutely breathtaking. Beautiful cathedrals and buildings, trimmed in lush vines and adorned with flamboyant flowers, line a picturesque harbor filled with trade and tourism. Cobblestone streets and alleys crisscross through hundreds of shops, outdoor markets, and restaurants all carrying the smells of freshly baked bread, pastries, and cakes. As I strolled along the waterfront admiring the turquoise waves waltzing with the shore, in the distance I noticed a large risqué silhouette standing guard over the harbor. The silhouette turned out to be a thirty-foot-tall statue of a woman with large bared breasts, belly and crotch exposed, and a long sleek leg flirtatiously bulging from her split dress. The woman's arms were raised in the air and, in the hollows of her hands, as if mounted on a pedestal, she displayed two trophies for all to see. As I drew near, I noticed the two figures were men, both naked. One wore an Imperial Crown and the other a Papal Tiara.

The statue (featured below) is called "Imperia" and lies at the entrance of Lake Constance. It was built by Peter Lenk to commemorate the Council of Constance from 1414-1418. Apparently, the statue refers to a story written by Balzac, suggesting that the adulteress Imperia had successfully seduced and conquered Emperor Sigismund who called the council and corrupted the Papal vote. The other figure in her hand is Pope Martin V, the Pope elected at the council.

Numerous kings, rulers, clergy, individuals, and marriages have fallen to the cunning schemes of the adulterer/adulteress. As Revelation 17:1-7 says:

> Then one of the seven angels who had the seven bowls came and said to me, 'Come, I will show you the judgment of the great prostitute who is seated on many waters, with whom the kings of the earth have committed sexual immorality, and with the wine of whose sexual immorality the dwellers on earth have become drunk.' And he carried me away in the Spirit into a wilderness, and I saw a woman sitting on a scarlet beast that was full of blasphemous names, and it had seven

heads and ten horns. The woman was arrayed in purple and scarlet, and adorned with gold and jewels and pearls, holding in her hand a golden cup full of abominations and the impurities of her sexual immorality. And on her forehead was written a name of mystery: 'Babylon the great, mother of prostitutes and of earth's abominations.' And I saw the woman, drunk with the blood of the saints, the blood of the martyrs of Jesus.

Regardless of whether the statue of Imperia and its story about the Emperor and Pope are true, it does signify the reality of those who commit adultery. The adulteress will flamboyantly display her trophies on Judgment Day and expose every person who drinks from her poisonous and polluted streams. The adulteress will utterly dominate all her victims as she brings them down to the chambers of hell: "Many are the victims she has brought down; her slain are a mighty throng. Her house is a highway to the grave, leading down to the chambers of death" (Prov 7:25-26). God's design for sex protects the marriage bed and honors marriage, forgoing the consequences that adultery and the adulteress levy on all victims both male and female.

I find it quite remarkable that the only reason for divorce in the entire Bible is adultery: "And I say to you: whoever divorces his wife, except for sexual immorality, and marries another, commits adultery" (Matt. 19:9).

In Job 31, Job makes a covenant with his eyes to never look upon a woman lustfully. Adultery usually begins with the eyes and is why in Proverbs 6:25, God says, "Do not lust after her beauty in your heart, and do not let her capture you with her eyelashes." Jesus said in Matthew 5:27-30,

> You have heard that it was said, 'You shall not commit adultery.' But I tell you that anyone who looks at a woman lustfully has already committed adultery with her in his heart. If your right eye causes you to stumble, gouge it out and throw it away.

It is better for you to lose one part of your body than for your whole body to be thrown into hell. And if your right hand causes you to stumble, cut it off and throw it away. It is better for you to lose one part of your body than for your whole body to go into hell.

I received an email one day from a married couple who attended one of my seminars wanting to set up an appointment. I did not know exactly what they wanted to discuss, but I presumed it was with regard to sex and the marriage bed. I met with the couple about a week later in my office. The husband and wife walked into my office and sat down. I greeted them and began with some informalities. I explained my level of confidentiality and then said, "So what's going on? What would you like to discuss today?" The wife immediately looked at her husband, who immediately looked at the floor. After several seconds of complete silence, the wife looked back at me and said, "Well, after your conference, we got in the car and were on our way home. While driving home, I said, 'That was so good. I have never heard anything like that and can't wait to get home and discuss . . .' when, all of a sudden, John[104] started crying. Go ahead John, tell him what you told me."

As John cried in my office, I just waited, and silence once again descended upon the session. John finally broke the silence and said, "During your conference, when you spoke on adultery, the Holy Spirit spoke to me, and as we were driving home, I knew I had to tell her—I just couldn't hold it in any longer. About two years ago, while on deployment, I had an affair with a girl on the ship. I knew it was wrong, and it has been tearing me apart ever since. As soon as you spoke on it and I heard the Holy Spirit speak to me, I knew now was the time to finally tell her."

The affair had kept John in a perpetual state of pawn and if he hadn't confessed and sought out professional counseling, both personally and with his wife, the marriage would have most certainly been destroyed. Fortunately, at the opportune time, the Holy Spirit, through my seminar, spoke to John, who finally obeyed, confessed, and found mercy from a loving and patient God—and wife. Proverbs 28:13 says, "Whoever conceals his transgressions will not prosper, but he who confesses and forsakes them will obtain mercy." John received mercy, and, I can happily announce, as I write this section (in 2020), this couple is still married and doing great. I am so proud of them.

Another passage in Proverbs highlighting the adulteress and the consequences left in the aftermath of adultery comes from chapter 5:5-14 (NKJV), saying,

> Her feet go down to death, her steps lay hold of hell. Lest you ponder her path of life—Her ways are unstable; You do not know them. Therefore, hear me now, my children, and do not depart from the words of my mouth. Remove your way far from her, and do not go near the door of her house, lest you give your honor to others, and your years to the cruel one; Lest aliens be filled with your wealth, and your labors go to the house of a foreigner; And you mourn at last, when your flesh and your body are consumed, and say: 'How I have hated instruction, and my heart despised correction! I have not obeyed the voice of my teachers, nor inclined my ear to those who instructed me! I was on the verge of total ruin, in the midst of the assembly and congregation.'

John heeded the instruction and correction I gave at my seminar and obeyed the voice of the Holy Spirit, thus restoring his honor and stopping the 'aliens' and 'little foxes' from stealing the bounty of his marriage bed. In other words, John redeemed his sexuality and marriage bed from pawn.

For all those reading my book right now whose sexuality and marriage bed have been pawned to adultery, I pray you hear the Holy

Spirit speak to you now. Confess and forsake your sin so you can find mercy and redeem your sexuality and marriage bed. Find a Christian counselor and start to piece your life and marriage back together. Trust can be restored, and your gardens and streams unblocked to flow naturally again the way God designed. If you don't, your sexual desire will be misplaced, and you will suffer all the consequences of adultery God lays out throughout the Bible.

As I close this section, I leave you with two powerful Scriptures as you move forward in life whether single or married. The first comes from Proverbs 5:1-4:

> My son, be attentive to my wisdom; incline your ear to my understanding, that you may keep discretion, and your lips may guard knowledge. For the lips of a forbidden woman drip honey, and her speech is smoother than oil, but in the end, she is bitter as wormwood, sharp as a two-edged sword.

The second comes from Psalm 128:1-4:

> Blessed is everyone who fears the LORD, who walks in His ways. When you eat the labor of your hands, you shall be happy, and it shall be well with you. Your wife shall be like a fruitful vine in the very heart of your house, your children like olive plants all around your table. Behold, thus shall the man be blessed who fears the LORD.

Medusa, Jezebel, and the adulterer/adulteress all lurk in the shadows, desiring you to pawn your sexuality and marriage bed. They desire to dominate you, steal your inheritance, and feed upon your soul for all eternity. "The wicked have set a snare for me, but I have not strayed from your precepts" (Ps 119:110, NIV). Don't get turned to stone. Follow the sexual compass found throughout the Scriptures and the one I give throughout this book. Enjoy the wells, streams, shoots, and gardens God gave you. Protect your marriage bed at all costs and stay off all paths leading to the adulterer/adulteress. Don't become a trophy put on display for all to see, and don't allow Jezebel to occupy holy ground. Cast the lies out of your church and start preaching and teaching the truth!

Cybersex

Cybersex always comes up at my seminars and is a hot topic among the crowd. "Dr. Foshee, is it okay to have cybersex with my spouse while on deployment or a business trip?" I believe this question is answered in Proverbs, and thus this section will be short and to the point. Proverbs 5:15-19 says:

> Drink water from your own cistern, flowing water from your own well. Should your springs be scattered abroad, streams of water in the streets? Let them be for yourself alone, and not for strangers with you. Let your fountain be blessed, and rejoice in the wife of your youth, a lovely deer, a graceful doe. Let her breasts fill you at all times with delight; be intoxicated always in her love.

In this passage, God reminds wives and husbands their "springs/streams of water" should never be "scattered abroad and flow in the streets" to be drunk and polluted by strangers. Although there are numerous advantages to technology, there are also disadvantages and extreme dangers as we see with the millions of men and women addicted to porn.

Today, smartphones, computers, watches, iPads, and cameras are all connected to the Internet, and the information on them, including all pictures and videos, can be hacked into and viewed by strangers. Although a married couple may think cybersex is a way to satisfy sexual desire while apart, nothing is private about the Internet. Thus, a married couple who uses technological devices to fulfill their sexual desires—even if the person on the other end is their spouse—has "scattered abroad their springs and streams of water" into the "street" for strangers to drink and pollute.

Numerous wives innocently think cybersex is a way to keep their husbands from committing adultery and to fulfill his sexual desires only to find out they have opened the door to pornography, which a lot of husbands find much more satisfying than masturbating to their wives over Skype, Messenger, WhatsApp, Zoom and other video apps. In chapters 4 and 5, I will explain the benefits of having only one sexual outlet, which means a married couple should never do anything sexual without the other being present.

I encourage married couples to stop participating in cybersex, taking nude photos of themselves, and to instead practice self-control. This will allow their libido to build up and be released only to their spouse during sex. People who practice self-control and have no other sexual outlet other than their spouse—and this goes for singles as well—will experience sustained sexual satisfaction more than those who spill their "springs and streams of water" into the streets to be polluted by strangers. I call this a "sexual fast." Couples who practice sexual fasts when away from each other will experience sustained sexual satisfaction more than couples who engage in cybersex and send nude photos of themselves for all the world to see. Remember, once you send a photo or video over the Internet, you can never get it back, and it could be viewed by millions of people around the world.

4

SEXUAL DESIRE: WOMEN

"He will fulfill the desire of those who fear Him; He also will hear their cry and save them" (Ps. 145:19, NKJV).

Concupiscence

Although some theologians believe concupiscence[105] is a sin, sexual desire in and of itself is not. As with most things, it depends on the context. Everyone post-puberty should have a natural sexual desire that they diligently work to understand and rule. Christians must learn to safeguard its positives, set boundaries for its dangers, and unbridle its passions only within the covenant of marriage, as the Shulamite suggests with love: "do not stir up nor awaken love until it pleases" (Song 2:7c, NKJV). Once love is stirred up or awakened, a natural stream of sexual desire will accompany, as Proverbs 5:19 says: "a lovely deer, a graceful doe. Let her breasts fill you (satisfy you) at all times with delight; be intoxicated always in her love." Different versions of the Bible translate "intoxicated" as "captivated, exhilarated, enraptured, and ravished." Married couples should naturally desire sexual relations with each other and have sex regularly.[106]

Singles should, once love has been awakened, naturally be drawn to the opposite sex and sexually desire their lover.[107]

Paul, in his address to the Corinthians, encourages singles and those widowed to remain unmarried, but if their natural sexual desire—what he calls "passion/to burn"—becomes "uncontrollable," i.e., if they "cannot control themselves," he encourages them to marry.[108] Why? Because the covenant of marriage is the conduit God established to satisfy and quench the sexual desires men and women naturally have. A scriptural example of sexually desiring someone is Solomon's passionate discourse with the Shulamite:

> A garden locked is my sister, my bride, a spring locked, a fountain sealed. Your shoots are an orchard of pomegranates with all choicest fruits, henna with nard, nard and saffron, calamus and cinnamon, with all trees of frankincense, myrrh and aloes, with all choice spices—a garden fountain, a well of living water, and flowing streams from Lebanon (Song 4:12-15).

A prominent sexual reference from this passage is "a spring locked," "a fountain sealed." These two water symbols are a direct reference and testimony to virginity. God desires that women and men remain virgins until they get married; thus, from the onset of the one-flesh union, innocent, pure, and holy vessels embark on an adventure together to explore and discover the beautiful and wonderful gift of sex God created.

Unfortunately, numerous couples pawn their sexuality prior to entering the covenant of marriage by becoming one flesh with multiple sexual partners,[109] which greatly affects sexual desire and causes significant problems that, without intervention, can end up destroying the marriage. Sex outside of marriage (fornication) is a sin, and sexual sins are the most devastating sins to the physical body as revealed in Corinthians: "Flee from sexual immorality. Every other sin a person commits is outside the body, but the sexually immoral person sins against his own body" (1 Cor. 6:18). Sin against the body corrupts, defiles, taints, and degrades. In other words, sin pawns the body, diminishing how individuals view the image of God they are responsible to keep holy.

For Christians, a sin against their body is a sin against the house of God and is why God instructs his children to seek wisdom regardless of the cost:

> Get wisdom, get understanding; do not forget my words or swerve from them. Do not forsake wisdom, and she will protect you; love her, and she will watch over you. Wisdom is supreme; therefore get wisdom. Though it cost all you have, get understanding (Prov. 4:5-7, NIV).

And again, with regard to wisdom, Scripture says, "But he who fails to find me harms himself; all who hate me love death" (Prov. 8:36). Sexual sins and pawned sexuality leave individuals laden with shame and guilt. This can cause wives and husbands to reject the sexual advances of their spouse, sparking a series of issues and arguments as chapter 3 discussed in the section, "Frequency."

I have heard the same complaint out of several couples during counseling. They say, "Before we got married, she/he wanted sex all the time, but now, she/he never wants it." This scenario plays out every day all around the world in both Christian and non-Christian marriages and often is a result of pawned sexuality, sin, or untreated sexual trauma/abuse. Sometimes it is a result of medical conditions, spiritual injury, or psychological issues, but often, it is the latter.[110] However, sometimes it is a direct result of the fall of Adam and Eve and the consequences that followed.

Sexual desire is one of the most wonderful, powerful, and intense desires a person will ever experience and is why God establishes boundaries for it. The tenth commandment says,

> You shall not covet your neighbor's wife. You shall not set your desire [Heb., *chamad*, "to delight in, covet, lust"[111]] on your

neighbor's house or land, his manservant or maidservant, his ox or donkey, or anything that belongs to your neighbor (Deut. 5:21).

In Galatians, God warns followers about the dangers of desire(s) or lust(s) of the flesh: "But I say, walk by the Spirit, and you will not gratify the desires [Gk., *epithumia*, 'a longing,' especially for what is forbidden, concupiscence[112]] of the flesh" (Gal 5:16). Ecclesiastes 6:9 says, "Better is the sight of the eyes than the wandering of desire [Heb., *nephesh*, from *naphash*, 'a breathing, to breathe'[113]]." This passage, although not directly referencing sex, does highlight the need to tether "wandering of desire," which is fantasy, and enjoy the real, touchable, tasteful, and physical things in life.

I reference this passage here as a reminder to wives and husbands: God wants you to be content with each other and enjoy the real and sustainable sexual relationship he instructs married couples to have[114] and never set foot on the path of fantasy or the virtual realms of porn and cybersex. This verse is also a prelude to what Solomon says in Song of Songs to his bride as he vividly describes her body and the sexual plan he desires to perform with her:

> How beautiful you are and how pleasing, O love, with your delights! Your stature is like that of the palm, and your breasts like clusters of fruit. I said, 'I will climb the palm tree; I will take hold of its fruit.' May your breasts be like the clusters of the vine, the fragrance of your breath like apples, and your mouth like the best wine (7:6-9).

And how does the Shulamite respond to his sexual innuendos? She acknowledges and welcomes his sexual advance and passionately reciprocates: "May the wine go straight to my lover, flowing gently over lips and teeth. I belong to my lover, and his desire is for me" (Song 7:10). She is delighted in the fact that her lover's desire is for her—a key factor in sustained sexual satisfaction in marriage. When the wife is the husband's only sexual outlet, wives are much more willing to open wide their wonderful "fountains, wells, and streams," to satisfy and quench their husband's sexual desires.[115] Women—can I get an AMEN! So what factor has the fall of Adam and Eve played on woman's desire?

Dominion

Most people around the world have heard the story of *Romeo and Juliet*, written by William Shakespeare. As the tragedy unfolds, Romeo falls in love with Juliet and sneaks into the orchard where he overhears Juliet pledging her love to him. Romeo, the prince in shining armor, climbs the rose-covered lattice without any regard for the danger to his own life. At the top, the lovers embrace and passionately kiss. Secretly, they marry and consummate the marriage the next day. Unaware of the hidden marriage, Juliet's father plans to give her in marriage to Count Paris, but Juliet refuses. The story ironically ends in a tomb with all three characters dead—thus, the tragedy of the story. Numerous theatrical plays reenact this famous occurrence in what is known as the "Balcony Scene."

Countless stories like Romeo and Juliet have circulated since the fall. Herein lies a tragedy and a mystery. Why is it always the prince/knight in shining armor who rescues the damsel in distress and *then* they live happily ever after? Where is the princess in shiny armor who courageously scales mountains, fords croc-infested rivers, battles dragons, beasts, thieves, and robbers, all the while facing the perils of Mother Nature just to rescue her lover—a peasant man locked away in some dark dungeon by an evil Queen?[116] It's because of the fall, that's why. The fall of Adam and Eve altered God's original purpose and place in the world, and the family, for women. Let me explain.

Before the fall, God allocated equal dominion to women, a fifty-fifty mutual partnership in governing the fish of the sea, the birds of the heavens, and every living thing on earth (Gen. 1:28). Notice the three-dimensional and mutual sovereignty women shared with men: supremacy over all of the heavens—the sky; all of the sea—the water; and over all of the earth—the land.

Next, there was unity, community, and fellowship with the serpent. The serpent's seed (offspring, children) and the seed of women lived in perfect harmony[117] as they worked toward mutual civility. Happiness and peace radiated like powerful sunrays from every woman's heart and mind as joyous celebrations accompanied the conception of every baby girl and boy. Birthing was as tranquil as water flowing from a calm natural spring; minimal vaginal pain; minimal abdominal discomfort; and no days and weeks of recovery. And, above all else, the most important and prominent attribute of woman before the fall was her desire to have dominion over the earth![118] The admonishments of the fall had residual and incessant effects on women, especially with the topic of sexual desire.

The Mystery of the Fall of Adam and Eve

The desire for more knowledge, and thus perpetually "more power/dominion," has enticed countless men and women to embark on precarious endeavors they inevitably regret. Knowledge is power, and although there are numerous passages throughout the Bible that encourage the quest and attainment of wisdom, there remains a substantial difference between wisdom (the ability to judge and make right choices) and knowledge (the collection of information). It was the lure of knowledge, not wisdom, that caused Eve to disobey God: The serpent dangled it before her like the notorious "carrot before the horse" metaphor. The serpent said, "For God knows that when you eat of it your eyes will be opened, and you will be like God, knowing good and evil" (Gen. 3:5).

Bedazzled by a carrot of knowledge and divinity, Eve pawned herself, her husband, and humanity. And for what? The meager possibility of acquiring more knowledge and the superfluous notion that she could be like God. Subsequently, the lack of wisdom had equal and imminent consequences for the serpent, which the Bible describes as more "cunning, crafty, sensible," than all the other animals. Satan easily deceived the serpent, thus causing its demise and accursed transformation. If gaining wisdom would have been Eve's and the serpent's desire, there would be no need for this book or for the Cross.

So what is the mystery of the fall for women? God said to Eve, "I will greatly multiply your sorrow and your conception; in pain you shall bring forth children. Your desire shall be for your husband, and he shall rule over you" (Gen. 3:16, NKJV). Two chapters before, in Genesis 1:28, God blesses Adam and Eve and bequeaths absolute dominion and blessings to both of them. However, Adam and Eve, in one selfish and foolish moment, received God's scourge, and for Eve, there were three aspects of the admonishments of the fall that had lasting sexual consequences on her and all women.

Conception Sorrow

First, God said, "I will greatly multiply your sorrow and your conception." Theologians and scholars usually bypass this important aspect of the admonishments of the fall and lump it together with the second part of the admonishments—an increase of pain during childbirth. However, I believe the multiplication of sorrow and conception is the first part of the four-part admonishments. The increase of pain during childbirth is the second part of the admonishments of the fall and deals with the end result of conception which is delivery of the infant. The first part of the admonishment deals with the first part of pregnancy, which is conception and this aspect of the fall has caused severe consequences for females and is ever present throughout the world still today.

Before the admonishment of "sorrow and thy conception" (Gen. 3:16, KJV), every conception was celebrated for the wonderful miracle of life it is. The sex and gender of the infant was insignificant compared to the joyous news of the newly discovered infant incubating within the womb.[119] After the admonishment, this changed. Now there are countless instances of couples, societies, and entire nations displaying sorrow at the news of the conception of a baby girl. Because of Eve's disobedience, the admonishment of "sorrow and '*thy*' conception," drastically shifted humanity's attitude and view of females. This new attitude and view of females caused suffering of epic proportions, incomparable throughout all recorded history.

Since that moment, females have suffered immeasurable and catastrophic consequences: they have been denied countless rights, pay, and privileges; they've been aborted, abandoned, sold, traded, sex trafficked, sacrificed, devalued, dishonored, neglected, and mistreated in every way imaginable—and the list goes on and on and on.

The effects of the first part of the admonishment also caused women to feel intellectually, physically, psychologically, and sexually inferior to men. It diminished their view of themselves, causing them to feel less attractive, sparking a constant pursuit of recognition, attention, and beauty (e.g., lotions, jewelry, makeup, clothes, shoes, hair styles, treatments, surgery, injections, implants, etc.). And now, with their "desire for dominion" taken from them and transferred to their husbands, they now long for the attention, approval, and affection of their husbands, contrary to God's original design. The serpent took advantage of the admonishments of the fall and used it to bruise the woman.

The Serpent's Thorn

Second, God said, "Your desire shall be for your husband and he shall rule over you." Now we come to the sexual mystery of the admonishments of the fall. As discussed above, I believe woman's prominent desire before the fall was for dominion, but after the fall, God transferred/shifted/supplanted her desire to her husband. I've already listed a few outcomes about feelings and the pursuit of attention, recognition, and beauty, so I will now address the sexual effects it had for females—the reason I wrote this entire chapter was for this single discovery.

I have counseled several thousand individuals and couples over the course of my life. I have also interviewed a variety of men and women, both Christian and non-Christian, about the topic of sexual desire and sex. I ask them, "When you think of having sex with your spouse, what comes to mind—how do you envision it? In other words, describe the event in detail." Without hesitation, a normal response I get from men sounds something like this, "I go into the bedroom, I start kissing her and touching her breasts. I undress her and kiss her all over her body—'I usually get a good laugh right here,' and I massage her vagina, and then I have sex with her, and yeah, something like that." Sometimes there are less details, sometimes more, but I think you get the point here.

For women, I get a similar account, but a completely different personal pronoun is used. The typical response I get from women goes something like this, "It depends if it is in the day or at night. In the day, he comes home, and he starts touching me, rubbing my shoulders, arms, and squeezing my bottom. He starts kissing me, and you know, letting me know he wants sex. Then we go to the bedroom, or maybe it just happens right there, but he starts to undress me, kiss me, and then we have sex. If it is at night when I am in the bed, he starts kissing me, rubbing me all over, touching my arms, breast, and butt. He then takes my clothes off and continues kissing me all over and touching me, and then we have sex."

Sound familiar? Although these two accounts may sound similar, this is a monumental and underlying effect of the fall undetected for centuries. I have never read or heard any other scholar or theologian discuss this observation of the fall and the way women view the sexual encounter. The use of the personal pronoun "he," which I believe is a result of the admonishments of the fall, is the direct and leading cause of several sexual issues within marriage leading to sexual frustration, dissatisfaction, adultery, sexually immoral behaviors, divorce, and the loss or lack of sexual desire. I have named this effect *The Serpent's Thorn*.

The Serpent's Thorn affects married women in three key areas, as seen in Genesis 3:16:

1. It alters their view of themselves and their place in society—"I will greatly multiply your sorrow and conception."
2. It supplants their sexual desire and needs—"Your desire will be for your husband."
3. It diminishes their desire for dominion—"And he shall rule over you."

Because men still have the command from God to "have dominion over the earth," sex is about what they get out of it or give, thus they typically use the personal pronoun "I" in their normal description of a sexual encounter. Likewise, and because of the admonishment of "your desire will be for your husband," women predominantly use the pronoun "he" in their descriptions. So what's the big deal, right? What does this mean, and what does it have to do with sex and, most importantly, sexual desire?

When women lost their place of authority and God shifted their desire to their husbands, not only did the world view them differently, but women viewed themselves differently, thus creating *The Serpent's Thorn* effect. Numerous authors bypass this effect of the fall and tell us the difference between men and women is because *Men Are from Mars, Women Are from Venus;* or *Men Are Like Waffles, Women Are Like Spaghetti;* or, they have different needs: *His Needs, Her Needs*, which can have unintended negative effects. Dr. James Mallory says,

> Some self-help books and marriage conferences have had a destructive effect on male-female relationships by giving women's needs and characteristics a higher priority than those of men. The female needs for communication, intimacy, encouragement, and nurture seem much more laudable than male needs to achieve, compete, feel strong, be respected, and have impulsive sexual needs met.

This bias toward the importance of women's needs may cause men to think they can never satisfy her need for closeness with its requirement of in-depth communication and intimacy that makes them uncomfortable. Such a bias may also cause women to believe that a man's needs, interests, and goals are childish, selfish, and superficial; and she may simply humor him, manipulate him, or belittle him.[120]

Other authors list all the ways the brains of women are different from men and how women and many theologians, scholars, and professionals go into great detail about all the other differences there are between men and women. However, they fail to take into account the residual and imminent effects of the fall still affecting women and men today.

Just as Paul's thorn was a constant source of agony that he wholeheartedly begged God to remove, *The Serpent's Thorn* is a constant reminder for women of the residual effects of the fall. Before the fall, Eve and Adam sexually pursued one another in an effort to rule over their sexual desire and needs, and this explains why single women, who have yet to come under the admonishment of "your desire will be for your husband," equally pursue men as men pursue them and do everything they can to win the attention, affection, and heart of their lover. And if the unmarried couple engages in fornication, the woman often and equally initiates the advances—something men love because it makes them feel confident, desired, wanted, etc.

However, once the couple marries, the woman comes under parts one, three, and four of the admonishments of the fall and begins to experience the effects of *The Serpent's Thorn*. Ironically, they end up in my office weeks, months, or years later saying, "But she wanted sex all the time before we got married," or the wife saying, "All he ever wants is sex." This is the effect that *The Serpent's Thorn* continues to have on married women, and because this discovery has been overlooked for centuries, it has led countless men and women to turn to sexual outlets other than their spouse. And when men or women have other sexual outlets other than their spouse, the marriage quickly falls apart.

There will, of course, be women who disagree with me on this topic and state they have no such feelings or thoughts, i.e. that they are physically, intellectually, psychologically, mentally, or sexually inferior or that their sexual desire has lessened since they got married; thus, I submit four theories why. First, at some point in their life, they pawned their sexuality and have yet to redeem it. Second, at some point in their life, someone trespassed and stole their sexuality, and they have never triumphantly taken it back. Third, they grew up in a home or religious tradition that taught sex is bad or sinful, and they learned early in life to repress all sexual feelings—in other words, they classically conditioned themselves. Fourth, women who remained virgins until they were married and have kept and maintained a pure marriage bed experience a purified sexual desire unlike all others. They did not "sin against their own body" (1 Cor. 6:18) and thus bypassed the consequences of sin that so many others endure. Even though they are susceptible to *The Serpent's Thorn* and the admonishments of the fall, the effects of both are minimal.

Obedience

God punished Eve because of her disobedience, and her punishment came in the form of admonishments as listed in Genesis 1:16. As with other forms of punishment, though, women and men have a long record of not obeying the punishments, rules, or restrictions imposed by God, parents, or anyone else in authority for that matter. Think about it: How many times did you get in trouble by your parents, and they implemented some form of punishment that, at the first opportunity, you did not obey? I am not pointing any fingers here because I, too, am guilty as charged. I am, however, making a point that God does expect women/wives to be obedient to his reprimands listed in the "admonishments of the fall."

The point here is that numerous women do not obey the instructions God put forth in the admonishments of the fall to Eve. Some women refuse to let/allow their husbands to rule over them. This is why Paul instructs wives to submit to their husbands.[121] God did not tell Adam to rule over Eve, nor did he tell men to rule over women—in Genesis 3:16,[122] he told Eve/women that her/their husbands would rule over them, which was God's way of saying to Eve/women, "Eve/women, you now need to submit to your husband. You are no longer to share fifty-fifty rule with him." Women most certainly have free will to disobey God and try to evade the consequences of the fall. Of course, like anything else, there are exceptions to this, especially in homes where husbands refuse to "rule" their homes or serve as "head of the house." In these instances, wives are innocent, and their husbands will have to answer to God for their blatant disobedience to his instructions.

When a wife obeys God's admonishments and submits to her husband and allows him to rule over her, and when the husband, in obedience to God, assumes his role as the "head" of woman, and if he rules over his wife and home in love, humility, grace, and wisdom, there are minimal effects, if any, of the fall because the admonishments are rendered powerless, ineffective, and/or non-applicable. Why? Because "love covers over a multitude of sin,"[123] and the love of a husband and wife, who live in obedience to God's admonishments, limit the effects of the fall just as Jesus's love limited the effects of sin, and the law, on the Cross.

In summary, women were and are created in the image of God. They were created to have equal share in ruling over the sky, water, land, and everything in and upon them. Because of sin, though, women came under a four-part admonishment altering the way they viewed themselves and the way society viewed them, and women have suffered enormous consequences ever since. Dr. Mallory believes the fall also caused men and women to develop adversarial relationships which caused changes in the brains of both men and women.

Dr. Mallory says, "Men and women need each other to balance their strengths, to compensate for their weaknesses, and to experience more completeness. However, due to our fallenness, we develop adversarial rather than complementary relationships."[124]

Thus, at the beginning and before the fall, women were physically, intellectually, sexually, and psychologically equal to men. Today, however, and because of the way women view themselves and societal attitudes toward them, refined differences are now noticeable in women than men in these areas. It was through the process of the admonishments that women began to use different parts of their brains; this is now viewable and quantifiable through research and studies on the brains, that they appear to be different from those of men. It is through the process of the admonishments that women have refined sexual, emotional, physical, and psychological needs.[125]

Women were not created different than men in these areas! The admonishments of the fall altered women's views and attitudes of themselves and their place in the family, society, and the world, but praise be to God, there is hope. Women who realize the effects of the fall, the effects that *The Serpent's Thorn* has on sexual desire, who submit to the admonishments, and who honor marriage and keep their marriage beds pure, can redeem their sexuality, and suffer minimal effects of the fall.

Thriving under the Fall of Adam and Eve

There are endless examples of women who live in obedience to the admonishments of the fall and have redeemed their sexuality and now experience the most lovely, harmonic, and blessed marriages in the world. Living under and in obedience to God's admonishments does not mean that a woman has to suffer. On the contrary, women who live in obedience to the admonishments experience increase, favor, blessings, and sustained sexual happiness and fulfillment much more than those who live in disobedience. God's admonishments to Adam caused the ground to produce thorns and thistles, and only by painful toil and the sweat of his brow was Adam allowed to eat of its bounty.

The fall may have altered sexual desire in women, but it doesn't stop them from enjoying the bounty of sex. Women need to realize the effects of the fall on their sexual desire, and by the sweat of their brow and by painful toil, work diligently to limit its effects in their lives and on their marriage beds. Your sexual desire can return, your "shoots, fruits, wells, gardens, and fountains" can satisfy your husband and quench his sexual desires, and his can quench yours as well.

My desire in writing this chapter is fivefold:

1. Make women aware of how the fall affects their sexual desire.
2. Remind women they are created in the image of God and are fearfully and wonderfully made.
3. Remind women that their beauty, value, confidence, meaning, and purpose comes from God and God alone.
4. Convince women they are not inferior to men in any way whatsoever: not physically, intellectually, psychologically, mentally, or sexually.
5. My desire in writing this section was to divulge the ultimate secret of men: Women, we need you! We need you by our side, helping us lead our marriage, our children, and our community. We need your prayers, supplications, and intercessions. We need you to complete God's plans for this world and our lives. And most importantly, we need your love, your affection, your support, your trust, and your sexual desire—we need you to pursue us sexually the way we pursue you. We need you to drop the personal pronoun "he," and take up "I." We need to feel handsome, valued, appreciated, strong, and we need to feel sexually desired.

If I were Doctor Seuss, I would have written point 5 as such:

> Men need to be sexually desired
> in the morn and most INDUBITABLY at night.

Whether wiry or plump, a midget or a giant.
Whether an artist or a lawyer, a preacher or Tom Sawyer;
Whether a prince or a pauper, a romantic or a scoffer.
Men most INDUBITABLY need women as women need men,
and most certainly and ALWAYS…
with a VERY BIG GRIN!

Women, when you realize the significance of this section and the discoveries within, when you meditate on the effects of *The Serpent's Thorn*, and when you live in obedience to the admonishments of the fall, your marriage, your view and attitude of yourself, your sexual desire, and your sexual satisfaction will forever be transformed. You have the power to render the effects of the fall powerless, which starts by honoring marriage and keeping your marriage bed pure.

4 Tips for Women to Enhance Their Husband's Sexual Satisfaction

Take the lead and initiate sex and physical touch more often. This will make him feel pursued, wanted, and desired. It's how he felt when you first met!

Change the "He" to "I." Think about what you will give during sex and the joy you will receive.

Let him see you naked more often. Don't let him know you are doing it on purpose, but let him see you naked, especially your breasts.

Speak openly with him about sex. What he does that you like, and most importantly, what he does that you don't like. Anything that makes you feel shameful, dirty, or guilty needs to stop immediately. This will allow you to accept his advances more often because you will trust him with your body. A win-win for both!

5

SEXUAL DESIRE: MEN

"For where your treasure is, there your heart will be also" (Matt. 6:21).

SEAL Team FOUR

One of the greatest honors and assignments in my life was serving as the Command Chaplain to Naval Special Warfare Group TWO. Although I had oversight of SEAL teams TWO, FOUR, EIGHT, and TEN, I personally served SEAL Team FOUR. I served with SEAL Team FOUR from 2017 to 2019 and traveled extensively all over the world visiting them during training exercises and deployment. This by far was my most challenging tour, mainly because of the time I spent away from my family and the dangerous places I visited during deployment.

The United States Navy SEALs are, without question, the premier war fighters of the world. I have never served with more disciplined, team-oriented, educated, tactical, and strategically minded professionals in all my years. Navy SEALs are committed to vanquishing evil, protecting the innocent, defending the Constitution, and serving their country with honor, courage, and excellence. When everyone else runs away from bombs, bullets, and danger, Navy SEALs charge headlong into suppressant fire to defeat the enemy, at all costs, and all without any regard for the dangers to their own lives.

When I first checked into the command, I was nervous, as I didn't know what to expect or how they would act toward an outsider—especially a chaplain.

The few times I had been around SEALs, though, I did notice they were mostly type A personalities, very self-confident, avid learners, and they loved to work hard and play hard.

So I knew I needed an edge. I needed to, like an Alpha dog, walk in, mark my territory, announce my arrival, and stake my ground. At the very first meeting, I stood up and said, "I'm Gary (SEALs go by their first name). I spent four years as a grunt marine in the early '90s. I have been a chaplain now for twelve years. I just finished my doctorate last summer, and I specialize in sex. I am 'The Most Sexually Satisfied Man on Earth,' and if you would like to talk, I will be here for the next two years." Then I sat down. The CO looked around the room, smiled, and said, "All right, thanks Chaps." And that was that. I became part of the team and ran, swam, skied, trained, sweat, froze, and deployed with them. I spent numerous hours counseling single and married SEALs about life, marriage, death, killing, stress, relationships, and, last but not least, sex.

I had ample time to study SEALs as I traveled all over the world with them. As I did, I asked myself what was different about these men? I say men because, as of 2020, there are no female SEALs yet. Why did these men make it through the training when so many others failed? Attrition rates at BUD/S (Basic Underwater Demolition/SEAL Training) are extremely high. What I concluded was this:

1. The men who make it through BUD/S and become SEALs are not faster, smarter, stronger, more athletic, coordinated, or skilled than others.

2. The men who become SEALs refuse to quit as failure is not an option—you would have to cut their arm off and take it to the bell for them to ring out.
3. The men who become SEALS have a tolerance for pain that is off the charts.
4. The men who become SEALs are more focused, disciplined, and determined than others.
5. The men who become SEALs are 100% committed to a Team mentality—meaning, they unequivocally believe in being a part of a team—living together, training together, eating together, socializing together, and most importantly, dying together.

God expects nothing less from single and married Christian men. Satan desires to steal your identity as a man, husband, and father. He desires to steal your sexuality, your marriage, your marriage bed, and use your pawned sexuality for his own ends.

Remember, 1 Peter 5:8 says, "Your adversary the devil prowls around like a roaring lion, seeking someone to devour." Satan desires for you to ring the bell, pawn your sexuality, forsake your marriage, defile your marriage bed, and give up on God.

Praise God, I have good news for you men. God never said you needed to be faster, smarter, stronger, or more skilled and coordinated than other men to be the man, father, and husband God wants and your wife desires. God does want you to remain focused, determined, and disciplined. He never wants you to quit on your marriage, and he wants you to tolerate pain, sorrow, and disappointment knowing he "will never leave you nor forsake you" (Heb. 13:5). And, most importantly, God wants you to commit 100 percent to your wife and the one-flesh union you share with her because God hates divorce.[126]

So how do you do that? Well, buckle up, you're about to go on the ride of your life. You may think I am being hard on you—I am! But keep reading, even though the Holy Spirit may be slapping you upside the head and knocking you to your knees.

Captain Jack Sparrow

Let me start by reminding you that you, too, are created in the image of God. You are not an animal, a product of evolution, or an out-of-control vessel designed to be blown and tossed around by every sexual desire. You are made in the image of God. You were and are created to rule over the air, land, and sea and everything in them, including yourself and your sexual desires. You were not and are not created to rule, dominate, or think you are superior to women in any form or fashion. Women are intellectually, mentally, physically, psychologically, and sexually equal. The third part of the admonishments of the fall for women required wives to submit to their husbands. This does not mean that all women are to submit to all men—even though throughout history and even today, men foolishly dominate women and thus suffer tremendous sexual consequences themselves.

I can't even begin to tell you how many married men I have counseled who have not had sex with their wives for several months or years. The only sexual experiences they have had come from masturbation, porn, strip clubs, adultery, and the hormonal indulgences of lust-filled fantasies.

Really? Come on, men, you can do better than this. Stop pawning your sexuality to the deceptive schemes of Satan. Redeem your sexuality and restore the sanctity of your marriage bed. Pray the prayer of Psalm 119:133, "Direct my steps by Your word, and let no iniquity have dominion over me" (NKJV). The deep feelings of shame, guilt, and disgust you feel after engaging in these activities will never sexually satisfy you the way God designed you to be sexually satisfied if you allow sin to have dominion over you. Just like Captain Jack Sparrow's compass pointed to what he wanted most, the Golden Compass will direct you to the most awesome, holy, pure, and sustainable sex of your life.

So how do you redeem your sexuality, restore the sanctity of sex, and keep your marriage bed pure?

Ouch

First, you must rule over *yourself*. Juliet longs for her Romeo, the princess longs for her knight in shining armor, and the Shulamite for Solomon her king. So too your wife waits eagerly for you to be a man of self-control worthy to receive the bounty she has locked and sealed[127] for you. This was the first step I took on my journey to become "The Most Sexually Satisfied Man on Earth," and it started when I was single. As mentioned earlier, when I rededicated my life to Christ, I stopped fornicating and masturbating. Thus, I stopped pawning my sexuality and started stockpiling it—protecting it for my future wife, lover, and "One-Flesh Covenant" soulmate.

The desires you have for sex are natural and designed by God to be stored up and presented to your wife alone. God also ordered you, "do not deprive one another" (1 Cor. 7:5), which means you are to have no other sexual outlet other than your wife. Every time you look at porn, lust after other women, masturbate, or visit strip clubs, chat rooms, sex hotlines, etc., you deprive your wife of what is rightfully hers. In turn, you pawn your sexuality to Satan, defile your marriage bed, and sin against your own body.

Cain's anger boiled, upset that God had rejected his offering, favoring the fat offerings of his brother, Abel. Feeling cheated and pouting, Cain heard the voice of God: "Why are you angry? Why is your face downcast? If you do what is right, will you not be accepted? But if you do not do what is right, sin is crouching at your door; it desires to have you, but you must rule over it" (Gen. 4:6-7, NIV). I counsel "Cain" all the time. Yes, that's right. Cain walks into my office daily. He stomps in, plops down, eyes lowered, droopy lip, arms crossed, heart racing, knee bobbing.

"What's the matter, Cain?" I ask.

"It doesn't matter what I do; she never wants to have sex with me."

"Why is that?"

"I don't know," replies Cain.

"What happens when you try?"

"She pushes me away and says, 'Just go watch your porn and masturbate.'" OUCH!

Sadly, this is a true story from one of my counselees. What's even more sad is that "Cain" just doesn't get it. He doesn't understand that by pawning his sexuality every night to porn and masturbation and other acts of sexual immorality, he, in turn, has lost the trust of his wife and wounded her deeply. She is absolutely disgusted with him, repulsed by his touch, and, in time, starts to reject all his depraved and abusive attempts to have sex with her. Unless "Cain" gets himself under control, redeems his sexuality, and restores the sanctity of his marriage bed, this scenario will play out until the marriage ends—and it will end.

Men, learn a tough lesson from Cain. Sin desires to have you. It's crouching at your door, and just like an old Alfred Hitchcock movie, it is crouched down looking through the keyhole waiting for the opportune moment to pounce from the shadows and overtake you. That's why God said to Cain, "You must rule over it [sin]" (Gen. 4:7, NIV). The Golden Compass I'm teaching you about yields significantly more returns and is sustainable, but it all starts by, "Ruling thyself" through the fruit of the spirit called "self-control."

Crosshairs

Second, you must take captive every thought and make it obedient to God.[128] The most powerful sexual organ is the mind. The temptations men experience every single day are normal:

> No temptation has overtaken you except what is common to mankind. And God is faithful; he will not let you be tempted beyond what you can bear. But when you are tempted, he will also provide a way out so that you can endure it" (1 Cor. 10:13, NIV).

Humankind, by design, is drawn to beauty, whether through art, jewelry, clothes, mountain landscapes, or beautiful sunrises and sunsets.

Above all else, though, humans—especially men—are drawn to beautiful bodies. A beautiful woman catches the eye of everyone and can stop a whole room dead in its tracks and cause the moon to skip until dawn. Single men and husbands, listen intently to what I am about to say next. It will free you from lust and give you a way out when tempted.

There is nothing wrong with admiring God's magnificent creation, and women are most certainly a magnificent creation of God. The problem though is when men stop admiring women as the image of God and give in to temptation and lust after every long-legged, big-busted woman in eyesight. The Bible says, "Each person is tempted when he is lured and enticed by his own desire. Then desire when it has conceived gives birth to sin, and sin when it is fully grown brings forth death. Do not be deceived, my beloved brothers" (Jas. 1:14-16). Temptation is not a sin. It's what happens during and after the temptation that matters. Admiring the beautiful creation walking by is normal; undressing it in your mind and going home and masturbating to it is the problem—and the sin.

God provides a way out for every Christian single and married man. However, he leaves the choice up to you. Do you take the high road or the low? Do you rule over temptations and sin, or do they rule over you? Do you take captive every thought, or do they run wild and out of control in your mind? When I was a young marine, my drill instructor taught me how to move under fire. He called the move, "I'm up, he sees me, I'm down." This means I have about three to four seconds to get to the next barrier before the enemy lifts his rifle, aligns the crosshairs, and pulls the trigger. I teach the same maneuver in counseling. I call it "3SL"—the Three-Second Look. When a beautiful woman walks by, a man has about three seconds to admire God's creation and then take cover before his head gets blown off. Anything beyond a 3SL, and temptation lifts its rifle, aligns the crosshairs, and pulls the trigger. Gentlemen, stay out of the crosshairs!

I stay out of the crosshairs by following a set of covenants all derived from God's Word. The following eight covenants I created and live by. These covenants help me honor marriage and keep my marriage bed pure. I print these out on laminated business cards and pass them out at my conferences for men and women to keep in their purse or wallet.

The One-Flesh Covenants

1. I make a covenant with my mind to never think sexually on anything other than my spouse (Song 7:10).
2. I make a covenant with my eyes to never look sexually at anything other than my spouse (Job 31:1).
3. I make a covenant with my ears to never listen sexually to anything or anyone other than my spouse (Luke 8:18a).
4. I make a covenant with my mouth to never speak sexually to anyone other than my spouse (Prov. 5:15-18).
5. I make a covenant with my hands to never touch anything sexually other than my spouse (Prov. 5:20).
6. I make a covenant with my feet to stay off all paths that lead sexually to anything other than my spouse (Ps. 119:101).
7. I make a covenant with my heart to never seal it sexually with anything other than the love of my spouse (Song 8:6).
8. I make a covenant with my God to honor the marriage bed and keep it holy (Heb. 13:4).

These eight covenants offer protection from the adulteress, keep marriage beds pure, and direct men down paths of sustained sexual satisfaction. The first covenant protects my mind and preserves my marriage bed.

Men must set healthy boundaries to protect their sexuality and marriage beds. Single men, now is the time to take captive every thought, stockpile your sexuality, and protect the "springs, wells, and fountains" God gave you. If you don't, you will enter marriage with your sexuality pawned, your "springs, wells, and fountains" polluted, and yourself experiencing severe sexual consequences. Married and single men, you need to start by redeeming your sexuality. Fall on your knees, ask God to forgive you, commit your life, your sexuality, and your sexual desires to him. Next, throw away and delete all pornographic material and files. Put controls on your computer and phone to block the adulteress from putting you in her crosshairs. Never again set foot on the path of the adulteress.[129] Stay off all paths leading to her door including all strip clubs, adult stores, websites, phone sex, chat rooms and cybersex sites, lustful thoughts, being alone with other women, and anything else that corrupts your mind, defiles your marriage bed, pawns your sexuality, and leads away from paths of righteousness, holiness, and self-control.

Body Trust

Third, you must never betray the trust of your wife, and you must convince her that she can trust you with her body. Men, if your wife suspects you are cheating on her, either with another woman or that you have other sexual outlets other than her, i.e., masturbation, porn, visiting strip clubs, etc., you will wound her deeply, and she will withhold her body from you, leaving you sexually unsatisfied.

I have my title because I have never, ever, betrayed the trust of my wife. She has never stayed up late at night wondering where I am or who I am with. She has never caught me hanging out with other women alone for reasons other than work or official business (obviously there are times at work I have to meet alone with women, i.e., counseling, performance reviews, etc.). And most importantly, I have never done anything sexual to her and her body causing her to feel shameful, guilty, or dirty. My wife knows that when I approach her to make love, to have sex, and to enjoy all her shoots, springs, wells, gardens, and fountains, I will not pollute, defile, or abuse them in any way. My wife can trust me with her body because I have earned and kept her trust.

Numerous men believe they can watch porn and act out the same abusive sexual acts on their wives, and then wonder why their wives don't respond to their sexual advances. Men, women know when you are making love with them and when you are using their bodies to masturbate yourself or live out some sadistic fantasy. I say this because there is an enormous difference in having sex the way God designed it and having the selfish and abusive sex you see in porn, which has nothing to do with unity, consummation, procreation, and holiness.

When husbands act out what they have seen in porn, they often trigger their wives without even realizing it. Numerous women have been sexually molested, abused, and raped. The trespasser often sodomizes the victim, and makes the victim perform degrading sexual acts on and to the trespasser, violating and traumatizing the victim, all for the selfish personal satisfaction of the trespasser. When a husband does the same selfish, abusive, and degrading things that the trespasser did (or pressures the wife to perform the same acts the trespasser did), without even realizing it, the husband triggers his wife, causing her to flashback to the trespass. This causes her to immediately shut down emotionally, physically, psychologically, and sexually.

The selfish sexual acts of the trespasser and the husband also cause some women to experience a medical condition called vaginismus, which causes the vagina to close, making sex difficult, if not impossible. Do you see now why your wife wouldn't want to have sex with you and why she rejects your sexual advances? She is not rejecting you *per se*, but the degrading, abusive, and selfish sexual acts you believe will satisfy you even though you know it won't!

Let me be blunt and honest—it is difficult for me as a counselor to counsel your wife and encourage her to have sex with you when you continue to have other sexual outlets, abuse her body, or ask her to do things to you (or allow you to do things to her) that make her feel shameful, guilty, and dirty, or that trigger her back to a trespass against her. I'm sorry, I just can't do it, and it wouldn't work anyway. Only a pure marriage bed where sex is mutual, loving, gentle, and holy will allow you to get back in the race for my title. Only a woman who trusts you and trusts you with her body will give herself to you when she is tired, upset, or not in the mood. Only a woman who feels like she is the "rose of Sharon"[130] will give you unconditional access to her shoots, wells, springs, fountains, and gardens, allowing you to gorge and drink until you are satiated with unadulterated sexual delight.

Mick

Fourth, men all around the world—and even some reading this book—are caught in the seductive web of the adulteress, for every time they lust after other women, look at porn, visit strip clubs, commit adultery, and masturbate, the adulteress wraps another string around them and slowly consumes their sexuality, marriage, money, happiness, health, and their precious life. To keep them alive and siphon every last drop of blood from their miserable lives, she feeds them a cheap, two-bit, pawned sexual experience that will never satisfy or quench their sexual desires. In the end, they lose everything, as Proverbs 7:21-27 says:

> With her enticing speech she caused him to yield, with her flattering lips she seduced him. Immediately he went after her, as an ox goes to the slaughter, or as a fool to the correction of the stocks, till an arrow struck his liver. As a bird hastens to the snare, he did not know it would cost his life. Now therefore, listen to me, my children; pay attention to the words of my mouth: do not let your heart turn aside to her ways, do not stray into her paths; for she has cast down many wounded, and all who were slain by her were strong men. Her house is the way to hell, descending to the chambers of death (NKJV).

Trust me, I watched this firsthand with my own father. I'll never forget the day I learned he was cheating on my mother. I was nineteen.

My mother had moved out of the house, which was nothing new and had happened several times over the course of my life. I was living with my dad in our house in Arkansas, and it was around dusk when a woman pulled into our driveway. Now, we lived down a long dirt road, and no one ever just pulled into our driveway, let alone a single female. I was on the front porch when she turned off the car and asked if Mick lived here. I said no. As soon as I said no, my dad stepped out and asked who she was looking for. I said, "Someone named Mick," and he said to me, "Ask her if she wants to come inside and have dinner."

My heart sank. I may have been only nineteen, but I wasn't stupid. I instantly knew something was up and that they knew each other. She came inside, and several weeks later she moved in. I didn't know what to do. *Do I tell mom, or do I let her find out on her own?* I was scared. Not wanting to be kicked out, I decided not to say anything. I will spare you all the details, but my mom eventually found out and filed for divorce. My dad married the woman a few months later, and slowly but surely, his life was stolen. The last twenty years of my dad's life were filled with alcohol, meth, and drugs.

In February 2018, he died of a meth overdose. He had no teeth, his body was frail and depleted, he was broke, and he didn't own a single thing. There was a point in my dad's life when he had everything a man could ever want: eighty acres of land, a nice house, a wife, two kids, a thriving business, and he was a very handsome man. At his funeral, I made a lot of people upset. I preached a message about adultery and spoke the truth about what had really killed him. My father didn't die from a meth overdose; he was killed through the sin of adultery. Thirty years of this lifestyle cost him everything.

Men, let this be a stark reminder of what happens to all who journey down the path of the adulteress. Proverbs 7:26 says, "All who were slain by her were strong men." However strong you think you are, trust me, the adulteress is stronger. She will reduce you to a crust of bread and feed upon you all the days of your life. At the end, you will die a lonely, miserable death.

Late one cold winter night, my dad, high on meth, stumbled out of the house and got lost in the fog. People looked all over the countryside for him for several days. I was living in Virginia at the time and serving with SEAL Team FOUR when I got the call that he was missing. I immediately booked a flight home to help look for him, as I suspected he was probably dead. I landed in Little Rock, Arkansas early in the morning, jumped into my rental car, and drove two hours to my uncle's house where Dad was living at the time. As I turned onto the road, I noticed a bunch of cars at the end of the road. I pulled into the driveway and asked my uncle if there was any new word and what all the cars were doing at the end of the road. My uncle said Dad was still missing and he didn't know about the cars.

I jumped back in my car and headed down the road. As I approached, I noticed the lights on the cars; it was the police. I pulled up, walked over, and introduced myself, "Hello, I'm Gary Foshee, the oldest son of Darrell Foshee. What's going on? Did you find him?" They looked at me and said, "Sir, I am sorry, but your father was found dead in the woods. They are bringing him out now. Do you mind staying and identifying him?"

Two hunters found him face down in the mud early that morning frozen to death. Darrell Warren Foshee was once a successful businessman, handsome, fun-loving, the life of the party, with numerous friends, and the world in his hands. Completely defeated and dominated by the adulteress, he died on a dark foggy night, deep in the woods, cold, disoriented, intoxicated, and utterly alone. As a man of faith, I hold out hope that with his last few breaths Darrell cried out to God. If so, the God I serve says all who call to him shall be saved.[131] If not, then I pray for mercy. May God have mercy on his soul.

Little Foxes

Fifth, you must keep the little foxes out of your garden.[132] When I first met my wife, her father (Mike) had a massive garden in their backyard. Mike spent hours in the garden pruning, pulling weeds, hoeing, fertilizing, and watering it. One of his biggest battles, though, was trying to keep out all the "little foxes" that kept destroying his fruits and vegetables, i.e., rabbits, squirrels, foxes, deer, and all other kinds of varmints. Being an old country boy from Louisiana who loved to hunt and fish, Mike could have grabbed his shotgun and, like Elmer Fudd, blasted the "wascally wabbits" and ate them for dinner. However, wisely wanting to stay married and enjoy the fruits of his labor, Mike, instead, built a fence around the perimeter. He lived in the city limits and didn't want to get fined; nor did he want his wife all over him for shooting cute furry animals from the neighborhood!

The same goes for the marriage bed. Men who honor marriage and keep their marriage beds pure must vigorously protect it. The adulteress cunningly and relentlessly looks for weakness in the fences you've built to protect your marriage bed. Satan prowls around like a lion continually looking for prey (men who lack self-control and fences). Single and married men who fail to build healthy perimeters around their sexuality, sexual desires, and marriage beds, and who fail to defend those perimeters at all costs, foolishly permit the "little foxes" of Satan and the adulteress to steal the tangible, enriching, fulfilling, and satisfying sex God designed. Uncontrolled sexuality, lustful desires of the flesh, and unprotected marriage beds allow trespassers access to forbidden ground where they plunder crops and pollute streams, wells, and cisterns—ultimately leaving individuals and marriages sexually bankrupt and woefully dissatisfied.

Goldminers do this every day. They search out the most fertile, promising land laden with gold and lease the property. Then they topple all the trees, shrubs, and grass, and strip off the top layer of soil until they hit bedrock. Once they've removed all the gold, they vacate the land, leaving it in utter ruin. Satan and the adulteress do the same thing. They steal all the good things God planned for you, and once they own the lease to your pawned gardens and streams, they force you to feed off cheap, moldy scraps of two-bit sexual experiences.

Single men and married men, listen to me. God has a better way and a different plan. When God finished disciplining Eve, he said to Adam:

> Because you have listened to the voice of your wife and have eaten of the tree of which I commanded you, 'You shall not eat of it,' cursed is the ground because of you; in pain you shall eat of it all the days of your life; thorns and thistles it shall bring forth for you; and you shall eat the plants of the field. By the sweat of your face you shall eat bread, till you return to the ground, for out of it you were taken; for you are dust, and to dust you shall return (Gen. 3:17-19).

It is hard work becoming a man. No male wakes up one day, looks in the mirror and says, "Well, would you look at that? I'm a man." It doesn't work like that. It takes years of trial and error to develop and mold these fleshly bodies into the kind of man a woman will trust, respect, follow, and most importantly, love and cherish. Like the Apostle Paul, I have to beat my body daily to keep it under control.

A male does not become a man at eighteen or twenty-one, or at some magical date and time in life. In fact, there are males of all ages who are still immature, who lack self-control, who don't honor their commitments, who don't protect their marriage bed, or who don't wisely save and spend money. The world has many men in it who cannot hold down a steady job and have not assumed the role as head of their household. There are males in their 20s, 30s, 40s, and older who act like adolescents. There are men so lonely and sexually frustrated, yet they refuse to undertake the arduous labor it takes to become the man who women are attracted to and will sexually desire. There are men who are the epitome of Proverbs 26:11, which says, "Like a dog that returns to his vomit is a fool who repeats his folly." There are men who continue to return to the same old depraved sexual acts, keeping them in a perpetual state of pawn. If this is you, throw the pornography in the trash, honor marriage, build a strong perimeter fence around your marriage bed, and get yourself under control.

How to Build a Strong Perimeter Fence and Keep Out the Little Foxes

1. **Take the One-Flesh Covenants Pledge**. Make all eight covenants of the One-Flesh Covenants your personal covenants between you, your wife, and God. These eight covenants will protect your marriage bed more than anything else I have ever seen.
2. **Commit to One Sexual Outlet**. Stop masturbating, going to strip clubs, watching porn, having phone sex and cybersex, committing adultery, lusting after other women, and flirting.
3. **Take Captive Every Thought**. Your mind is your most powerful sexual organ. Control it, and you've already won half the battle.
4. **Don't Be Alone with Women**. Set professional boundaries at work and outside of work. There will always be exceptions, but control the exceptions to the best of your ability, and keep temptations at bay.
5. **Add Security Apps and Programs to Your Electronics**. Your computer, phone, tablet, and TV are direct portals the adulteress can use to get to you. Block the portals before she finds a way in. Remember, she is a "Little Fox" and will try to climb, dig under, and chew through the fence you build.
6. **Don't Go Out Alone**. Dancing, drinking, and partying without your wife has caused men to succumb to adultery than almost anything else.
7. **Keep Your Marriage Bed Pure**. Don't ever do anything to your wife or ask her to do anything to you that makes you or her feel shameful, guilty, or dirty.

Abraham cast Hagar and Ishmael out of his home with only a skin of water and a loaf of bread, and she wandered in the wilderness until the water and bread ran out. Thinking there was no hope, she laid little Ishmael under a small bush and walked away as she could not bear to see her son die. Distraught and crying, Hagar was heard by God, and, in a miraculous turn of events, he opened her eyes, revealing a fresh well of water a short distance away. Hagar sprung to her feet, filled the skin with water, and refreshed her son, thus saving his life. Some of you men have crawled up under a similar bush, thinking there is no hope for you and are simply waiting to die. God is watching and waiting for you to cry out. When you do, he will open your eyes to a well of living water that will radically transform your life and marriage, and you will be sexually refreshed in ways you never imagined. Cry out now. Redeem your sexuality and restore the sanctity of sex. This is the Golden Compass to sustained sexual satisfaction.

Golden Nugget

I can spot a Navy SEAL from a mile away; he's the one walking with his chest in the clouds and golden rays of sunshine dancing radiantly off the trident pinned over his heart. The trident is a treasure he will risk everything to honor and maintain. Matthew 6:21 says, "For where your treasure is, there your heart will be also." Are you willing to risk everything, endure immense amounts of pain, build and fortify perimeter defenses to win the trust of your wife and to protect your marriage bed at all cost? Then, let me leave you with one last Golden Nugget.

When you make love to your wife, and she looks long and deep into the depths of your eyes, she knows whether or not your heart is hers. Your secrets may still lie undiscovered, but she knows whether or not you are making love to her or just having sex with her as men have sex with prostitutes.[133] However, if, when she looks into the depths of your eyes, she sees her reflection, bravo! I tip my hat to you, my brother. You will enjoy a bountiful supply of sustained sexual delight that most men will never experience.

If not, I have one more word of encouragement for you. There are several men who don't make it through BUD/S the first time due to injury, sickness, and several other reasons. But SEALs don't quit. At the first opportunity, those men fly back to San Diego to compete once again for the title and honor of being an elite warfighter of the world. Are you willing to risk everything to be the man, husband, and father your wife desires and God created? Are you willing once again to put in the hard work to truly become a man and earn the love, trust, and respect of your wife? If so, fall on your knees right now, repent of your sins, ask Jesus to redeem your life and sexuality from pawn. Build the best perimeter fence ever built. Follow the Golden Compass I've disclosed throughout this book. It will change your life and marriage.

4 Tips for a Man to Enhance His Wife's Sexual Satisfaction

1. **Protect the Garden**. At all costs, you must keep out all the "little foxes" trying to steal, devour, and pollute your marriage and marriage bed. Throw away the porn, delete the files, stop lusting after other women, visiting strip clubs, masturbating, and everything else that keeps you from enjoying your own private garden.

2. **Cultivate the Garden**. God wants you to have the best sex of your life. Speak to your wife about sex. Find out if there is anything you are doing to her or she is doing to you that makes her feel shameful, guilty, or dirty. And, whatever you do, don't ever do anything sexually to her and her body that's abusive, degraded, or humiliating. If something is discovered during your conversation, ask her to forgive you and stop the sexual act immediately. Remember it is all about body trust. Can she trust you with her body?

3. **Eat and Drink Only from Your Private Garden**. God created your wife to satisfy you sexually. Don't have any other sexual outlet other than your wife. Allow your libido to well up inside, be a man of self-control, and never deprive your wife of her conjugal rights.
4. **Don't Overfertilize Her Garden**. The number one thing men do, and that they think women like, is apply lots of pressure to the vagina and clitoris and to caress those areas hastily. Slow and gentle is the key.

My desire in writing this chapter is fivefold:

1. Remind single and married men that they, too, are created in the image of God and created to have dominion over the air, land, and sea and everything in them including themselves. Men must learn to rule over themselves before they get married, have children, and become leaders.
2. Convince single and married men of the importance of building healthy, fortified perimeters to protect their sexuality, marriages, and marriage beds. Follow the One-Flesh Covenant at all cost and never set foot on the path of the adulteress.
3. Just like Navy SEALs, Christian men must work hard, endure pain, and never ever "ring the bell" on your marriage. God hates divorce. He expects all men to honor marriage and keep their marriage beds pure. Put no confidence in your flesh. Beat it into submission, and be the husband your wife desires.
4. Convince married men that their wives must be their only sexual outlet. If a husband has any other sexual outlets other than his wife, he pawns his marriage bed, sins against his own body, and will pay a huge price.

5. Teach husbands—A wife must trust her husband with her body. A husband who fails in this area will earn a title he will deeply regret—"The Most Sexually UNsatisfied Man on Earth." A wife should never leave the marriage bed feeling shameful, guilty, or dirty. Trust me, men, when you follow the sexual compass I've laid out in this book, when you convince your wife she is "The rose of Sharon," and when your wife trusts you with her body, she will give you the Golden Key to her garden and you will have unconditional access to her garden, streams, wells, shoots, and cisterns.

6

THE HEART OF SEX

"Then Samuel explained to the people the behavior of royalty, and wrote it in a book and laid it up before the LORD" (1 Sam. 10:25, NKJV).

Introduction

The previous five chapters laid out God's plan for sex, provided the Golden Compass to sustained sexual satisfaction, explained the importance of understanding sexual desire and the lasting effects of the fall of Adam and Eve, and described what pawned sexuality looks like. This chapter provides the icing on the cake. To redeem sexuality and restore the sanctity of sex, a person must truly understand the meaning of sex that God designed for humanity—which is the heart of sex.

The heart of sex and the meaning of sex begins and ends with God and his design for coitus. The Lord God said, "Therefore a man shall leave his father and his mother and hold fast to his wife, and they shall become one flesh" (Gen. 2:24). The meaning of sex resides exclusively in the divine character and supernatural design of God to unite a man and a woman into one flesh. It is the foundation on which all relationships must be established to receive God's approval and blessing. David Jeremiah notes, "Sex and passionate, romantic love are God's ideas!"[134] For Hollinger, the meaning of sex does not lie within the framework and opinions of society, the will of humans, or the natural process of love between two people. He says,

> It [the meaning of sex] is a meaning rooted in the very character of God and his designs for creation. The meaning of sex is made explicit in the Christian worldview of creation, fall, redemption, and consummation. . . . Redemption is not freedom from sex, but a freedom within our sexual beingness. . . . The ultimate intimacy and communion with God will fulfill all that we have longed for sexually in this world.[135]

A sexual relationship originating from any foundational principle other than uniting a man and a woman into a "One-Flesh Covenant" is outside God's design and meaning for sex. Although consummation, love, intimacy, and procreation are central to understanding sex, these do not define its meaning but merely emanate from the "One-Flesh Covenant" God established.

John Piper believes that God uses sexuality to allow Christians to know "God in Christ" more fully and the oneness they share. Knowing and understanding how God and Jesus are one, he notes, guides, and guards Christians as they explore the deep passions and desires of sexuality and the one-flesh union God established:

> God created human beings in his image . . . with capacities for intense sexual pleasure and with a calling to commitment in marriage and continence in singleness. And his goal in creating human beings with personhood and passion was to make sure there would be sexual language and sexual images that

would point to the promises and the pleasures of God's relationship to his people and our relationship to him. In other words, the ultimate reason why we are sexual is to make God more deeply knowable.[136]

The word "to know" in Scripture refers both to sexual intercourse and to knowing God more fully. Genesis 4:1 says, "Now Adam knew his wife, and she conceived and bore Cain." In Jeremiah 24:7, God says, "I will give them a heart to know me." The heart of sex begins with God's design for a one-flesh covenant and is sustained by a new heart God gives when a person is born again. Several Scriptures warn about trusting in a heart untransformed by God's divine grace (Ps. 78:8c, 37; Prov. 11:20; 28:26; Jer. 17:9; Hos. 4:8, 11). A new heart leads people to the truths of God's Holy Word. The Bible serves as the moral and ethical compass pointing humanity to holiness and righteousness.

The heart of sex is also found in the purpose of sex. Boteach concludes that three possibilities exist with respect to the purpose of sex: pleasure, procreation, or oneness:

> Judaism . . . rejects the far-right extreme of sex is only for babies. Neither does Judaism embrace the extreme secular view that sex is for fun and pleasure. Rather, Judaism says that the purpose of sex is to synthesize and orchestrate two strangers together as one. Sex is the ultimate bonding process. God, in His infinite kindness, gave a man and a woman who are joined together in matrimonial holiness the most pleasurable possible way to call forth their capacity of joining onto another human being and feeling permanently attached.[137]

Boteach highlights sex as an infinite kindness of God that helps married couples feel permanently attached.[138] God's plan for the heart of sex does the same. Godly sex strengthens the covenant of marriage, allowing couples to know each other the way God intended.

Another way married Christian couples can strengthen the covenant of marriage through the heart of sex, according to Doug Rosenau and Michael Wilson, is by becoming "soul virgins." For them, a soul virgin is "one who continuously seeks to value, celebrate, and protect God's design for sexuality—body, soul, and spirit—in oneself and others."[139] Rosenau and Wilson believe that a soul virgin desires to learn "God's viewpoint" and then enjoy that viewpoint as they guard God's original design for sexuality. They also believe that soul virginity "begins in single adulthood, and the concept continues to apply into married, single-again, or widowed life as well. This makes the pledge of soul virginity a lifetime commitment."[140]

The Song of Solomon renders a beautiful example of the heart of sex and the intimacy God designed for humankind. Solomon's affection and passionate interaction with the Shulamite is a tutorial every man should emphatically emulate. Solomon whisks away a proletariat girl, soiled with dirt, darkened from the sun, and fragranced by nature, and develops her into a confident princess adorned with jewels, shadowed by love, and bathed in myrrh. Immersed in gardens of love, the Shulamite develops into a confident bride who believes she is "the rose of Sharon, and the lily of the valleys" (Song 2:1, NKJV). Solomon's loving affection toward the Shulamite could be the key to unlocking a fountain of sensual passion and desire in lovers. Lovers who invigorate each other with constant praise, affection, and a healthy dose of unveiled sexual intentions significantly increase their coital encounters and sexual satisfaction as they enjoy the heart of sex. Jack and Judith Balswick conclude:

> God created us as sexual beings and pronounced it good. By design our sexual nature moves us toward intimate knowing. Through mutual exchange and engagement, our sexuality deepens relationship meaning. . . . It's not merely the sexual encounter that drives us; it's the complete one-flesh experience

of two persons becoming one through mutual vulnerability and responsiveness.[141]

The sexual compass of society lures individuals into dark dungeons of hedonistic ideologies where perfunctory desires lead to superficial bodily encounters and one-dimensional relationships. Untethered indulgences sever the deep spiritual bonds of a one-flesh union from the covenant of marriage God predestined for the heart of sex. Winner states,

> Just as scripture's vision of bodies begins in Genesis, scripture's story about sex also begins in Genesis. God's vision for humanity is established in the Garden of Eden, and the uniqueness and one-ness of the marriage relationship . . . this relationship is the context in which sex is first understood. One-fleshness both is and is not metaphor. It captures an all-encompassing, overarching one-ness—when they marry, husband and wife enter an institution that points them toward familial, domestic, emotional, and spiritual unity. But the one flesh of which Adam speaks is also overtly sexual, suggesting sexual intercourse, the only physical state other than pregnancy where it is hard to tell where one person's body stops and the other's starts.[142]

To know a person fully is to know a person's nakedness. Immoral sexual practices may intermingle bodies.[143] However, they subsequently circumnavigate unity, intimacy, consummation, and sacred one-flesh unions. Impetuous sensuality generates enmity, leaving individuals spiritually and sexually isolated.[144] Circumspect sensuality, navigated by God's sexual compass, generates oneness, sequentially unveiling the true heart of sex. The heart of sex is oneness—with one's spouse, with God, and with the body of Christ. Shame and guilt subside, and innocence returns. Adam and Eve stood before God naked and unashamed. God's sexual compass protects sexuality, allowing lovers to passionately make love on an unadulterated marriage bed before God—naked and unashamed.

Six Excuses Obstructing the Healing Process of Sexual Trauma

Before I write this section, let's open with a prayer.

> Father, you are the God of miracles, the God whose breath allows the blind to marvel at sunsets, the lame to dance, and the mute to sing glorious melodies of praise. You are the God who disintegrates cancer, heals infirmities, and calls the dead back to life. You are the God whose wisdom reconciles marriages, purifies marriage beds, and restores the "One-Flesh Covenant."
>
> Father, I humbly come before you now and ask you to heal the gardens, shoots, streams, wells, and springs of every man and woman devastated by the crippling effects of sexual abuse and trauma. In the name of Jesus, let the miracle of redemption redeem their sexuality and restore the sanctity of sex in their lives. Amen!

Healing from sexual abuse and trauma is a delicate matter. There is no "one size fits all" treatment plan because treating sexual trauma depends on the degree of trauma experienced, e.g., the level of violence, duration of abuse, and time elapsed since the incident occurred, etc. The effects of sexual abuse are unlimited, and it is paramount to seek professional and spiritual help to heal, restore, and redeem the pawned sexuality often experienced in the aftermath.

Victims who don't seek help often encounter depression, eating disorders, self-inflicted wounds, anxiety, distrust of people and God, homosexual ideations and actions, control issues, addictions, and come to fear intimate relationships. Rosberg and Rosberg report that victims come to believe that if they enjoy sex, they condone what their trespasser did to them. Gary Rosberg says,

> People who have been sexually abused will see sex as wrong, dirty, and shameful. They feel that if they enjoy sex, they are

condoning what their abusers did to them. And if they don't enjoy sex, they are a bad spouse. So they become paralyzed. They're frozen and scared, and they may unknowingly disconnect from their marriage relationships.[145]

A few years ago, I was on vacation when a woman asked if she could speak to me about an issue from her childhood still causing her pain. Not wanting to miss what God had ordained, I agreed to listen. The woman said,

> I was sleeping one night in my bed and woke to find one of my brother's friends, who was spending the night, on top of me. I was only five and I froze and didn't know what to do. He raped me that night and a few days later I told my mom. To my horror, my mother called me a liar and told me to never speak of this again.

The woman was in her fifties at the time of our encounter, but the crippling effects of the sexual abuse and trauma still haunted her, especially the deep wound of her mother's betrayal. The woman stated she had forgiven her mother; nevertheless, that moment severed her relationship and trust in her mother and was never restored—her mother had passed away a few years before we met.

Sadly, stories like this and stories much more violent, abusive, and prolonged, happen every day all around the world. It wasn't until I specialized in the subject of sex that I realized how frequently males and females are sexually assaulted. I won't even quote a statistic here because the reported numbers of sexual abuse don't come close to the actual number of unreported cases never reported or disclosed. No matter the level of sexual abuse and trauma a person experienced, the message of this entire section is to convince every victim of sexual assault reading this book that there is hope and healing from the trespass. Sexuality can be redeemed, and the sanctity of sex can be restored.

The following sections address six excuses that keep victims from healing.

But It's My Fault

Healing from sexual abuse and trauma starts by admitting that it was not your fault. Survivors of sexual trauma can subconsciously blame themselves for what happened. Every so often, when I counsel victims of sexual assault, I hear, "It was my fault. I shouldn't have done this; I shouldn't have done that." Really? When that little five-year-old girl was woken up in the middle of the night, scared, and all alone, what options did she have? Scream? Fight? Run? Children don't have the cognitive abilities to process such horrific moments the way adults do. That little girl did what every other kid does: she froze. Paralyzed with unimaginable fear, she just tried to survive the moment and live to see another day. It is easy, with an adult mind, to reflect back and process all the options available. However, for everyone sexually abused as a child, they didn't have the luxury of an adult mind to help process all the options available in that horrific moment.

Numerous children, teens, and adults blame themselves for the sexual abuse they endured. They blame themselves because, as adults, they think about all the things they "shoulda, woulda, coulda" done to stop the abuse, not realizing they are using an adult mind to process the incident. When victims of childhood or adolescent sexual abuse use their adult minds to render solutions for past incidents, they unfairly hold themselves captive to unrealistic solutions unavailable at that point and time in life. Child and adolescent minds are vulnerable and undeveloped, and extreme fear or trauma can significantly alter the brain's ability to make sound cognitive decisions.

If this is you, the last thing you need are self-inflicted wounds unfairly imposed by adult cognitive abilities unaccessible as a child. You've been wounded deeply by a trespasser, but the surface wounds you keep treating are self-inflicted. You deserve better. Do you hear me? **YOU DESERVE BETTER!** Victims become their own worst enemy and blame themselves for something absolutely not their fault. As an adult, you can think about all the things you should have done, but you will never triumphantly redeem your sexuality or restore your gardens and springs by holding yourself captive to unrealistic solutions for a trespass that happened years ago by thinking about all the "shoulda, woulda, couldas."

Let me stop here and address all those shaking their heads right now and saying, "Dr. Foshee, this doesn't pertain to me because I was older when the sexual abuse happened, and it was my fault. I shoulda, woulda, coulda done something." Once again, I must confess my bewilderment at how paralyzing sexual abuse is, even to adults. Never having been sexually abused myself, I have no idea how terrifying it must be, but I am amazed at the crippling effects sexual abuse and trauma have on full-grown adults and their cognitive abilities. I hear every excuse in my office as to why "it was the victim's fault," and how, "I shouldn't have drunk that much, worn that outfit, went to that party, been with that person, etc." The list of excuses goes on and on.

No one has the right to trespass on forbidden land—period! There is no excuse to trespass on another person's sexual gardens and springs. It doesn't matter how much you had to drink, what you had on, who you were with, or where you were. Let me say it again, no one has the right to trespass on the private gardens and springs God gave you. It's not your fault. When you correctly place the trespass on the trespasser, it will free you from the continuous cycle of unwarranted shame, guilt, and unforgiveness—all self-inflicted wounds keeping you from healing.

But It Felt Good

Before you start casting stones at me, please wait and hear me out. This section may not pertain to you at all, but for some, it is an important section that they need to hear and meditate on. The guilt and shame some victims continue to experience years after the sexual abuse occurred stems from the issue that, when they were sexually molested as a child or adolescent, or even as an adult, their smooth, cunning, and deceptive trespasser actually made the abuse pleasurable for the victim (notice how I said *abuse*). Every so often in counseling, victims report that the trespass felt good, which becomes a source of deep conflict and confusion significantly disrupting the healing process. When this issue isn't addressed and processed correctly and professionally, it can lead victims to become sexual predators themselves, and, if and when that happens, they naturally gravitate to pedophilia. This is so sad, devastating, and completely avoidable with professional and spiritual help.

The fact that sexual abuse felt good is a moot point. Whether you were young or an adult, intoxicated, or didn't say no, trespassers are highly skilled at the art of deception and can coax you into thinking you willingly participated and allowed yourself to enjoy the abuse. I don't know many tricks, but I do know one card trick, and it is a good one. I love to play it on innocent and gullible bystanders, and it is always a crowd pleaser. The trick is simple. I deal out twenty-one cards in a line of three rows of seven. I ask my "victim," who I will name Scott, to pick a card in his mind and tell me what row it's in. After a few seconds, Scott says a row, and I scoop up all the rows and place the row he picked in the middle of the pile. I deal out the cards again and repeat the process until I know which one is his. (There is a spot his card will end up and never move again no matter how many times I deal the cards.) This is where the trick happens. Once I know his card, I turn the cards over so no one can see the cards, and I deal out four piles of four cards each, two on top and two on the bottom. (As I deal, I count the cards because I know what number his card is in the deck.)

I then turn to Scott and say, "Pick two piles." Scott picks two piles, and I either remove them or keep them. Once again, this is the trick! This process is then repeated until there are two cards left. Once Scott picks the final card, and depending on if it is his card, I keep it or take it away and then turn it over. Then, behold, there lies Scott's card. The look on Scott's face and the faces in the crowd are priceless. The people I play this trick on can't believe *they* picked their card, but that is the trick. I made my "victim" believe he or she picked the card, but in all reality, I picked the card. I led Scott right to it without him ever realizing what I was doing.

A cunning, smooth, and deceptive trespasser does the same. He tricks his or her victims into believing they like and/or even desire what took place, but it's a lie, and the victim was deceived. The victim's innocence or situation was exploited to the fullest extent possible. The fact that it felt good and that the victim may have experienced an orgasm is once again a moot point. The victim was tricked and taken advantage of! If this sounds familiar, don't let the fact that it felt good or that you liked it stand in the way of healing. Triumphantly take back your sexuality by realizing you were exploited, and your innocence or situation were taken advantage of.

But I Can't Find the Key

On June 5, 2002, an innocent fourteen-year-old girl named Elizabeth Smart was sound asleep in her house in Salt Lake City, Utah when a trespasser snatched her from her bed in the middle of the night. For the next nine months, the trespasser held Elizabeth captive in the woods, raping and molesting her repeatedly. Her story of sexual abuse, intimidation, and survival are chronicled in numerous documentaries, articles, books, and even a movie. I watched the documentary about Elizabeth and couldn't believe my eyes. I didn't see a wounded, angry, man-hater who wanted revenge on her trespasser and the world. I saw a beautiful, gentle, articulate woman, wife, and mother who had triumphantly taken back her sexuality and redeemed the sanctity of sex in her life.

Elizabeth Smart is a hero and champion of what it means to triumph over the trespass and trespasser. She now travels all over the world speaking out against sexual assault and is an advocate for missing persons and victims of sexual abuse and trauma. But how did she triumphantly take back her sexuality and become the woman, mother, and wife she is today?

Elizabeth first started by taking back the key to her garden and springs that her trespasser, Brian Mitchell, had illegally stolen from her. Although Mitchell trampled Elizabeth's choice fruits and shoots, and polluted her streams, wells, and springs, after her rescue, Elizabeth sought professional help and took back the key to her private garden and springs. With professional and spiritual help, she pulled the weeds, removed the trash, tilled the ground, cleaned out the wells, and replanted seeds. Most importantly, she built a strong perimeter fence and locked the gate, reserving her private garden and springs for her future husband alone.

You can do the same. Stop stalling and making excuses, and take back the key to your private garden and spring that someone illegally stole. This is why so many victims never again experience sex and sexual desire the way God designed it. They never triumphantly take back the key from their trespasser and, in turn, their garden and springs lie blocked and in utter ruin. Sadly, when and if they get married, they build a tower overlooking their abandoned garden and shoot anyone who approaches, even their spouse.

Clifford Penner and Joyce Penner believe that sexual desire is in every person and something they have to allow to surface. Clifford Penner says,

> Sexual desire or interest is not something someone else can provide for you. It is something already in you by creation that you have to allow to surface. ... If you don't freely and spontaneously have sexual interest, there is some distraction, hormonal imbalance, anxiety, or barrier blocking its free expression in you. You need to uncover and correct the problem to free the natural desire that is in you.[146]

Victims who don't take back the key end up in my office saying, "Dr. Foshee, we haven't had sex in weeks, months, or years." Believe me, I counsel a lot of husbands and wives shot full of holes by their spouse.

7 Advantages of Taking Back the Key

1. The meaning and purpose of sex is identified, understood, and accepted.
2. Your view of yourself, others, and sex is restored.
3. The beautiful gift of sex is once again yours to lovingly and honorably share with your spouse.
4. You view sex as holy and sacred.
5. You can receive sexual foreplay, touch, and intercourse from your spouse without being triggered.
6. With full restoration and absolute ownership of your sexuality, the deep wellsprings of love, passion, and sensual desire return—unblocked and clear to flow freely the way God designed.
7. You are no longer a victim! You are a Triumphant Overcomer!

But I Can't Trust God

One of my favorite passages of Scripture and one I quote more than any other comes from Proverbs 3:5-6, "Trust in the Lord with all your heart, and lean not on your own understanding; in all your ways acknowledge him, and he will make your paths straight" (NIV). When God called me into the ministry, I thought I had to have all the answers to every question and situation, and to tell the truth, I was absolutely terrified. Since I am an old country boy from Arkansas and the son of an alcoholic and drug addict, I didn't think I stood a chance in ministry. Thank goodness, I was wrong and besides, that is utter foolishness. No one has all the answers. No denomination has God all figured out; nor does any person, preacher, or prophet correctly interpret every passage of Scripture. God is infinite! Humans are finite. God is omnipresent. Humans are limited. God is omniscient. Humans have restricted knowledge. God is omnipotent. Humans have limited power, except in Christ where "all things are possible" (Matt 19:26). Amen!

Nevertheless, this excuse rises to the top and keeps sexual assault survivors from coming to God and trusting that he can heal, restore, and redeem their sexuality. The deep wounds of sexual abuse and trauma also cause survivors to experience what is called a spiritual injury. A spiritual injury, defined by Timothy Mallard, is:

> The intra and inter-personal damage to souls brought on by significant trauma, including the rupture to foundational religious values, beliefs, and attitudes, the inability to healthfully participate in an immanent human faith community, and the temporary or permanent loss of a transcendent relationship to God (manifested particularly in questions about forgiveness, doubt, truth, meaning, and hope).[147]

Spiritual injury due to sexual trauma and abuse is often an invisible injury that Christians, pastors, and pastoral counselors are untrained to recognize or screen for. Undiagnosed spiritual injuries also keep victims from true healing and closure, and they remain distanced from God and the body of Christ.

Anger and transfer of blame are two major factors I see during counseling that keep victims from healing the invisible spiritual injury deep within. First, anger is often misinterpreted and mislabeled as sin. People believe that if they get angry, and especially if they get angry at God, they have sinned. The Bible does not say anger is a sin. It says, "In your anger, do not sin" (Eph. 4:26, NIV). God created anger as a healthy emotion to signify or sound the alarm that something is not right, as witnessed when Jesus entered the temple and found people buying, selling, and exchanging money, and not using it the way God designed (Matt. 21; John 2). Most people I see who are angry have every right to be upset. There are most certainly instances of unjust anger—I'm not overlooking that, but I believe victims have every right to express anger at the trespasser, God, themselves, and the world, etc. Kevin Doll says that true healing from spiritual injury begins when people honestly admit they are angry with God:

> Spiritual healing begins when we are honest with ourselves and with God. When we honestly admit that we are angry with God, we feel abandoned by God or we even question the existence of God. These are the feelings and struggles David admits to in [Psalm] 69. We must address the reality of our spiritual injury, we cannot hide it, stuff it down, ignore it or self-medicate. Spiritual healing is only resolved when we [become] honest with God about our spiritual injury. In doing so, we must approach God on His terms, not ours. We must lay aside our bitterness, anger, and resentment towards God and accept the love, forgiveness, and acceptance of God. David's healing began when he admitted his pain and focused on the reality that God does indeed hear the cries of the needy. Once he took his eyes off his emotional feelings and placed them upon the reality of God's unfailing love, he found the spiritual peace he longed for.[148]

The important thing to remember about anger is, "in your anger, do not sin." Use the good side of anger to take action and turn what the enemy meant for evil into something good and positive.

Second, the transfer of blame to God instead of the trespasser causes more spiritual injuries than anything else I have seen. Keep blame in its rightful place: on the right offender. This does not mean that victims can't be angry with God; it simply means that blame is placed on the right entity responsible for the trespass. Spiritual injury, when not appropriately identified and addressed, moves victims away from God, religious people, and institutions, and makes them highly skeptical of anything religious and spiritual. This is exactly what Satan wants and desires, because, in the end, he wins when the victim stays away from the Divine Healer, Comforter, and Redeemer. By transferring blame back to the offender, true healing and reconciliation will allow the victim to approach God and receive his love, comfort, healing, and protection.

Dawn Wilson, a sexual abuse survivor, says that the most amazing changes in her life came as a result of rekindling a relationship with God and trusting him with her past wounds. Wilson offers eight lessons learned that help heal spiritual injuries incurred by sexual abuse:

1. God saw my abuse and did not condone it. Neither should I. I do not have to stay silent or bury the pain and trauma. The Lord hates all wickedness, including my abuser's sinful actions (Ps. 11:5).

2. I can, as a member of the Body of Christ, be a part of holding abusers accountable—especially within the church (Matt. 18:15-17).

3. As I run to the Lord who sees, heals, and comforts, I can use what the enemy meant for evil to bring glory and praise to God (Gen. 50:20).

4. Knowing my thoughts will control my actions and responses, I must allow God to transform my thinking so I can make daily choices to please Him (Rom. 12:2).

5. I will grow and heal as I rub shoulders with godly women who model how to respond with the pure love of Christ and trust the Lord to help me stand in dignity and strength (1 Peter 3:3-5).

6. God loves me. Deeply and completely. The enemy loves it when I feel shame, condemnation, and self-loathing, but God's Word says I am precious in God's sight—accepted and valued (Isa. 43:4).

7. I can pray for wisdom and entrust true justice to the righteous heart of God. He always has the last word—He brings justice to the unrepentant and great mercy to the repentant (Ps. 103:6).
8. I can also encourage those who still struggle toward freedom from the pain and insecurities that arise out of sexual abuse (Gal. 6:2).[149]

Wilson encourages victims to focus on God and not inward. Inward-focused victims tend to concentrate on the wounds inflicted by the abuse. However, by rekindling a relationship with God and focusing upon his promises, victims lose focus of their scars, and once again, acknowledge the scars of Jesus and that "he died to make us (them) whole again."[150] When this happens, victims can trust the God who loved the world so much he gave his only begotten Son to redeem it (John 3:16).

Spiritual injury can also be accompanied by moral injury, keeping a person in a cycle of anger, guilt, shame, distrust, and unforgiveness, which leads victims to addiction (both substance and sexual). Sexual assault survivors suffering from spiritual injury feel that God will not forgive them, even though their sexual abuse was completely out of their control when they were children (e.g., sibling incest, child molestation, child rape).

Adults experience spiritual injury as well. Adults who grew up in a religious or spiritual home or environment may engage in sexual behavior condemned by their religious community and find themselves overwhelmed with feelings of shame, guilt, and unforgiveness. According to Gardner, "Shame forces us to act in opposition to what we need."[151] Victims who address the spiritual and moral injuries caused by sexual abuse and trauma no longer live in isolation fearing God or the things of the world. They are finally free to exalt God and praise him for his wonderful creation and grace.

The great theologian, pastor, and author, A. W. Tozer, says exalting God allows people to acquire a new viewpoint (even a new psychology) and is the key to unlocking the door to the great treasuries of God's grace:

> The moment we make up our minds that we are going on with this determination to exalt God over all, we step out of the world's parade. We shall find ourselves out of adjustment to the ways of the world, and increasingly so as we make progress in the holy way. We shall acquire a new viewpoint; a new and different psychology will be formed within us; a new power will begin to surprise us by its upsurgings and its outgoings. . . . "Be thou exalted" is the language of victorious spiritual experience. It is a little key to unlock the door to great treasures of grace. It is central in the life of God in the soul. Let the seeking man reach a place where life and lips join to say continually "Be thou exalted," and a thousand minor problems will be solved at once. His Christian life ceases to be the complicated thing it had been before and becomes the very essence of simplicity.[152]

By exalting God, Tozer says, the complicated things in life cease, returning the chaos back to simplicity. I may not understand everything God does or allows, but I don't have to. As Proverbs 3:5-6 says, all Christians need to do is trust God, and he will make their paths straight. Stop going around in circles blaming God, the world, and yourself. Control your anger, place blame on the offender, and allow professionals to help heal the spiritual injury incurred from the trespass. Stop allowing the excuse of, "But I can't trust God" to keep you from the rich treasuries of grace eagerly awaiting your return to God.

But I Thought It Would Just Go Away

My family and I were boating around the islands of Procida and Ischia in southern Italy when I spotted a large cave nestled in the steep cliffs of Ischia. The boys and I jumped in the water and swam deep into the cave until we ran out of light—okay, the truth, until we got scared. On the way out, I swam over to the wall and tried to climb up when a wave knocked me back, scraping my hand against the rocks. Unaware of the barnacles and a sea urchin hiding beneath the waterline, I shredded my left hand and approximately eight to ten spines pierced deep into my palm.

I arrived at the ER and, after treating the cuts in my hand, the doctor proceeded to remove the spines. She removed several surface ones without much difficulty or pain. However, when she went for the deep ones, I couldn't take the piercing pain. I pulled my hand away and didn't give it back. I said, "Sorry doc, but I will dig the rest out on my own." She laughed and said, "You sure?" "Yes!" She ended up giving me some antibiotics and creams and sent me home. It took me a couple of days, but I finally got most out except for two deep ones. I tried desperately to get them out, but once again, I couldn't take the pain. After trying for a few more days, I realized I had to make a decision. I either had to leave the spines in and allow them to work themselves out on their own, or I had to go back to the ER. (The doctor told me that foreign bodies like spines, splinters, and thorns eventually work themselves out; however, it can take a long time.)

The choice of leaving the spines in or going back and allowing a professional to remove them wasn't easy. Regardless of the choice, pain was inevitable. The same is true for everyone whose lives have been turned upside down by sexual abuse and trauma. Some victims choose to leave the spines of sexual abuse in, what I will refer to as "thorns" from here on out in this section, hoping someday the thorns will work themselves out on their own, not realizing that sexual abuse and trauma do not work like that. Nonetheless, countless victims leave the thorns in and instead choose to cope, manage, and deal with the pain. Unfortunately, there are severe consequences for leaving in the thorns of sexual abuse and trauma.

4 Consequences of Leaving in the Thorns of Sexual Abuse and Trauma

1. The victim never experiences true healing. The thorns continue to fester and throb deep within the victim.
2. The victim never sees the true beauty of God's creation. The thorns cloud the vision of victims leaving them with negative views of themselves, men, women, sex, and God.
3. The victim never attains true autonomy. The thorns continue to influence the decisions of the victim.
4. The victim remains a victim, as the individual tightly holds on to their victim status.

First, if the thorns are left in, they become infected. A few days after I left the ER, the cuts in my hands scabbed over and started to heal. The skin around the two thorns in my palm, however, became red and tender and sensitive to touch. I naturally started to shield my left hand from further injury and use it less. Victims who leave the thorns of sexual abuse in never experience true healing, and intimate issues and relationships can easily trigger the victim, causing them to shut down emotionally, physically, and sexually.

Second, the thorns of sexual abuse and trauma eventually infect the victim's view of themselves, men, women, sex, and God, and cause victims to shield their sexuality from others and/or use it in ways contrary to God's design. Once again, the constant throbbing of the thorns causes victims to withdraw from intimate relationships because they become afraid that someone may accidentally bump into or discover the thorns, which could cause them to view the victim differently and think the victim is damaged or unworthy of love. Even though this is a lie, the lie becomes a truth and reality (the same message Michael Jackson sings about in his song, "Billy Jean"). The victim never triumphantly overcomes by using the excuse of, "But I thought it would just go away."

Third, when the thorns of sexual abuse are not professionally and spiritually removed, they slowly begin to control every decision victims make: where they go, who they associate with, what activities they engage in, and the filter they use to interpret everything around them. Without even realizing it, they use a tainted filter that, instead of filtering out impurities and untruths, it filters out good, natural, and pure things that God meant to heal and restore. Thus, their sexuality remains in a perpetual state of pawn, and their tainted filter blocks true healing, restoration, and redemption.

I love to go to the beach with my family and throw a football, a frisbee, or just lay out and take in some good ol' vitamin D. Something happens every time, though, that catches me by surprise. My glasses film over with a thin layer of seafoam gently blown in by the wind and waves. Without realizing it, things darken, my vision blurs, and my depth perception becomes skewed. It usually takes me a while to realize it, as I am busy enjoying time with my family, but once I do realize that my glasses are fogged, I clean them, thus restoring my vision back to normal. Victims must realize that the thorns of sexual abuse and trauma subtly fog their minds and hearts with views and ideologies that blur and skew the truth of God and his design for sex.

It takes action on the part of the victim to clean out the thorns and return to normal. Don't let the fact that there will be pain involved keep you from seeking professional and spiritual help. Pain is already present, and it needs to stop. Sometimes professionals need to open the wound to get to the source. They are not intentionally hurting you. The pain is necessary to remove the thorns and return the person back to health and normalcy.

A victim who accepts the truth that the thorns of sexual abuse do not just go away on their own and seeks professional and spiritual help will finally experience three important factors they've never experienced before: (1) a renewed vision of sex and sexuality; (2) a renewed vision of themselves, men, women, and God; and (3) possession of the key to their private garden and springs. However, this starts by making the choice to seek help and remove the thorns, regardless of the pain involved to open the wound, dig down deep, and extract the foreign bodies deposited by a trespasser.

So back to my thorn story. I made the choice to remove the two remaining thorns burrowed deep within my palm that were keeping me from using my left hand the way God designed. I walked into the ER, checked in, and when the doctor entered my room, I said, "Doc, there are two thorns too deep for me to get out. I tried, but I couldn't take the pain. Can you numb my hand first and then take them out?" She smiled and said, "Sure." The doctor ordered a vial of lidocaine and injected a dose into my palm close to the thorns, which hurt. She waited several minutes and then started to dig around in the first spot. I flinched and breathed in deep. "Did you feel that?" she asked. "Yes," I responded, disappointed that the medicine didn't work. She stopped digging and immediately injected me with another dose of lidocaine, which hurt. After several more minutes, she tried again, and to my disbelief, the medicine worked and my hand went completely numb. The doctor tried for several minutes to dig out the thorn, but it wasn't budging as it was deep. She asked for a scalpel and made a tiny slit in my palm. She then opened up the cut with a pair of forceps, finally exposing the top of the thorn. Using another pair of forceps, she clamped down on the thorn and gently pulled it out. As she removed the thorn, I breathed out deeply, thankful to have it out.

The choice to remove the thorns of sexual abuse will hurt, but the short-term pain of having them removed doesn't compare to the benefits of removing the thorns once and for all. Once the thorns of sexual abuse are removed, the journey of healing and full restoration truly begins. Although a scar will always remain at the extraction point, the scar now serves as a reminder of an event over which the victim triumphed. This brings me to the most important point of this entire section. Once the victim takes action and removes the thorns, the victim is no longer a victim. A person who realizes that sexual abuse and trauma do not just go away on their own moves from being a victim to a brand-new title: Triumphant Overcomer! Don't remain a victim for one more second. Triumphantly take back your sexuality and become the man or woman God created. When that happens, God will renew your vision, restore your gardens and springs, and hand you back your key.

4 Benefits of Removing the Thorns of Sexual Abuse and Trauma

1. The Triumphant Overcomer takes back control of his or her life. The sexual abuse no longer controls the individual's life and decisions.
2. The Triumphant Overcomer's wounds heal. With the thorns finally removed, the constant throbbing of the trespass stops, allowing sexual desire to return. The Overcomer can, once again, give and receive intimate touch and relations without being triggered.
3. The Triumphant Overcomer gets a new filter. The Overcomer no longer views themselves, men, women, sex, and God through tainted filters. A clear filter of truth and healing leads the Overcomer to a new normal filled with happiness, fulfillment, and sustained sexual satisfaction.
4. The Triumphant Overcomer takes back the key to their garden and springs. With possession of the key to his or her private garden and springs, the Overcomer can till the ground, unblock the springs, build healthy perimeters, and then give their spouse unlimited access to eat and drink of the beautiful gift of sex the Creator of the universe designed.

I end this section with a lesson from Scripture. In Ezekiel 16, a little babe is thrown out into an open field left to die in the scorching sun. No one took pity on the helpless toddler kicking about in the amniotic fluid and blood of its birth until the young child's cry reaches the ears of an almighty, all powerful, all merciful God. I pick up in verse 6:

> Then I passed by and saw you kicking about in your blood, and as you lay there in your blood I said to you, "Live!" I made you grow like a plant of the field. You grew and developed and entered puberty. Your breasts had formed and your hair had grown, yet you were stark naked. Later I passed by, and when I looked at you and saw that you were old enough for love, I spread the corner of my garment over you and covered your naked body. I gave you my solemn oath and entered into a covenant with you, declares the Sovereign Lord, and you became mine. I bathed you with water and washed the blood from you and put ointments on you. I clothed you with an embroidered dress and put sandals of fine leather on you. I dressed you in fine linen and covered you with costly garments. I adorned you with jewelry: I put bracelets on your arms and a necklace around your neck, and I put a ring on your nose, earrings on your ears and a beautiful crown on your head. So you were adorned with gold and silver; your clothes were of fine linen and costly fabric and embroidered cloth. Your food was honey, olive oil and the finest flour. You became very beautiful and rose to be a queen. And your fame spread among the nations on account of your beauty, because the splendor I had given you made your beauty perfect, declares the Sovereign Lord (Ezek. 16:6-14, NIV).

Victims who believe the thorns of sexual abuse and trauma will just go away miserably kick about in the blood of wounds inflicted by a trespasser, emotionally, physically, and sexually bankrupt, until they cry out for help. David Jeremiah says,

> We know what it's like to feel emotionally bankrupt. There in the desert, David looks across the parched wasteland and sees it as a mirror of his own soul. And what can he offer in such a situation other than the response of any child who has stumbled and injured himself? David cries out to his Father to come, pick him up, and care for his hurts.[153]

The miracle of redemption eagerly awaits all who cry out to God.[154] Call out now. Get professional and spiritual help and become a Triumphant Overcomer ready to experience the true sexuality God designed before you were created.

When you do, God will cover your nakedness, put a bracelet on your arm, a necklace around your neck, and a crown on your head. A crown that crushes shame, guilt, and the tainted filter keeping survivors of sexual abuse and trauma in a victim status. Come receive your crown. The crown of a Triumphant Overcomer! Before an individual can receive his or her crown, though, there is one last excuse that must be addressed—the excuse of unforgiveness.

But I Can't Forgive

I worked at Naval Medical Center San Diego from 2013 to 2017 as a Board-Certified Clinical Chaplain. I worked in numerous wards over the course of four years, but one of my favorites was Mental Health. I taught a spirituality group every Tuesday and Thursday and covered a wide variety of topics. One day, I decided to talk about forgiveness. I opened up by talking about what forgiveness is, how important it is to forgive others, and how sometimes the hardest thing to do is to forgive yourself. All of a sudden, the girl sitting across the table from me slammed her fist on the table and yelled right in my face, "You mean

God wants me to forgive the &*!%# who did what he did to me!?" She jumped up and abruptly left the room.

All eyes locked on me, and I knew the next few words coming out of my mouth would quite possibly be the most important words I ever spoke. I hesitated, looked everyone straight in their eyes and said, "That's an excellent point." You may not think those four words were profound, but trust me, in that moment and context, they were. Why? Because the group wasn't expecting it. Nonetheless the young woman was right. I wish she had said it in a different way and stayed in the room, but, ironically, she was right. How could a good God, who punishes sin and is supposed to protect his children allow horrible things to happen to them? And as if that's not complicated enough, God then expects victims to forgive their trespassers? Seems absurd, doesn't it?

The conversation following the outburst was absolutely amazing. When the group saw that I didn't react to the outburst, that I remained calm, and that I even validated her point, it turned what could have ended in disaster into the most beautiful discussion on God and forgiveness I've ever heard or been a part of since. This leads me to my next question: What does God mean when he says, "But if you do not forgive others their trespasses, neither will your Father forgive your trespass" (Matt. 6:15)?

Sexual abuse and trauma leave a deep, deep wound in the hearts, minds, and bodies of both Christians and non-Christians. To truly be healed and take back the key to your private garden, a person must forgive the trespasser. However, considering that an overwhelming amount of instances of sexual abuse occur from a family member, friend, or colleague, forgiveness is often misunderstood. Forgiveness frees both the victim and the trespasser from the trespass, allowing both to find true healing and closure. For the trespasser, it opens the door to true repentance and the realization of their sin.

Dawn Wilson offers five lessons learned about healing from sexual abuse and the power of forgiveness:

1. I know I can forgive others because I have been so greatly forgiven. Bitterness will only make my pain worse and continue to wound others (Heb. 12:15).
2. I can pray for my abuser's change of heart and repentance—that my abuser will seek the Lord, turn from wickedness, and learn to live a godly life so God will be glorified (Luke 6:28).
3. I do not have to live in fear like a victim. Peace and victory come as I study and rest in who I am in Christ (Eph. 1:3–8).
4. I can learn how to communicate clear, pure boundaries in all relationships and speak truth in love (Eph. 4:15).
5. I must be aware of the enemy's schemes to control my responses and defeat me. I must saturate my life with Scripture and remember God's grace is greater than the condemnation I feel (1 John 3:20).[155]

Forgiveness does not mean that the victim ever has to be around, talk to, like, the trespasser ever again.

With that said, though, it becomes complicated when the trespasser is a family member. The Word of God says that Christians must never hate our brothers and sisters, either by blood or in Christ.[156] However, like, love, talk to, or ever see again is left up to the heart of the victim. The choice is the victim's alone. If the victim wants to rekindle a relationship with the trespasser, they are free to do whatever they decide. The trespasser will always technically occupy a title: father, brother, uncle, aunt, etc., but the important thing to remember is that the person has lost the rights and privileges that accompany the title. That's okay. Because now the victim is in control of his or her life and decisions. Forgiveness frees the victim from the trespass, allowing the victim to move from a victim to a Triumphant Overcomer who is in control of their present, future, and, most importantly, his or her sexuality. Now the Triumphant Overcomer has ownership of the key to his or her private garden. The trespasser no longer has any power, control, or influence over the victim. Forgiveness is the key to true healing and closure.

6 Steps to Healing Sexual Trauma

1. **Believe and Accept It Wasn't Your Fault**. If you keep blaming yourself, then you, your sexuality, and your marriage bed will perish from self-inflicted wounds. Allow your innocence to return—innocence is what God desires the most.

2. **Admit You Were Tricked and Exploited**. Innocence is precious and greatly desired by both adversary and foe. The cunning pawn broker pays top dollar for innocence. Whether the trespass felt good or not, you were tricked and exploited. Once you redeem your sexuality, your view of sex will be renewed and your sexual desire restored.

3. **Take Back the Key**. No one has the right to trespass in your private garden. When you marry, your spouse is the only one who should ever have a copy, allowing him or her unlimited access to your choice fruits, shoots, wells, and springs. Your marriage bed will never experience the heart of sex God designed if you don't take back the key. Take ownership of it now and never look back.

4. **Trust God**. Anger is not a sin and being angry with God is normal and acceptable. Rule over your anger, address the spiritual injury, and once again commune with a loving Heavenly Father who wants to redeem your sexuality and restore the sanctity of your marriage bed. Don't allow your spiritual injury to keep you from God. Embrace and use it to draw near to God!

5. **Remove the Thorns**. The thorns of sexual abuse and trauma do not come out on their own with time. Stop managing the pain and get professional and spiritual help. Take control of your sexuality and no longer allow the thorns of sexual abuse to influence your decisions.

6. **Forgive the Trespasser**. The wound of the trespass should no longer keep you from healing and the wonderful gift of sex God gave humanity. Once the wound heals, a scar will remain. However, the scar will signify a pivotal moment of transformation and transition. The scar will signify an incident over which you triumphantly conquered. Forgiveness is the key to healing the wound.

7

THE HEART OF SEX IN THE OLD TESTAMENT

"Speak to all the congregation of the children of Israel, and say to them: You shall be holy, for I the LORD your God am holy" (Lev. 19:2, NKJV).

Introduction

The perfunctory indulgence in Eden and the residual effects of the fall have diminished cultural and individual views on the meaning of sex and human sexuality. Divine principles set forth by God designed to protect sexuality and the marriage bed have been discarded and replaced with progressive ideologies of self-expression, sexual exploration, and instant gratification. Relentless attacks against traditional marriages have capitulated malapropos unions separating sex from the one-flesh union God predestined. God had different plans when he created Eve and presented her to Adam, her covenantal soul mate. To fully understand God's extraordinary plan for sex and sexuality, a person must incline his or her heart to wisdom and understanding. Christians, who seek wisdom like silver, find the hidden treasures of sexual intimacy.[157]

This chapter examines the heart of sex by exploring God's divine plan for human sexuality in four stages. The first stage begins at creation and examines God's original design for humanity. The second investigates coitus practices taking place in the lands of the Bible before the Law was written. The third follows the teachings of Moses found in the Pentateuch and studies the parameters intended for coitus. The fourth reviews the reoccurring themes throughout the rest of the Old Testament (OT) regarding sex and sexual immorality.

The Heart of Sex at Creation

On the sixth day the earth, moon, and sun brightly spun in the galaxy. Trillions upon trillions of star clusters illuminated the night sky. The sea teemed with life, and reptiles, animals, and dinosaurs filled the earth. Lush tropical vegetation covered the earth, and trees, with giant leafy boughs and tops touching the clouds, drank morning dew straight from the fountains of heaven.

God still had a few things to finish, though.[158] He knelt down and scooped up a small clump of dirt and gently formed it into his own image. Staring into the lifeless molded image lying in his unscarred hands, God drew a deep breath and blew the breath of life, sparking a relationship that would cost him his only begotten Son.

The story of creation does not end with the creation of man, though. At this point, the plot thickens as the majestic Creator debuts one of his most precious gifts to man—woman! God then blesses them and says, "Be fruitful and multiply and fill the earth" (Gen. 1:28). Remarkable. The first commandment God gave humanity was to have sex! I bet you didn't learn that in Sunday school.

The Gift of Procreation

To "be fruitful, multiply, and fill the earth," Adam and Eve would inevitably engage in a lot of sex. When God gave his blessings and charge, Adam and Eve remained innocent, holy, and pure. God set them apart from the rest of creation by forming them in his image, which he repeats three times in Genesis 1:26-27. God bestowed knowledge, righteousness, and holiness upon them, and when "God looked at what He had done, all of it was very good" (Gen. 1:31, KJV). Before the fall, Adam and Eve remained sinless. The innocence they shared allowed them to stand "naked and unashamed" (2:25, KJV) before each other and God. Innocence unlocks the doors of the heart, allowing people to fully understand the heart of sex.

God gave all creatures, including humans, natural sex drives that, when kept within the healthy boundaries he established, lead to feelings of holiness and happiness. God created one man and one woman, establishing the covenant of marriage for all generations. According to Tikva Frymer-Kensky, "In the Bible, the appropriate locus of sexuality is the monogamous nuclear family, the ideal human relationship."[159]

The union between Adam and Eve stands as the only family model for raising children in a loving, nurturing environment where a child can observe both the masculine and feminine nature of God's original design for humanity. The child, after completing puberty and entering the covenant of marriage, can then continue the natural cycle of procreation, thus fulfilling God's charge to "fill the earth" (Gen. 1:28). Jewish tradition understands God's charge to "be fruitful and multiply and fill the earth" as the first commandment (*mitzvah*) of the Torah. Thus, rabbinical teachings make procreation obligatory for all Jewish families.[160]

However, God's purpose for sex extends far beyond mere propagation. God also gave males and females the ability to experience an orgasm,[161] which induces physical and emotional sensations and the release of sexual tension.[162] The intense contractions in the prostate of men and the vagina and uterus in women, flood the body with endorphins in the form of peptides, distributing euphoric sensations throughout the body. Matthew Fox asked a group of mostly men and a few women about sperm: "Was it a metaphor or a literal gift of sexuality we share with another?"[163] One of the responses he received reveal the poetic harmony humans share during coitus: "The orgasmic moment is the momentary experience of the Immense and Intense Divine Love of the Creator; so intense, that if it lasted for more than a few moments it would cause a total systemic overload in the human person—to feel so loved so totally by the Divine One who created us."[164] This description showcases the splendor and intensity people feel during orgasm, an experience, undeniably, created by God.

Studies have shown a normal male ejaculates enough semen over the course of his life to generate nearly one trillion human lives.[165] Another study on women found the clitoris, located near the front juncture of the labia minora (inner lips), just above the urethra, has over eight thousand sensory nerve endings and is the most sensitive erogenous zone for females. The clitoris serves one purpose and one purpose only; it is the primary source of sexual pleasure for females. Sexual intercourse and the orgasm were designed by God for purposes of procreation and pleasure ultimately uniting male and female into one flesh.

Becoming One Flesh

Genesis 1 ends with God proclaiming everything "good." However, in Genesis 2:18, God proclaims, "It is not good that the man should be alone. I will make him a helper fit for him." God then ushers all the animals before Adam, but no suitable helper emerges.[166] Hence, God subsequently brings a deep sleep upon Adam. As Adam sleeps, God removes one of his ribs, and uses it to fashion a woman.[167] After Adam wakes, God presents the woman to Adam, who says, "This at last is bone of my bones and flesh of my flesh; she shall be called Woman, because she was taken out of Man" (Gen. 2:23).

This verse leads to the second paradox in Genesis regarding humanity. The name that Adam gives her reflects the identity they share in each other, "for she alone is his true counterpart in the creation."[168] This reality lays the foundation for Genesis 2:24, for a man to leave his mother and father and unite with his wife and in doing so the two become one flesh. Remarkably, the rib God took from Adam to form Eve, God now gives back to Adam, making him whole again. The verb "to leave" (*azab*) also means to forsake, abandon, reject, or desert.[169] To forsake mother and father and reject the authority of parents signifies the birth of a new relationship, a new covenant united in marriage, and is never to be seen or viewed as a capricious relationship of convenience.[170]

Genesis 2:24 establishes the covenant of marriage and defines the meaning of sex. This account of humanity deviates from other mythologies regarding the origins of man. Victor Hamilton writes, "The only man-woman relationship in view here is marriage, and it is presented in the biblical narrative with a respectful tenderness unknown elsewhere in ancient Near Eastern accounts of human origins."[171]

Contrary to Augustine of Hippo, who thought that sexual desire was unnatural, a result or punishment imposed due to Adam and Eve's original sin, the desire to become one flesh and engage in sex is perfectly natural and acutely willed by God.[172] Sex consummates the marriage and supernaturally unites two individuals, making them one flesh. Paul's message to the church at Corinth likewise warns against unholy one-flesh unions with prostitutes (1 Cor. 6:15-16).

The crowning point of two people falling in love and entering into a covenant of marriage and the one-flesh union is the wedding night. After the ceremony, the bride and groom consummate the final marriage act by having sexual intercourse.[173] The blood caused by the act bears witness to the bride's virginity and is a source of respect, honor, and dignity for her, as well the bride's family and community.[174] John Whalen proposes that God actually braced marriage with the character of a Sacrament:

> Christ has endowed marriage with the character of a Sacrament, making it something holy and a source of special graces. This confers a completely new dignity on the bodily union.

> Though marriage is validly established by the consensus, it is consummated only by the marriage act, assuming through it the character of a strictly indissoluble union. Its essential role in the consummation of the Sacrament clearly reveals the dignity to which the conjugal act has been elevated.[175]

God created man and woman, and he blessed and charged them with filling the earth with children. Thus, "Sex is made the means of obeying the divine command."[176] Everything God created, including the heart of sex for procreation and pleasure and for becoming one flesh is good: "For everything God created is good, and nothing is to be rejected if it is received with thanksgiving" (1 Tim. 4:4, NIV). Lewis Smedes suggests humans should love things made by God:

> Keeping the good of creation separate from sin's distortions of creation is no easy job. . . . Seduction and rape, unbridled sensuality, sadism and masochism, and personal exploitation are not difficult to identify as sexual distortion. But how do we know whether the early stirrings of sensual pleasure in a child, the genital excitement in an adolescent, the erotic passions of an adult are native to God's good creation or a mangled parody of it. . . . We are to love what God has made, feel good about anything that is human, and hate only what sinful human beings and devils have unmade.[177]

The heart of sex at creation remained innocent and good. Unfortunately, Adam and Eve disobeyed the one recorded rule God gave them: "You may surely eat of every tree of the garden, but of the tree of the knowledge of good and evil you shall not eat, for in the day that you eat of it you shall surely die" (Gen. 2:16-17). Death brought unintended consequences and distortions to God's original creation, and humankind has suffered ever since.[178] With the one rule broken, and without any laws or written rules in place, sexually immoral practices continued to lead humanity further away from God and holiness.

The Heart of Sex before the Law

After the fall, and after Adam and Eve were kicked out of the garden, the next chapter of humanity began. Adam and Eve could no longer approach the tree of life and live forever. Because of their disobedience, Adam, Eve, and the serpent suffered under God's admonishments as life for them changed dramatically. Humankind would no longer gather food without struggle or give birth with minimal pain, and they now had an archenemy waiting to kill, steal, and destroy them.

Adam and Eve, banished from the garden, inaugurated the charge of filling the earth. They bore children, and their children grew and bore children, proliferating the cycle of procreation, a direct result of God's blessing (Gen. 1:28). By Genesis 6, thousands, if not millions of people, populated the earth. Venturing farther from the garden, they spread out across the land (v. 1) and built villages, towns, and cities without divinely written laws and regulations. The heart of sex, in the meantime, had degraded severely from creation, and the imminent consequences reveal the visceral enmity God has against sin.

Sodom and Gomorrah

The communal aspects of the story of Sodom and Gomorrah reflect the dangers of social ethics (a collection of behaviors and values of a culture or group of people). Evil does not discriminate. It embraces every willing vessel, and once it takes hold in a village, town, or city, it spreads like leprosy. Genesis 18 and 19 record the deplorable actions of a community enthralled with the evil behavior of sexual immorality.[179]

The immoral sexual lust of the men from Sodom and Gomorrah, referred to today as "sodomy," is the practice of anal copulation or intercourse by a man with another man or woman. Mosaic Law would later forbid the practice and participation of sodomy (Deut. 23:17; Lev. 18:22; 18:29; 20:13). A Sodomite (Hebrew: *Qadhesh*) refers to an unclean male temple prostitute and is mentioned several times in 1 and 2 Kings.[180] In Scripture, "sodomite" and its plural denotes a negative connotation of anyone, male or female, who engages or participates in immoral sexual acts to include anal intercourse (1 Kgs. 14:24; 15:12; 22:46; 2 Kgs. 23:7). Several Scriptures instruct the Israelites to remove from the land and have no interactions with "shrine prostitutes, prostitutes, sodomites, whoremongers, and those who lusted after strange flesh" (both male and female) throughout the Bible.[181]

The practice and participation of sodomy caused the complete destruction of several towns and all the inhabitants except one family (Gen. 19:12-29). In one moment, entire bloodlines and countless generations received in themselves the due penalty for their sins (Rom. 1:27). God's judgment and punishment on the sexual sin of sodomy and all who engaged in it (and all those who knew about it and chose to do nothing) continues as a stark example of social ethics and what happens when people follow the crowd in doing evil (Ex. 23:2a). The account of Sodom and Gomorrah, which takes place before the writing of the Pentateuch, highlights the practice of an evil, unnatural vice and its condemnation by God. This story also reveals the prevalence and supremacy of God's judgment upon all creation, even before his eternal divine laws were written down.

These examples stand as a witness of what life was like before the writing of the Law. Without written divine law, humanity returned to their vomit of immorality,[182] just as they had before the flood. Sensual and social sin devastated men and women, which ended in the destruction of the earth and Sodom and Gomorrah, not to mention the numerous lives the Bible does not record. The need for divine laws coupled with God's divine grace is the only way humanity will redeem the heart of sex.

The Heart of Sex in the Pentateuch

The Law brought atonement for sins and instruction, regulation, and peace to a troubled and lost civilization.[183] The nations discarded the image of God for worthless idols unable to see, hear, or speak, let alone rescue and redeem from sin, shame, and deep feelings of meaninglessness. The nation of Israel experienced the glory of God unlike any other nation. Israel witnessed firsthand the mighty acts and miracles of the Creator of heaven and earth. God chose Israel as a conduit for holiness. Unfortunately, the Israelites' lust for sexual exploration with neighboring nations caused them to sin, bringing judgment once again.[184]

Moses authored the first five books of the Bible, commonly referred to as the Pentateuch. Parameters regarding sex and sexual practices promulgate a message of holiness. God established these boundaries in an attempt to redeem human sexuality while protecting the covenant of marriage and the integrity of the family; these parameters also instruct singles, people committed to celibacy, and eunuchs. The Pentateuch outlines the meaning of sex and the oneness God intended for the heart of sex.

God Establishes Healthy Sexual Boundaries

In the book of Leviticus, God establishes healthy sexual boundaries by giving detailed instructions concerning coital practices. God confronts Israel and warns them about the evil sexual practices of the nations around them (Lev. 18:3). The premise of God's instructions in Leviticus 17-26 pertain to holiness.[185] God's aspirations for Israel constituted a holy nation and royal priesthood. The nations inhabiting the land defiled themselves by engaging in sexually immoral acts which caused their eviction.[186] Sexual defilement apparently causes the land to vomit out the people (Lev. 18:24-30).

John Oswalt addresses the implications of God's warning to Israel about following the practices of the nations they would eventually drive out of the land:

> The rationale behind that ethic (of Lev. 18 and 20) is not simply a reaction to a life style that happens not to be Hebrew. . . . Rather these activities are prohibited because they grow out of

and lead to a world view that is radically opposed to that of the Bible. . . . They represent one common outlook on sex and the world, that is, the denial of boundaries.[187]

The message directly following Leviticus 18 highlights the true reason why God gave Moses laws concerning the establishment of healthy sexual boundaries. The second verse of chapter 19 says, "You shall be holy, for I the LORD your God am holy." Holiness is repeated again in 1 Thessalonians 4:3, "For this is the will of God, your sanctification: that you abstain from sexual immorality."

God establishes healthy sexual boundaries predominantly for reasons of holiness. Holiness protects the covenant of marriage and the sexuality God assigns to individuals. Sexual immorality degrades the image of God and leaves people feeling alone, insecure, shameful, and empty. Sexual immorality is counterintuitive to the life of holiness and love God designed for the heart of sex.

Exodus 20:14 records another example of a healthy boundary God establishes for Israel. The commandment forbidding adultery transcends the marriage bed. It protects children, family, and society. Throughout history, the family has been foundational to the health of any society.[188] Adultery breaks the covenant of marriage between the husband and wife, and it breaks apart the family bond God meant to stay united.[189] The disintegration of marriage often led to divorce and remarriage in Mosaic Law (Deut. 24:1-4) and was a dispensation to the condition of the human heart and its vulnerability to sin.[190]

God Confronts Sexual Immorality

Sexual immorality played a significant part in the corruption of the human race before the flood and the writing of the Law. Sexual sins and promiscuity corrupt every dimension of humanity, leading humankind away from a vibrant relationship with God and into a realm filled with dark, evil thoughts all the time. When sin remains unchecked in an individual, it completely corrupts the image God originally planned for that person, and the end result will be one of utter dismay and turmoil where sin controls every action and thought, leaving the individual emotionally, physically, mentally, and spiritually empty.

Sin, especially sexual sin, affects every facet of a person. Christopher Wright describes humans as multidimensional beings made up of physical, social, rational, and spiritual parts.[191] He describes humans as physical because they come from the created order of the earth. Humans have social aspects, and their gender plays a significant factor in all other relationships, including their relationship with God. He believes humans are rational by having the ability to communicate, show emotions, and have memories, but, most importantly, they are spiritual because they can have a personal and direct relationship with God.[192]

When Eve approached the forbidden fruit in the garden of Eden, she approached it rationally. The fruit was good for food and pleasing to her eyes; by eating it she could gain knowledge and become like God. That was what she rationalized, and in her rational mind, she was correct. The forbidden fruit was good for food, it looked great, and she did gain knowledge. However, she was deceived into doubting God's command, and she was lied to by the serpent, who told her she would not die. Wright says,

> All the capacities of the human intellect are good in themselves, commended as highly prized gifts of God. There was nothing wrong with Eve using her mind; the problem was she was now using all its powers in a direction that was forbidden by God.[193]

The mind desires to have no boundaries when it comes to human sexuality. A phrase often repeated in today's culture is, "If it feels good, then do it." When humans doubt the truth of God and approach life rationally, they are deceived by societal ideologies[194] and practices that lead to death and eternal separation from God.[195]

Paul instructs the church at Corinth to "flee from sexual immorality" (1 Cor. 6:18). He continues, "Every other sin a person commits is outside the body, but the sexually immoral person sins against his own body." The Book of Proverbs affirms, "He who commits adultery lacks sense; he who does it destroys himself" (6:23). God confronts the detestable practices of sexual immorality to keep people from making themselves unclean and perverted and to keep them from sinning against their own body, which completely corrupts their own sexual identity. When sexual identity is lost, blurred, and confused, sexually immoral acts like bestiality and sodomy can lead people further into sin, which can lead to gender dysphoria,[196] transgender recognition, homosexuality and lesbianism, orgies, and numerous other acts.

The sexual laws God gave Moses were not intended to keep people from enjoying sex. Intimate relationships have always been a part of God's plans for humanity. God's laws and instructions concerning sex protect children, adolescents, women, and men from rape, sodomy, victimization, sex trafficking, prostitution, sexual exploitation, and sexual abuse. God's sexual laws protect humanity against diseases from incest, inbreeding, and sexual intercourse.

Sex throughout the Old Testament

After taking possession of the Promised Land, the Israelites moved on with life and enjoyed the good land God gave them. They planted vineyards and dug wells. They cleared land and grew crops. They built houses, towns, and cities, and they continued to carry out the charge of God to "fill the earth." God gave specific instructions to the Israelites about intermarrying with the nations around them (Deut. 7:3-4), but these instructions were ignored, and before long, Israel fell back into the sexual sin so prevalent in the surrounding nations.

The consequences of these actions once against caused the Israelites to defile themselves by intermarrying with nations that served other gods and engaged in sexually immoral acts. These acts caused the children of God to turn away from him, so God sent prophets to confront Israel and her detestable practices and to remind them of their humble beginnings and the promises God made to Abraham, Isaac, and Jacob (Ezek. 16).

Eugene Merrill acknowledges that God's original covenantal purpose for Israel, traced through Abraham, called people out of sin to a better life of holiness and ultimately the redemption of the world:

> God created Israel by calling Abraham out of paganism and through him eventually establishing a people who would serve him in the task of redeeming the world. This gracious act of making a non-people the elect and gifted servant of the Lord should also do away with any spirit of hostility of one toward the other.[197]

Unfortunately, the Israelites forgot God's call of holiness and redemption and became hostile toward each other and the surrounding nations.

In Ezekiel, God equates Israel's rebellion to that of a prostitute. The sexual insinuations God uses in chapter 16 testify to the power sexual immorality has in turning people away from the living God and to idolatry, pagan sacrifices, and as in Israel's case, even sacrificing their own children. When sexual immorality and power intermingle, lives and kingdoms become pawns in a battle to distort God's plan for his children. The story of David and Bathsheba and the story of the nation of Israel during the times of the Old Testament prophets show how sexual immorality distorts God's plan for human sexuality and the heart of sex.

David and Bathsheba

David will forever be known as "a man after [God's] own heart" (1 Sam. 13:14). David's life is an intriguing story of humble beginnings as the youngest of eight brothers to one of infamy as the king of Israel.

David's story follows the life of a man chosen by God at a young age to fulfill God's plan of redemption through God's only begotten son who would come from David's lineage. David's story of adultery with Bathsheba testifies to the weakness of the flesh and showcases the power of sexual lusts.

It was probably a normal day for David. He attended to his daily duties as king, and as the sun dropped below the mountains, he retired to his quarters. After supper, he took a stroll on his balcony to survey his kingdom when suddenly he noticed a beautiful woman bathing in the open air on her roof. David had to make a quick decision. Would he walk back inside and respect the young woman's privacy, or would he gaze lustfully at her naked body? David unfortunately allowed his flesh to make the decision, and he watched her bathe.

As he did, he had another thought: "I am king, and I can have sex with her tonight." Countless men and women have been taken advantage of by people in powerful positions. David used his position and power to indulge in adultery, which resulted in the death of two individuals. David sent for the woman, who was the wife of Uriah, a soldier serving in David's army. David had sex with Bathsheba, and unbeknownst to them, the sexual union impregnated her. When David received word that Bathsheba was pregnant, he tried to cover up the pregnancy by bringing Uriah home, thinking Uriah, after having been gone for an undisclosed amount of time, would surely want to have sex with his wife. Uriah turned out to be a man of great integrity and leadership and refused to have sex with his wife on account of his men who were still at war (2 Sam. 11:11). When David's plan failed, he had Uriah killed on the battlefield.[198]

This story is a reality for many. Numerous men and women innocently become intrigued by their natural sexual passions and normal attraction to beauty.[199] The Apostle Paul, in writing to the Corinthians, says, "No temptation has overtaken you that is not common to man. God is faithful, and he will not let you be tempted beyond your ability, but with the temptation he will also provide the way of escape, that you may be able to endure it" (1 Cor. 10:13). Everyone has a choice when tempted. David had a choice. He did not plan to see Bathsheba that evening taking a bath. He was taken by surprise and, in a moment of sexual lust, chose to disobey the laws of God. Sin deceived David into committing adultery, which ended in murder and eventually led to the death of the child.

Fortunately for David and his kingdom, God did not allow David's story to end like this. God sent David a prophet named Nathan, who rebuked David and confronted him about his sin. David repented and fell into the hands of a loving and merciful God who only desires the best for his children. The beauty of this story is God desires the same for every single person living today.

The story of David and Bathsheba reveals the tragedy of an unguarded moment of sexual desire and the consequences of not following the sexual boundaries God put in place for all humanity. God created humanity to be sexual, to experience orgasms, and to be captivated by each other. To understand the true beauty of the heart of sex, one must turn to the most profound book on sexuality in the Old Testament—Song of Solomon. The vivid sensual accounts in this book alone portray the creative splendor of God and his plan for sexuality.

The Shulamite and Solomon

The romantic courtship of two young lovers is forever captured in the eloquent prose of Song of Solomon, which covers every phase of a relationship, from dating and courtship to engagement and marriage. The Shulamite and Solomon's relationship displays the natural sexual desire God intricately wove into the heart of every human being, especially those preparing for the covenant of marriage. Throughout the duration of this adoring love story, God records[200] the sensual fondness and passionate sexual innuendos the love-struck couple extol upon one another.

The Shulamite, a servant girl who works by day in the fields, catches the eye of King Solomon. Her beauty and endearing passion for life, love, and romance captivates the king, sparking a love story unparalleled in Scripture. Solomon's passionate affection releases a flood of legitimate sexual desires in the Shulamite everyone should experience when interacting with their prospective true love and covenantal soul mate. According to William Loader, these feelings are strong sexual emotions the Apostle Paul likened (1 Cor. 7:9) to the intensity of "burning" (*pyroo*—to burn, to be inflamed [with lust])[201] and are experienced outside and before marriage.[202]

The Shulamite recognizes the intensity and passion of falling in love and wisely cautions others about the dangers of awakening love prematurely. She says not to "stir up or awaken love until it pleases" (Song 2:7, 3:5, 8:4). Love is powerful and, when carelessly roused and consigned, breaks more hearts than anything else in all creation. Counseling centers throughout the world fill each day with broken hearted individuals who stirred and awakened love prematurely. The Shulamite warning serves as a beacon to all who venture into the throes of love. Love is a double-edged sword. It can protect and serve, and it can cut and destroy. Thus, the Shulamite says, wield it wisely and wait "until it pleases."

Several metaphors dramatize sensual passions deep within the Shulamite and Solomon, who apparently are overflowing with sincere fidelity for each other. However, none are more powerful and revealing than verses 4:12-5:1. Finally, the courtship is over and vows are exchanged. Solomon now refers to her as "My bride/spouse." Thus, the final consummation of the wedding night has arrived. Both lovers waited patiently, as well as passionately, for this moment, and as the marriage will soon be consummated, the Shulamite reveals one last gift to her husband—her virginity—an honored and cherished gift from a bride to her groom, or a groom to his bride. Solomon acknowledges her priceless gift by stating, "A garden locked is my sister, my bride, a spring locked, a fountain sealed" (4:12). David Jeremiah writes,

> Shulamith now stands before her husband for his loving delight, and his only. The blocked fountain is unblocked, and

the waters can flow. Since water is the physical basis of life on our planet, no symbol could be more powerful. Solomon can now take a refreshing drink from this private stream. He can be cooled from the desert heat by bathing in it, and these 'living waters' will rinse away the dust of daily living. He will be baptized into the newness of his marriage identity.[203]

Solomon highlights her purity in the previous passage and in the next three verses joyfully celebrates the pleasant abundance she protected and reserved for him by stating, "Your shoots are an orchard of pomegranates with all choicest fruits . . . a garden fountain, a well of living water, and flowing streams from Lebanon" (Song 4:13-15). Her love and virginity are a well of living water and an orchard Solomon will enjoy for the remainder of his life as he "come[s] to his garden and eat[s] its choicest fruits" (v. 16).

The expressive and passionate sexual dialogue between the Shulamite and Solomon reveals God's intimate plan for the heart of sex. When people fall in love, they should naturally experience a wellspring of sexual desires for each other. When those feelings become mutual and lead to courtship, engagement, and marriage, the two become one flesh and experience the fullness of their sexuality under the blessing of the covenant of marriage. If the couple stays within the healthy sexual boundaries found throughout Scripture, they will enjoy an orchard of sexual love and gratification for the duration of their life and marriage.

Unfortunately, numerous Christians never experience the full extent of the heart of sex God intended for humanity because leaders rarely address sexuality from the pulpit. Or, if they do, the message usually addresses sexual immorality and not the heart of sex God designed for purposes of enrichment, holiness, pleasure, etc. The sensual message of Song of Solomon and others like it helps Christians embrace sexuality the way God designed it and helps Christian couples keep the marriage bed pure, passionate, and undefiled.

The Nation of Israel

Israel inherited a land flowing with milk and honey. The land thrived with an abundance of lakes, streams, and mountains filled with gold and copper. The people settled down and had children and built towns and cities as their flocks and herds increased. Trees laden with olives, figs, and all kinds of fruits scattered across the mountains. Fields thick with barley, wheat, and rye stretched as far as the eye could see, but the complacent hearts of the people once again caused Israel to engage in sexual wickedness. The people rebelled against God, who in turn exiled them to Babylon by the ruthless hand of King Nebuchadnezzar. However, even in a foreign land God's original charge to "fill the earth" remained.

The prophet Jeremiah proclaimed an encouraging message to Judah in the days of captivity in Babylon:

> Build houses and live in them; plant gardens and eat their produce. Take wives and have sons and daughters; take wives for your sons, and give your daughters in marriage, that they may bear sons and daughters; multiply there, and do not decrease. But seek the welfare of the city where I have sent you into exile, and pray to the Lord on its behalf, for in its welfare you will find your welfare (Jer. 29:5-7).

God gave the Israelites everything they needed to live productive lives of increase, but it wasn't enough in their minds. Social ethics, power, wealth, and sexual lusts corrupted them, causing the people of Israel to once again turn from God and experience decrease.[204] By the time God sends the prophet Malachi to speak to his people, Jewish men have turned from God and their wives. God sends Malachi to confront Israel so they will return to him and be forgiven, so they will increase and be blessed.

Malachi lived in the days of the prophet Nehemiah, who rebuilt the walls of Jerusalem. Malachi prophesied to the nation of

Israel because of the detestable practices of the people. Divorce, infidelity, and mixed marriages plagued the people, making the people and the land defiled.[205] In Malachi 2, Malachi confronts the people and the priests who had failed to uphold the Word of God:

> But you say, 'Why does he not [regard our offering]?' Because the Lord was witness between you and the wife of your youth, to whom you have been faithless, though she is your companion and your wife by covenant. Did he not make them one, with a portion of the Spirit in their union? And what was the one God seeking? Godly offspring. So guard yourselves in your spirit, and let none of you be faithless to the wife of your youth. 'For the man who does not love his wife but divorces her,' says the Lord, the God of Israel, 'covers his garment with violence,' says the Lord of hosts. So guard yourselves in your spirit, and do not be faithless (vv. 14-16).[206]

C. F. Keil and F. Delitzsch emphasize the importance of cherishing the marriage of "the wife of your youth" because the Lord himself is a witness to the marriage. Faithlessness to one's wife was considered faithlessness to God and his commands, but the real emphasis in this passage is more than just an appeal to remain faithful to one's wife and to God. Keil and Delitzsch also think that this passage is an attempt by Malachi to pierce the very hearts of Jewish men by reminding them that their wives had been with them through joy and sorrow and were their true companions. Their wives alone should be their love for all of life:

> With the expression 'wife of thy youth' the prophet appeals to the heart of the husband, pointing to the love of his youth with which the marriage had been entered into; and so also in the circumstantial clause, through which he brings to the light

the faithless treatment of the wife in putting her away: 'Yet she was thy companion, who shared thy joy and sorrow, and the wife of thy covenant, with whom thou didst made a covenant for life.'[207]

The message Malachi brings to the people concerning divorce goes all the way back to Genesis and the creation account of the covenant of marriage (Gen. 2:18-25). His message to Israel continues to show the union God wants a husband and wife to have, a union God meant to keep the marriage bed pure and to never be broken (Heb. 13:4). The marriage union between a husband and a wife parallels the union God desires to have with his children, a union filled with love, acceptance, forgiveness, and most of all faithfulness, so how did divorce, infidelity, and mixed marriages become so prevalent in their community?

The answer to this question lies within the message of the prophets throughout the Old Testament. The prophet Ezra confronts Israel about its unfaithfulness to God and its detestable practices, and he links this to mixed marriages (Ezra 9:2). The Israelites had mingled the holy nation with the nations around them, leading them away from the living God and to idol worship, pagan rituals, and sexual immorality. Ezra goes so far as to record the names of every priest who had intermarried. This same message is repeated in the New Testament. Paul warns the Corinthian church about being unequally yoked with unbelievers.[208] His message to them directly relates to Ezra's. Both Paul and Ezra attempt to keep the holy from becoming unholy, the clean from becoming unclean.

The prophet Nehemiah rebukes the men of Judah for marrying women from Ashdod, Ammon, and Moab. He relates their mixed marriages to being unfaithful to God just like Solomon was led away from God by the many wives he took from the surrounding nations (Neh. 13:23-29). As stated earlier, Moses confronted the Israelites and forbade them from intermarrying (Deut. 7:3).

The laws regarding sexual relationships in the Old Testament seem to revolve around the central theme of marriage, uniting a man and woman for a lifelong, exclusive union.[209] Malachi's statement, "For the man who does not love his wife but divorces her . . . covers his garment with violence" (2:16), speaks to the harm divorce brings upon a man (and to his wife, children, and others) and the harm brought upon the nation of Israel.[210] Divorce, infidelity, and mixed marriages led the men of Israel away from their wives and away from their children. It brought decrease to families, it caused Israel to become defiled, and it ultimately led the people away from God.[211]

Common themes in all of the Old Testament references about marriage and sexual immorality were unfaithfulness, uncleanliness, defilement, and idolatry. God often connected idolatry with immorality, which spawned from a wicked and perverse heart. The people were unfaithful to God, unfaithful to their spouses, and in many instances throughout Scripture, unfaithful to the marriage bed. Sexual sins brought severe consequence upon the Israelites and corrupted the nations around them. Sexual sins also brought decrease. Sexual sins took finances away from the home, and sexual sins were a major factor leading to divorce, disease, and sex acts so degrading that God's punishment was death.[212] Sexual sins caused the nation of Israel, and the pagan nations they lived among, to pawn their sexuality, which ended up diminishing their view of sex, men, women, children, marriage, and undermining the basic dynamics of the family.

J. Lanier Burns suggests that creation itself was lost with the introduction of sin and would need to be redeemed:

> The order of creation was lost in the chaos of sin; everything that had been created in a harmonious paradise was thrown into an evil absence of romantic ideals. The problem now was a problem of posterity, the 'seed of the woman' pointed to a Son who would reconcile God and humanity in fulfillment of God's stated will for the earth.[213]

With the coming of Christ and the fulfillment of the Law, humankind would finally experience the power of grace. A look into the New Testament will help usher in the new plan for sexuality in the lives of Christian believers.

8

THE HEART OF SEX IN THE NEW TESTAMENT

"This is the will of God, your sanctification: that you abstain from sexual immorality; that each one of you know how to control his own body in holiness and honor, not in the passion of lust like the Gentiles who do not know God" (1 Thess. 4:3-5).

Introduction

The books of the New Testament continue the motif of the heart of sex. They record how Jesus and his disciples responded to issues of marriage, sex, adultery, prostitution, orgies, homosexuality, and numerous other acts of sexual immorality. These books help believers understand the sexuality God assigned to them. Believers in the New Testament faced the same struggles, temptations, and desires that the children of Israel did in the Old Testament. Christians lived among nations involved in sexual practices forbidden by God.

The following sections will explore how Jesus and his disciples responded to the topic of sex and how they spoke against sexual immorality.

The Gospels

In the Sermon on the Mount, Jesus reminds the crowd about the seventh commandment: "You shall not commit adultery" (Matt. 5:27). He then takes this command deeper into the real issue of this sexual sin and says, "But I say to you that everyone who looks at a woman with lustful intent has already committed adultery with her in his heart" (v. 28).[214] Finally, the real truth about sexual sins comes to the surface. Sexual sin comes from deep inside humanity—it comes from the heart.

Jeremiah the prophet warns the people of his time about this, saying, "The heart is deceitful above all things, and desperately sick; who can understand it?" (Jer. 17:9). The Book of Proverbs concurs, "Folly is bound up in the heart of a child, but the rod of discipline drives it far from him" (22:15). Jesus goes on to say in his sermon to the crowd gathered on the mount, "For out of the heart come evil thoughts, murder, adultery, sexual immorality, theft, false witness, slander. These are what defile a person" (Matt. 15:19-20; Mark 7:21-23). And again, Jesus, speaking about divorce, says,

> Because of your hardness of heart Moses allowed you to divorce your wives, but from the beginning it was not so. And I say to you: whoever divorces his wife, except for sexual immorality, and marries another, commits adultery (Matt. 19:8-9; cf. Mark 10:5).

Jesus refers to the Mosaic Law and emphasizes that it was because of the hardness of their hearts that Moses gave them permission (and not a command) to divorce their wives.[215] Jesus then highlights the covenant of marriage God established from the beginning, which also has connotations to the supernatural power that sex plays in uniting male and female into one flesh.

Throughout the New Testament, the noun "heart" (*kardia*) is the center for all physical and spiritual life. Johannes Behm explains, "The heart is the main organ of psychic and spiritual life, the place in man at which God bears witness to Himself."[216] According to Behm, throughout the NT, the "heart" is affirmed in several ways:

> (1) In the heart dwell feelings and emotions, desires and passions. (2) The heart is the seat of understanding, the source of thought and reflection. (3) The heart is the seat of the will, the source of resolves. (4) Thus the heart is supremely the one centre in man to which God turns, in which the religious life is rooted, which determines moral conduct.[217]

The heart of humanity needs reconciliation from the powerful fog of sexual idolatry society casts over the heart of sex. The heart of humanity needs redemption from sexually immoral ideologies and practices destroying Christian singles and couples.[218] And the heart of humanity needs to return to innocence, which only happens at the cross and by the divine miracle of confession and forgiveness.[219] The key to breaking the bondage sexual immorality holds over humanity starts with the heart. After all, it was the heart that first got humanity destroyed in the first place:

> The Lord saw that the wickedness of man was great in the earth, and that every intention of the thoughts of his heart was only evil continually. And the Lord regretted that he had made man on the earth, and it grieved him to his heart (Gen. 6:5-6).

God desires holiness in his people. He is just as much a God of justice as he is a God of love and forgiveness. This is evident when the people bring Jesus a woman caught in adultery (John 8). Jesus does not condemn her, nor does he validate her actions. He offers her forgiveness with a warning, "Go, and sin no more" (v. 11, KJV).[220] This scene shows the love of God and his desire to commune with his children. Jesus's reply to the people about lustful looks and adultery in the heart also served to dispel rabbinical views concerning good deeds. Rabbis generally believed if a person had good intentions, those good intentions would bring forth good deeds, and if a person had evil intentions, those intentions would only count if the person succumbed to them.[221]

Sexual sins destroy the relationship God intended for marriage. They destroy families, they corrupt the heart, and they keep humanity from being reconciled to God.[222] The first commandment speaks to the truth of what God really desires from his children. Christians can't "love the Lord their God with all their heart" if their hearts are darkened by sexual sins.

The Writings of Paul

Paul speaks of sexual practices several times in his writings. The first time he mentions sex is in the Book of Romans. In chapter 1, Paul confronts the Romans about their ungodliness and unrighteousness which he attributes to their "foolish hearts" becoming "darkened," leading them to exchange the glory of God for idolatry (vv. 21-23). The people of Rome were so engrossed in idolatrous practices that they ended up corrupting their own sexuality.[223] Men lusted after other men, and women lusted after other women; in the process, they exchanged natural sexual relations for unnatural sexual relations (vv. 26-27). These sexual practices came from "the lusts of their hearts" (v. 24) and caused the people to become unclean and guilty of idolatry. As John Stott explains,

> The history of the world confirms that idolatry leads to immorality. A false image of God leads to a false understanding of sex. Paul does not tell us what kind of immorality he has in mind, except that it involved *the degrading of their bodies with one*

another (24). He is right. Illicit sex degrades people's humanness; sex in marriage, as God intended, ennobles it.[224]

Therefore, Paul says God "gave them up" or "turned them over" to their own lust, which eventually led to the degrading of their bodies.[225] Paul, in writing to the saints in Ephesus about Gentiles, states,

> You must no longer walk as the Gentiles do, in the futility of their minds. They are darkened in their understanding, alienated from the life of God because of the ignorance that is in them, due to their hardness of heart. They have become callous and have given themselves up to sensuality, greedy to practice every kind of impurity (Eph. 4:17-19).

The heart and the mind in this passage both play a role in the demise of God's original plan for human sexuality.

Contemporary brain research provides helpful insights for understanding this verse. Studies on the brain and its correlation to sex show that the hypothalamus is the principal regulator of hormone flow throughout the body and controls how reproductive behavior and sex are structured. Jo Durden-Smith and Diane Desimone, in their book, *Sex and the Brain*, point out, "The hypothalamus is almost certainly differently stamped by sex hormones before birth. It's like a photographic plate that is exposed before birth and then developed by a fresh rush of hormones at puberty."[226] This could explain why males tend to be more aggressive and prone to "acting out sexually" than women.[227] Other studies have indicated that testosterone levels in men increase behavioral reactivity which may explain why young males, who have higher levels of testosterone, engage in risky behavior, and commit almost all of the violent crimes, especially sexual crimes.[228]

The Diagnostic and Statistical Manual of Mental Disorders defines this type of aggressive behavior as an Impulse-Control Disorder (ICD). It refers to an individual's inability to resist a drive, temptation, or impulse to carry out an action harmful to the individual and to others. This manual further states that other disorders like "Impulse-Control Disorder Not Elsewhere Classified" possess the characteristics that the individual experiences an increasing sense of arousal or tension before executing the act and feels relief, gratification, or pleasure when executing the act.[229]

No matter what excuse or label people place on deviant sexual behaviors, sexual sins make the children of God and society unclean, and this same message reverberates throughout the Bible. Paul instructs the Romans to refrain from this type of behavior while encouraging them to present their bodies as instruments of righteousness to God (Rom. 6:13). Romans 1:20-27 highlights how the heart played a significant role in the demise of God's original plan for sexuality and how the consequences for humanity were and are universal. According to Stanford Mills, "Verses 26 and 27 should be taken together, for they portray the debased condition and the wickedness and degradation of humanity. This is perversion in its lowest aspect."[230] Men and women turned from the natural sexual desire for heterosexual sex and were inflamed with shameful lust for homosexual/lesbian relationships and sexual practices (vv. 26-27).[231] What started out as sexual in nature ended with an overflow of sins and evil behavior, e.g., wickedness, covetousness, maliciousness, disobedience, and faithlessness (vv. 28-31).

The result of sexual sin, as heartbreaking as it is, is heartlessness. Maybe this is the reason why so many people aren't satisfied with their sexual life as well as life itself. Heartless people will never be satisfied because the fruit of sin is shame and eventually death. As Paul says, "But what fruit were you getting at that time from the things of which you are now ashamed? For the end of those things is death" (Rom. 6:21).

Paul speaks about celibacy, fornication, marriage, and conjugal rights in 1 Corinthians 7. He begins this chapter by saying, "It is good for a man not to have sexual relations with a woman" (v. 1); the verb *haptomai*—to touch—means "of carnal intercourse with a woman."[232]

This verse refers to a question the Corinthians posed to Paul. It is okay to be single and celibate, or married and refrain from having sex for a time (e.g., during a woman's menstrual cycle, fasting, sickness, during a military deployment or on a trip when married couples are not physically together). God created humans in his image. The image of God in humans does not deteriorate because a person decides to refrain or engage in sex.[233] Paul goes on to recommend that it would be better, though, for singles to marry than to engage in sexual immorality. Corinth was a city filled with paganism, which was closely associated with fornication. Throughout the city, every temple housed slave-prostitutes.[234]

God placed natural and normal sexual desires inside the body. A lack of sexual desire once a person has gone through puberty would be abnormal. For married couples, sex should be a normal and frequent act of love and sharing that keeps the marriage bed "verdant." Unless a medical condition exists, a married couple should strive to fulfill what Paul says is a God-given right/concession, not a command.

In 1 Corinthians 7:3, Paul supports a monogamous marriage where both husband and wife render affection to each other. However, verses 4 and 5 showcase the true beauty of God's design for the heart of sex. Paul encourages married couples to share their bodies with each other by saying, "Do not deprive one another" (v. 5). Once again, this is a concession, not a command. Paul basically asserts that each spouse should fulfill his or her conjugal rights to each other. A basic definition of conjugal rights is, "The sexual rights or privileges implied by and involved in the marriage relationship: the right of sexual intercourse between husband and wife."[235] Husbands and wives should fulfill their conjugal rights and share their bodies regularly with each other.

Revelation and New Creation

The book of Revelation continues to reveal the fallen state of humanity with regard to human sexuality. Chapter 2 highlights the church at Pergamos and reports that people in the church were following the teaching of Balaam by eating food sacrificed to idols and committing sexual immorality (v. 14). Ironically, Paul's theology comes from his teachings on freedom from the law. While some leaders at Corinth accepted the "freedom" of a man living with his father's wife, Paul, in his letter to the Galatians, warns the people about using their newfound freedom as an excuse for immorality (5:13).

In Numbers 25, Israelite men indulged in sexual immorality with Moabite women. The Moabite women enticed the men to offer sacrifices to the Baal of Peor, and soon all Israel followed in the idolatrous action. The Lord did not allow Balaam to curse Israel, so Balaam suggested that King Balak corrupt Israel by tempting them to intermarry with pagan women, and it worked.[236] Balaam's principle of corruption for Israel (sexual immorality) had now crept into the church at Pergamos.

Balaamism is alive and well in Christian churches and families today. God promised to bless and save all who accept the sacrifice of Jesus and follow him. Because Satan has no power to curse what God has blessed, he resorts to the only thing he has left—corruption. And to his delight, Satan goes right to the core of humanity and attacks people at the very essence of who they are—their sexuality. When a person's sexuality is compromised and corrupted, a trickle-down effect occurs. The individual suffers, his or her marriage suffers, kids and family members suffer, the body of Christ suffers, and collectively, society suffers. In the end, Satan wins.

Later in the same chapter of Revelation, John confronts the church at Thyatira about allowing the self-proclaimed prophetess Jezebel to teach the people to commit sexual immorality (Rev. 2:20). Even though God gave them time to repent, the people of Thyatira refused to change their ways. God sent an angel to the churches at Thyatira and Pergamos to warn them about the severe consequences of sexual immorality, once again relating it to the heart and the mind. In verse 23, God reminds the church that he is the one "who searches mind and heart," highlighting his interest in the condition of his children's hearts and minds.[237] Sadly, even in the midst of the last days when the trumpets sound, and the plagues of God unleash upon humanity, Revelation 9:21 says that people will not repent of their sexual immorality.

The fog of sexual idolatry darkens and deceives the hearts and minds of humanity just like the serpent deceived Adam and Eve in the garden of Eden. Paul writes a similar message to the Corinthians: "The god of this age has blinded the minds of unbelievers, so that they cannot see the light of the gospel of the glory of Christ, who is the image of God" (2 Cor. 4:4, NIV).

All the way to the end of creation, humanity remains blind to God's original design for human sexuality. The beautiful art of coitus God intended to unite male and female, along with the euphoric experience of the orgasm, ended up corrupting humanity, and it even ends up corrupting many in the church. The consequence for sexual immorality will be eternal separation from God.[238] The book of Revelation emphasizes humanity's role in sexual immorality, and it also highlights the role that leaders in the church play in promoting this immoral behavior. Church leaders and Christians who teach heretical and unbiblical sexual practices (i.e., fornication, adultery, homosexuality, anal sex, and other sexual sins) will be held accountable before God for their teachings.[239]

The plagues God sends in the last days are meant to bring humanity to repentance and back to a life of holiness.[240] But because of the condition of hearts and minds, humanity remains stubborn and continues to engage in sinful acts that will ultimately cast them into hell. Sexual immorality seems to always be at the forefront of leading people away from God and straight into a life of sin and death. Sin and death were not God's original plan for humankind. God planted the tree of life in the garden of Eden and encouraged Adam and Eve to eat of it, have a lot of children, and enjoy the good land. Remarkably, Adam and Eve chose death, and humanity has done the same. Praise be to God, however, that in his foreknowledge, he did not leave humanity to its own devices. God wrote into creation the plan of salvation, which Christians know can only come through the blood of Jesus, the only begotten Son of God.

Conclusion

The heart of sex was meant to be a beautiful act of intimate love between a man and a woman, uniting them as one flesh. It was meant to consummate the marriage and protect it from sexual immorality, disease, and adultery. God implemented parameters for sex to protect the marriage bed while providing a safe and secure home to raise healthy and holy children.[241] Unfortunately, sin seized the opportunity (Rom. 7:8) and caused human sexuality to become distorted by minds and hearts given over to depravity.

God's message to humanity is the same from Genesis to Revelation. God searched the hearts of humankind before the flood and found every thought evil all the time (Gen. 6:5-6). The prophets challenged the people to repent and turn their hearts back to God.[242] Jesus taught the crowds adultery starts in the heart (Matt. 5:28). And again, Jesus said, "Because of your hardness of heart Moses allowed you to divorce your wives, but from the beginning it was not so" (19:8).

Paul wrote to the Romans about their ungodliness and unrighteousness, which contributed to their "foolish hearts" becoming "darkened" (Rom. 1:21), and he warned them about "the lusts of their hearts" (v. 24), which kept leading them into sexual immorality.[243] Maybe this is why Moses told the Israelites, "circumcise therefore the foreskin of your heart, and be no longer stubborn" (Deut 10:16).

Unless people return their hearts and minds to God and his divine guidance about the act of coitus found in the Holy Scriptures, human sexuality will continue to fall further from God's original plan for man and woman and the covenant of marriage. God's desire for humanity is clear when he says in Scripture to them, "love the Lord your God with all your heart and with all your soul and with all your mind" (Matt. 22:37). The true love and intimacy that God desires comes by living a life of holiness and righteousness—a life where a husband and wife honor the marriage bed and keep it holy, and a life fully devoted to God that diligently stays within the parameters God set forth in his Word.

9

SEXUAL IDOLATRY

"If you do what is right, will you not be accepted? But if you do not do what is right, sin is crouching at your door; it desires to have you, but you must rule over it" (Gen. 4:7).

Introduction

This chapter is predominantly written to health care and pastoral professionals who counsel people struggling with sexual addiction.

Scripture affirms the goodness of creation: "And God saw everything that he had made, and behold, it was very good" (Gen. 1:31). However, freewill conceived a parasitical virus of sin that infiltrated humanity, infecting the goodness of God's creation. At times, it feels almost impossible to imagine the perfection of Eden and naked innocence Adam and Eve enjoyed before the fall. As John Mahony writes:

> Sin arose through willful choices made by creatures whom God created. The only avenue through which sin appears in

creation is the open door of free choice. Consequently, sin is parasitic, a negative quality that has no actual existence in the created world but usurps the moral structure that God has instituted. In the similar case of viruses, the parasite requires a host to live. In the same way, sin is a moral virus and exists only in the context of the good purposes of God.[244]

Influenced by social and cultural norms, the degenerate plight of sexuality in society obscures the meaning of sex in a fog of sexual idolatry.[245] The fog conceals the oppressive spirit sexual idolatry holds over everyone bewitched by the mind-altering seductions of an "everything is permissible" philosophy. The world labels this as "sexual addiction." One of the challenges Christians encounter while working in a hypersexualized culture where interpretations of Scripture vary considerably is their own understanding and knowledge of the epidemiology of unhealthy sexuality. Without sound, biblical training on unhealthy sexuality as well as healthy sexuality, Christians and non-Christians may compromise, rationalize, and empathize the social ethics prevalent in progressive ideologies deeply ingrained within modern culture.[246] And if not careful, they can themselves become infected by the parasitical virus of distorted sexuality. The following sections address some key areas of unhealthy sexuality and offer recommendations for navigating issues related to them.

Sexual Addiction

This section focuses primarily on sexual addiction (SA), a result of compulsive sexual practices. The following material informs health care professionals, pastoral counselors, pastors, Christian singles, and married couples, how to recognize the signs of SA and explores how SA contributes to deeper issues of spiritual injury. Subsequent sections examine recommended treatments available for Christian leaders who make professional referrals.[247] Understanding sexual addiction, recognizing its symptoms, coming to realize how nefarious sexual behaviors circumvent God's design for the heart of sex, and referring for treatment remains vital for Christian leaders who counsel individuals trapped in this life-crippling mania.

Sexual addiction emerges from unhealthy compulsive sexual behaviors and has been viewed negatively throughout history. Roxanne Dryden-Edwards exclaims,

> Sexually addictive behaviors have been described in modern times for more than a hundred years. During the 19th century, people were described as frenetic masturbators and as having nymphomania, compulsive sexuality, and sexual intoxication.[248]

Throughout history, a lack of sexual discipline/sexual control and an enslavement to pathological needs and passions has been alluded to by different names: perversion, decadence, sexually immorality, licentiousness, lust, immodesty. Most recently, these behaviors have been referred to as hyper sexuality, sexual addiction, compulsive sexual behavior, and paraphilic-related disorders. The American Society of Addiction Medicine (ASAM) defines addiction as "a primary, chronic disease of brain reward, motivation, memory, and related circuitry. Dysfunction in these circuits leads to characteristic biological, psychological, social, and spiritual manifestations. This is reflected in an individual pathologically pursuing reward and/or relief by substance use and other behaviors."[249] ASAM also proposes that people suffering from addiction may pathologically chase relief or gratification by using some type of a substance or behavioral engagement which can manifest adverse implications spiritually, socially, biologically, and psychologically.[250]

According to An-Pyng Sun, Larry Ashley, and Lesley Dickson, there are five elements of addiction: engagement in the behavior to achieve appetitive effects, preoccupation with the behavior, temporary satiation, loss of control, and suffering negative consequences.[251] These five elements lead to feelings of hopelessness, shame, and guilt, which often lead to other compulsive behaviors such as sexual addiction. Dryden-Edwards defines sexual addiction as a condition where a person becomes excessively preoccupied with sexual behaviors and thoughts in order to achieve a desired effect. The addict excessively thinks about sex, cruises for sex, or engages in sexually addictive behaviors.[252]

These behaviors often involve paraphilic behaviors such as one-night stands, multiple sexual encounters, sex with prostitutes, watching pornographic pictures or videos, and excessive masturbation. The addict may also frequent sexual chat rooms, post personal ads seeking sex, or make inappropriate phone calls.[253] As McIlhaney and Bush point out, "People engaged in short-term sexual relationships cheat themselves out of authentic, fulfilling, and meaningful sex."[254] Recent statistics show approximately 10 to 17 percent of college students suffer from sex addiction. In the general adult population, sexual addiction and compulsive sexual behavior is around 3 percent, which translates to 17 to 37 million people.[255] Once again, this is pawned sexuality at its prime.

Patrick Carnes, author of numerous books on sexual addiction and a clinical director of sexual disorders, describes sexual addiction as

> '. . . the athlete's foot of the mind.' It never goes away. It is always asking to be scratched, promising relief. To scratch, is to cause pain and to intensify the itch. The 'itch' is created in part by the rationalizations, lies, and beliefs about themselves carried deep within the sexual addicts.[256]

Sex is essential to life and paramount to the survival of the human race. Sex remains a beautiful expression of love and intimacy God designed to consummate a marriage for the purpose of oneness, procreation, and mutual pleasuring. After sex, a person should feel good about the act and about their willingness to give of themselves unselfishly to their spouse. To the sex addict, however, sex leads to feelings of shame, guilt, and unfulfillment, and "when sex produces feelings of regret, depression, suicidal ideation and other emotional problems, it is not good."[257] These things are not what God had in mind when he created the gift of sex.

George Collins, director of Compulsion Solutions, an outpatient counseling service in San Francisco that specializes in treating sexually compulsive behavior, says,

> You can't get enough of what won't satisfy you! Objectifying and sexualizing people is a never-ending, negative process that yields a few minutes of excitement, a brief orgasm, then hours, days, weeks, months, and years of fear, pain, shame, self-doubt, self-criticism, judgment, and anger.[258]

God never intended this type of behavior and emotional distress for the heart of sex. Again, a prime example of pawned sexuality and its long-term effects.

A study conducted by Harvey Milkman and Stanley Sunderwirth reveals an interesting idea about how sex addicts use the excitement of drugs and the orgasm to simply feel normal and how the orgasm may have to do more with the brain than the genitals. Their research shows the brain is what controls the orgasm and not the genitals, and opium ingestion could cause impotence and decreased sexual activity.[259] Harvey Milkman and Stanley Sunderwirth suggest opiates can alter the nervous system:

> Opiates occupy endorphin receptor sites on the presynaptic terminals of neurons in the central nervous system. In this way opiates mimic the painkilling and the euphoric effects of our own endorphins. The inference is obvious: endorphins must somehow be involved in the ecstasy of sexual activity and orgasm.[260]

Opiates may intensify the sexual experience at first, but impotence and decreased sexual activity from long-term abuse can have lasting effects.

There are ten common characteristics shared by sex addicts that indicate the presence of sexual addiction. Pastoral counselors, pastors, Christian singles and married couples who observe the following characteristics, and Christian leaders working with individuals who display these types of behaviors should refer out for professional treatment and care:

1. A pattern of out-of-control behavior.
2. Severe consequences due to sexual behavior.
3. Inability to stop despite adverse consequences.
4. Persistent pursuit of self-destructive or high-risk behavior.
5. Ongoing desire or effort to limit sexual behavior.
6. Sexual obsession and fantasy as a primary coping strategy.
7. Increasing amounts of sexual experience because the current level of activity is no longer sufficient.
8. Severe mood changes around sexual activity.
9. Inordinate amounts of time spent in obtaining sex, being sexual, or recovering from sexual experiences.
10. Neglect of important social, occupational, or recreational activities because of sexual behavior.[261]

Recognizing these common characteristics early assists in making timely referrals to treatment facilities and follow-on care. Failure to recognize these characteristics could result in misdiagnosis. Failure to recognize sexual addiction when masked by chemical addiction could also be a contributing factor to the large number of relapses in drug and alcohol programs nationwide.

Just because a person engages in questionable or illicit sexual activity does not mean that he or she is a sex addict or suffering from a paraphilic disorder. Generally, people who have abnormal sexual interests do not have, nor are they labeled with having, a mental disorder. According to the Diagnostic and Statistical Manual of Mental Disorders (DSM-5), "A paraphilic disorder is a paraphilia that is currently causing distress or impairment to the individual or a paraphilia whose satisfaction has entailed personal harm, or risk of harm, to others."[262] The DSM-5 tried to clarify abnormal sexual interest and disorder by revising the names to differentiate between the behavior itself and the disorder stemming from the behavior (i.e., Sexual Masochism in DSM-IV was titled Sexual Masochism Disorder in DSM-5).[263] Sun, Ashley, and Dickson suggest that sexual addiction is an intimacy disorder and a compulsion:

> Sexual addiction is an intimacy disorder manifested as a compulsive cycle of preoccupation, ritualization, sexual behavior or sexual anorexia (excessive control over sexual behavior), and despair. Repetitive increased/decreased sexual behaviors are used to escape and soothe feelings of significant shame, stress, pain, or trauma in a person's life. Sex addicts will sexualize feelings and experiences that are not meant to be sexual and often lack sexual boundaries.[264]

The major difference between sexual addiction and chemical addiction is the lack of external chemicals. Internally, sexual addictive behavior produces a cocktail of endorphins in the form of peptides (dopamine) which parallels drugs like heroin and cocaine, thus producing a natural high. This natural high can be just as addictive and more difficult to stop because, unlike heroin and cocaine which are introduced to the body by external means, endorphins are produced internally and natural to the body but harmful when they continue to overload the bloodstream.

Professionals struggle to define sexual addiction, and new research is surfacing every day. Sexual addiction continues to materialize as sexual idolatry in the lives and careers of individuals caught up in this sin. By understanding the epidemiology of sexual addiction, Christian singles, couples, and leaders can help people get to the root cause of their idolatry.[265] Sexual idolatry tears people away from God, as David Calhoun says:

> In whatever shape it comes—the desire for illicit sex, the love of money, prideful ambition—temptation moves us to reject God's Word and deny his rule over our lives. Rather than seeking first the kingdom of God and His righteousness, we seek first our kingdom and our own way.[266]

By yielding to temptation, Calhoun says, "We remove God from the throne of our lives."[267] God has a right to the highest place in the hearts and lives of his children. Sexual addiction usurps God's plan for the heart of sex, leaving addicts isolated and spiritually void.

Trying to spot the signs of sexual addition can prove difficult, since addicts are good at hiding pain, stress, emotions, addictions, and secrets from other people. Like other addicts, sex addicts become experts at hiding their compulsive sexual behavior from their spouse, family members, and friends. Just like chemical dependency, definitive signs accentuate behaviors a person exhibits, that if not treated, end up destroying their bodies.[268] Carnes opens his book *Don't Call It Love* with eleven examples or signs of a sex addict.[269] These examples show how devastating this addiction is and the ultimate consequences it has on individuals, their families, and society.

Psychologists, psychiatrists, pastoral counselors, and chaplains who counsel people suffering from some form of trauma often notice the visible signs of trauma—post-traumatic stress disorder (PTSD), traumatic brain injury (TBI), and other stress-related injuries and addictive behaviors—and may overlook the hidden signs of sexual addiction masked by chemical dependency. Recognizing the inward and outward signs of sexual addiction allows professionals to treat and address the correct addiction or multiple addictions people hide and are extremely difficult for them to talk about. A husband or wife who witnesses these signs in their spouse should seek professional help immediately. Chris Lee, a writer for *Newsweek*, believes SA has become a national epidemic:

> Sexual addiction remains a controversial designation often dismissed as myth or providing talk-show punchlines thanks to high-profile lotharios such as Dominique Strauss-Kahn and Tiger Woods. But compulsive sexual behavior, also called hypersexual disorder, can systematically destroy a person's life much as addictions to alcohol and drugs can. And it's affecting an increasing number of Americans, say psychiatrists and addiction experts. 'It's a national epidemic.'[270]

This article should come as no surprise. Sex and sexual misconduct alike are seldom talked about by general society, let alone sexual addiction. The church has not helped much in this area either. It is rare to hear a sermon about healthy sexual practices in a person's life let alone a message about behavior as taboo as sexual addiction. Pastors deal with this topic in their congregations and would benefit by becoming more aware of the signs of sexual addiction. Pastors who have been properly trained offer much more effective counsel and can make appropriate referrals for screening, diagnosis, and treatment.

There are several signs or identifiable characteristics of sexual addiction. Because of the secrecy, guilt, and shame, one of the signs addicts exhibit over the course of SA is known as self-distancing; they slowly distance themselves from friends and family for fear of being caught or exposed. Studies show that sex remains secondary to the real issues involved, creating a greater "high," which comes from secrecy, lies, power, control, and the thrill of engaging in dangerous and risky behavior.[271] According to Carnes,

> Risk does seem to be one of the prime ingredients to the mood-altering addictive process. To violate cultural and legal norms

can enhance the sexual excitement. Risk, which is involved in the violation, is central to the escalation process so often described by addicts.[272]

Sex addicts are not trained "007s," though, and are left to deal with the emotional consequences of their compulsive behavior. Addicts often suffer from anxiety, stress, and high levels of shame and guilt. They can even suffer from pain experienced during a traumatic sexual incident from their past (e.g., childhood sexual abuse, incest, or rape).[273]

Spiritual injury can also happen as a result of sexual abuse and addiction and finding its origin remains paramount for healing to begin. Pastors, Christian leaders, and pastoral counselors should gently instruct while exploring the person's faith background. Journeying with a person as he or she discovers the road to spiritual recovery will assist them as they slowly reconnect to God. There are also traits of positive sexuality that religious leaders can use to help people identify and heal spiritual injuries. Ginger Manley lists seven positive traits on the road to spiritual recovery for sex addicts:

1. Believing that sexuality is a gift of God/higher power.
2. When the addict chooses to reject family's sexual shame.
3. When the addict believes that one is capable of receiving sexual grace in one's life.
4. When the addict affirms that sex is a source of goodness in one's life.
5. When the addict experiences the meaningfulness of sexual moments.
6. When the addict relates from one's heart regarding sexual meaningfulness.
7. When the addict has a defined sexual value system that is the basis for consistent behaviors.[274]

Cycles of Sexual Addiction

Jennifer Schneider, a physician certified in internal medicine, addiction medicine, and pain management, lists ten common patterns sex addicts are involved in. Being engaged in one, two, or any number of these activities does not constitute sexual addiction. She highlights common behaviors practiced by sexual addicts that indicate sexual addiction.[275] These signs or patterns generally progress through a four-step cycle that, over time, intensifies with each recurrence to the point where addicts become hostages of their own preoccupation. The addict gets so caught up in fantasy and obsession that every person who passes by, every person they meet or have a relationship with, passes through their sexually obsessive filter. This obsession eventually affects their work performance, keeps them from relaxing, and even affects their sleep—it's as if they are in a constant trance, unable to return to reality. To understand this trancelike state, Carnes uses the analogy of two young lovers caught up in the intense passion of courtship to the point they forget about everything else around them:

> The intoxication of young love is what the addict attempts to capture. It is the pursuit, the hunt, the search, the suspense heightened by the unusual, the stolen, the forbidden, the illicit that are intoxication to the sexual addict. The new conquest of the hustler; the score of the exposer, voyeur, or rapist; or the temptation of breaking the taboo of sex with one's child—in essence, they are variations of a theme: courtship gone awry.[276]

According to Carnes, the four stages of the addiction cycle intensify with each repetition:

1. *Preoccupation*—the trance or mood wherein the addicts' minds are completely engrossed with thoughts of sex. This mental state creates an obsessive search for sexual stimulation.

2. *Ritualization*—the addicts' own special routines that lead up to the sexual behavior. The ritual intensifies the preoccupation, adding arousal and excitement.
3. *Compulsive sexual behavior*—the actual sexual act, which is the end goal of the preoccupation and ritualization. Sexual addicts are unable to control or stop this behavior.
4. *Despair*—the feeling of utter hopelessness addicts have about their behavior and their powerlessness. [277]

Countless stories describe the addiction cycle of those caught up in sexual addiction. The following stories capture what sexual addiction or compulsive sexual behavior looks like in the life of an addict. The first story is of Mark, a physician, married, successful, and an avid runner—eight to nine miles a day. Mark's sexual behavior started long before his addiction. Mark started to masturbate at the age of five, and his first sexual encounter was at sixteen. When Mark eventually married, he had sex with his wife several times a day, he started masturbating compulsively, and then started experimenting in homosexual relations, which soon spiraled out of control. Mark explains his compulsive sexual behavior:

> I started having lover after lover. It was getting too complicated at times. Then I started getting this gift as a jogger: I had this ability to pick people from the street, I would not even go to gay areas. I'd bring them to my office in the evening or in the late afternoons. I started discovering bookstores, then buying male prostitutes. When the male prostitutes weren't around, I went to the girlie shows and I bought the gals. The pattern was the same: one wasn't enough, I'd need two guys at a time. It finally got to two women at a time. These people would call my house. They'd bug me for money. My last lover I figured cost me about $30,000. I was not a wealthy man. My addiction cost me a fortune. And time.

> I was spending hours a day pursuing lust objects, either going to pornos, picking people up, trying to get my wife in bed, or masturbating. A great deal of time and money.
>
> It was as if I thought I was invisible and I'd go to the pornos in the middle of the daytime. Here I was in a relatively small city, practicing a psychiatric profession and acting out my lust in broad daylight.[278]

Mark's life reflects a pattern of what happens when sexual compulsive behavior takes over. This type of behavior sparks the onset of addiction—the individual no longer has control and the compulsive behavior no longer serves as an experiment with life, things, or substances. The behavior becomes the controlling factor and negatively starts to impact every part of a person's life. Mark's life finally became overwhelming as collection agencies chased him over his debt. He also contracted several diseases and was spotted by one of his patients while cruising for sex at a YMCA.

Another story highlighting the cycle of addiction comes from Bill. Bill is married with four children and is a supervisor at his company. Bill suffers from alcoholism and is a regular exhibitionist. Bill sought out help for his sexually compulsive behavior/addiction and tells his story about how his addiction almost cost him everything:

> I think of all the Saturday and Sunday mornings that I would sneak off, sometimes in the afternoon or evenings. But the sneakiest way was before anybody got up. That way I did not have to explain where I was going—only the lie as to where I had been when I got back home. 'Where have you been all morning or all day?' Some of the lies were, 'Oh, I was over to a friend's house,' sometimes even making up a friend. Or the countless times that I had car trouble and how hard and long it was to fix. If asked about the friend, it was somebody from work: 'You would not know him, anyway you never met him.'

Sometimes I got mad because she asked where I was. I said, 'None of your business.'

There were countless times where I came to work late, left early, or did not show up at all. I told my boss I was sick or something happened at home. Spending endless hours driving around. I would leave the house on the spur of the moment with a lie to get in my car and go.

I could be driving down the street with good intentions. Just a thought or the sight of a pretty girl would set me going. I would tell myself it is not going to happen, but did not have any control to stop it. Completely powerless, a feeling of being taken over by a strong emotionally uncontrollable power that I did not understand. Afterward, I would feel so ashamed of what I had done and then start right over again, maybe even staying out all night or even looking for a prostitute. You can well imagine how apart I was from my family because of the guilty feeling; shamefulness for time away from home; sad because of all of it. Angry at myself for not doing anything about it or being able to control it. Why am I this way, why me? Dear God, help me.[279]

Bill's story reiterates the cycle of addiction that could happen to anyone who decides to partake in these types of activities. Sexual addicts find it difficult to navigate the internal conflicting feeling when society so conspicuously accepts their behavior as normal (e.g., masturbation, pornography, fornication). Millions of innocent men and women start out by engaging in socially acceptable sexual practices, not realizing the devastating consequences that follow.

Things that used to be "socially unacceptable" are regularly embraced by society today. There was a reason why certain behaviors were condemned throughout history by governments, society, organizations, and the church. Several times in the Bible, God instructs people to refrain from sexual immorality, debauchery, homosexuality, incest, adultery, and orgies.[280] Jude 1:7 says, "Sodom and Gomorrah and the surrounding cities, likewise indulged in sexual immorality and pursued unnatural desire, [they] serve as an example by undergoing a punishment of eternal fire." In this text, God not only mentions sexual immorality along with punishment by eternal fire, but he also mentions "unnatural desire." With the mention of Sodom and Gomorrah in the same sentence, the reference to unnatural desire is a direct reference against the practice of homosexuality. This unnatural desire has become normal to many sex addicts—even ones married to women. As in Mark's story, he practiced both sexual immorality and homosexuality while married to a woman.

Treatment

By the time sex addicts reach out for help, they are often in severe crisis in life, career, relationships, and health. Addicts tend to be distrustful (they don't even trust themselves); they have poor communication skills, experience lots of anger and resentment, and are usually in great financial debt. Treatment for sexually compulsive behavior differs from treatment for chemical dependency. The goal in treating sexual addiction is not abstinence from sex but abstinence from compulsive sexual behavior. Once an addict establishes a healthy view of his or her sexuality, the process of recovery and healing begins.

In treatment, addicts must abstain from all sexual activities for thirty to ninety days, and this includes masturbation, so they can exhibit control over sexual impulsiveness. Since masturbation is a fundamental compulsive behavior in sex addicts, it must be avoided so it doesn't trigger acting out and relapse.[281]

One treatment option for sex addicts is Cognitive Behavioral Therapy (CBT), which helps them recognize triggers (thoughts and feelings influencing their behavior) in an attempt to keep them from acting out and relapsing. CBT helps identify triggers and helps the addict brainstorm how to cope with or block them. An-Pyng Sun, Larry Ashley, and Lesley Dickson state,

> Psychoeducation pertaining to intimacy and the differences between degrading and enriching sex can benefit the therapeutic process. Examples of CBT strategies are forming an abstinence contract, carrying an index card with therapeutic phrases or sentences, changing negative self-talk to positive self-talk, counteracting irrational thoughts, and relapse prevention."[282]

George Collins, in *Breaking the Cycle*, lists several ways to help sex addicts stop the triggers causing them to act out. He uses the acronym HALT (Hungry, Angry, Lonely, Tired), which his clients say aloud when they encounter a trigger. The acronym HALT attempts to stop the "euphoric recall" that triggers create and turn the experience into a negative recall. Some examples of this treatment are the following:

- One of his clients was walking down the sidewalk and noticed a *Hustler* magazine lying on the ground and it triggered him. The client called Collins and confessed he was triggered and struggling with the temptation to act out. George said, "Steve, I want you to piss on the magazine." The client responded, "What if someone sees me or the police come by?" George replied, "If the police come by, hand them the phone, and I'll talk to them." Steve pissed on the magazine and created a negative recall of pornographic magazines.[283]
- He made another client go to the street where the client used to meet prostitutes and pick up a prostitute. George sat in the back seat and explained to the prostitute that they wanted to speak to her and were going to pay her but did not want to have sex with her. After some persuasion, the prostitute got in the car. George then talked to the prostitute about how she really felt

about the men she slept with. The woman was of course reluctant to talk at first but then broke down and screamed how she hated them, hated herself, and hated what she did. This helped stop the euphoric recall that the prostitute really wanted to have sex with his client.[284]

Collins helped his clients create negative memories of objects triggering them. These methods helped his clients block the euphoric recalls associated with the triggers, turning the recalls into negative ones. This helped his clients to stop focusing on the pleasure of a trigger and to focus on the adverse consequences of acting out.

Not every healthcare professional or pastoral counselor can take their patients on such excursions, but I wanted to present this to help professionals who deal with sex addicts understand the importance of stopping the euphoric recall which can be triggered very unexpectedly. Another way Collins treats his patients is by a technique he calls "Confronting Your Addict in the Amphitheater." Collins has his clients give names to the voices speaking to them inside their head: Porn Guy, Addict, Hotshot, Loser, Mr. Jerk Off, Prostitute Pete, Stripper Club Guy, Chat-Room Charlie, etc. He suggests, "By dialoging with your addict in your amphitheater, you can change the dynamic so that the addict is no longer in control. In fact, the whole idea of imagining the amphitheater allows you to eventually run the show instead of the stories you tell yourself of being in charge."[285] The following is an example of confronting your addict:

> Anthony: I'm in the amphitheater.
>
> Addict: It's Friday night, and every Friday night we go out and cruise. So let's get going.
>
> Anthony: I'm not even gay. Why do you want to be with trannies?
>
> Addict: Well, they know what a man likes. We'll have fun.

Anthony: But I don't have fun. Sure, it can be exciting and even scary. But the police can pick us up, like we've seen happen with other men.

Addict: You worry too much. We'll have fun.

Anthony: Those hooker trannies have difficult lives.

Addict: Yeah, but you know how much difficulty we have finding a woman to be with. And the trannies act like they really care about you.

Anthony: And I never got that from my own father. Is that what this is about?

Addict: No. This is about you getting what you need and having some fun with a man.

Anthony: No. This time we're not doing it. I'm taking a stand.

Addict: No, you can't. We have to do this. We always do this.

Anthony: Not this time. This time you're going to back off. I've heard enough. This time you're going to shut up and leave me in peace.

Addict: (Silence)[286]

Another treatment used with sex addicts is "Object Relations Theory." Because sex addicts are developmentally deficient, they need to go through four stages of therapy to restore the deficiency lacking. The four stages are the following:

1. Autistic Stage—The goal of this stage is to cope with anxiety, develop therapeutic bonds, to be in the here and now, and focus on the development of healthy relationships. Focus

on interpersonal relationships is crucial as long-term recovery depends on their satisfaction with their relationships with other people.
2. Symbiotic Stage—This deals with their need for attachment which they find by engaging in sex so they won't feel alone or abandoned. This stage focuses on their need for nurturing and to reduce anxiety while developing alternative and healthy ways to get their needs met.
3. Separation-Individuation Stage—This stage addresses narcissism and borderline personality traits that many addicts exhibit due to being separated from their parents as a child. This stage addresses their hypersensitivity to criticism, unconscious dependency needs, and feelings of inferiority.
4. Shame Reduction—This stage deals with shame which is the core of sex addiction. In this stage professionals help addicts reduce their levels of shame by understanding the origin of the shame and its function in the addictive system. They help them to differentiate between shame and guilt and to identify the defenses utilized to deny the painful feelings created by the shame. Professionals utilize specific shame reduction strategies at critical points in the treatment process to help change negative core beliefs that reinforce shame.[287]

Psychopharmacology is another way professionals treat sexual compulsive behavior, but this method is not typical. Research has shown antidepressants can decrease the intensity of the sexual experience and drugs like serotonin can help reduce sexual desire and regulate the intensity of the orgasm. There are numerous treatment centers available for treating sexual addiction, hypersexuality disorder, and compulsive sexual behaviors. The following is a list of several treatment facilities around the nation that treat a variety of compulsive sexual behaviors and addictions.

COSA
9219 Katy Freeway
Suite 212
Houston, TX 77024
866-899-2672
http://www.cosa-recovery.org

Incest Survivors Anonymous (ISA)
PO Box 17245
Long Beach, CA 90807-7245
562-428-5599
http://www.lafn.org/medical/isa/home.html

Recovering Couples Anonymous (RCA)
PO Box 11872
St. Louis, MO 63105
877-663-2317
http://recovering-couples.org

Sexual Recovery Anonymous (SRA)
PO Box 73
Planetarium Station
New York, NY 10024
212-340-4650

Sex Addicts Anonymous (SAA)
PO Box 70949
Houston, TX 77270
713-869-4902
https://saa-recovery.org

S-Anon
PO Box 17294
Nashville, TN 37217
615-833-3152
http://www.sanon.org

Sexaholics Anonymous (SA)
PO Box 3565
Brentwood, TN 37024
615-370-6062
http://www.sa.org

Survivors of Incest Anonymous (SIA)
World Service Office
PO Box 190
Benson, MD 21018-9998
410-877-1779
http://www.siawso.org

Sexual Compulsive Anonymous (SCA)
PO Box 1585
Old Chelsea Station
New York, NY 10113-1585
800-977-4325
http://www.sca-recovery.org

Sex and Love Addicts Anonymous (SLAA)
1550 NE Loop 410 Suite 118
San Antonio, TX 78209
210-828-7900
https://slaafws.org

Recognizing Childhood Sexual Abuse

Christian married couples, pastors, and pastoral counselors also need to recognize the signs of childhood sexual abuse. Parents, and professionals who counsel and treat children, must be aware of the physical as well as the behavioral and emotional signs that indicate sexual abuse in the life of a child. Harry Schaumburg points out the early physical signs of childhood sexual abuse:

> Unexplained torn, soiled, or bloody underwear; disruption of normal eating patterns; health problems, such as vomiting, headaches, allergies, rashes, unusual vaginal discharge, and unusual urinary tract infection; physical complaints such as stomachache, pain in the genital area, genital or anal irritation; sexually transmitted disease; soreness or injury to the genital area, anus, or mouth.[288]

Schaumburg says the behavioral and emotional signs of childhood sexual abuse are the following:

> unexplained irritability; unable to get along with others; sleep disorder, with or without bad dreams or nightmares; depressed, despondent, withdrawn, inactive, daydreaming, lack of concentration, unusually quiet; destructive behavior toward things or people; fearful of certain people or places; pleas of not being left alone or with someone or someplace, or becoming indifferent to being left with others; sexual awareness beyond what is age appropriate or what has been taught; inappropriate sexual behavior or play with other children; inappropriate childish behaviors or regression such as bedwetting and thumb sucking; aggressive behavior toward others; fearful of activities that were previously enjoyed, such as bathing, undressing, or playing somewhere or with someone.[289]

When parents, Christian leaders, and pastoral counselors identify childhood sexual abuse early in the life of a child, they can help get the counseling and treatment the child needs. Early identification and treatment greatly reduce the chance of the child's view of their own sexuality being distorted and can help detour them from a cycle of sexual addiction and confusion when they get older. According to Joan Ellason and Colin Ross, "Recidivism among sex offenders may be due in part to an unresolved childhood trauma that has been compartmentalized and remains untreated by traditional interventions."[290]

The signs of addiction are always present. Healthcare and pastoral professionals can uncover this debilitating addiction during the preliminary screening/assessment stage of care and counseling. Knowing what to look for and asking the right questions can make all the difference as the addict moves toward recovery. Defining sexual addiction, identifying the signs of sexual addiction, knowing what assessments and types of treatments are currently available allows leaders to offer thorough care while making appropriate referrals for treatment.[291]

Though research is still being done on the proper treatment needed for sexual addiction, healthcare professionals, pastors, and pastoral counselors can find a wealth of knowledge and support on this subject online. This knowledge helps direct patients to treatment facilities actively engaged in up-to-date treatment and care plans and gives addicts the best care available for recovery.

With treatment and follow-up care and counseling, people suffering from this addiction can continue on in their relationship with Christ as he helps them regain control of their compulsive sexual behavior. Once control is restored, individuals may begin to celebrate their recovery as they rediscover a new life free of compulsive sexual behavior. Being set free and restored with family, friends, and a faith community allows addicts to slowly regain hope and confidence as levels of shame and guilt decrease and normalcy is restored.

CONCLUSION

"Now may the God of peace himself sanctify you completely, and may your whole spirit and soul and body be kept blameless at the coming of our Lord Jesus Christ" (1 Thess. 5:23).

As this book comes to an end, and I write these last few lines, I must confess I am overwhelmed with a flood of emotions. It has been a long and arduous journey filled with self-reflection, confession, and revelation. God is faithful and so far ahead of us. I never dreamed I would specialize in a subject so sensitive and divisive and yet feel so fulfilled and validated. The material covered in this book has already touched numerous lives and marriages. I rejoice in the victory that countless singles and couples have experienced and the freedom they now share. With time, God will use this subject to touch and change countless more.

I give all glory and honor to God and the power of the Holy Spirit working and living in my life. Without the power of God's Spirit working through the calling he placed on my life, I would have never completed this book. God's Word has truly been a light unto my feet directing me to paths of holiness, while helping me honor marriage and keep my marriage bed pure and holy. God's laws, statutes, and ordinances are good and lead to godly sexuality, healthy and sustainable marriages, vibrant communities, personal holiness, and, inevitably, to eternal life.

The heart of sex is oneness—oneness with spouse, oneness with God, and oneness with the body of Christ. God's ways are truly higher than ours and Christians should thank him every day and trust his plans far exceed theirs.

The heart of sex and the meaning of sex starts and ends with God and his design for sex. When Christian married couples bring their sex and sexual practices into harmony with God's Holy Word, they will experience a verdant marriage bed. When Christian singles view sex as a gift from God that should be protected and shared only in the context of a covenant marriage, they will have a healthier view of themselves, others, God, and the act of sex itself. The benefits of living a biblical sexual life are immeasurable and can impact society in ways the church may never fully understand.

The Bible says, "Everything that was whispered in the ear will be shouted from the rooftops, and everything that was done in the dark will be brought into the light," and "Whoever conceals their sin will not prosper, but whoever confesses and relents will find mercy." The time for God's imminent return is near. I pray you take the opportunity afforded in this book to redeem your sexuality and allow God to restore the sanctity of sex in your life and marriage. By following the sexual compass taught in this book, you can redeem your sexuality and restore the sanctity of sex.

A Closing Meditation from
Matthew 7:24-27

"Therefore everyone who hears these words of mine and puts them into practice is like a wise man who built his house on the rock. The rain came down, the streams rose, and the winds blew and beat against that house; yet it did not fall, because it had its foundation on the rock. But everyone who hears these words of mine and does not put them into practice is like a foolish man who built his house on sand. The rain came down, the streams rose, and the winds blew and beat against that house, and it fell with a great crash."

This is the Golden Compass leading to Sustained Sexual Satisfaction!
GOD BLESS – Dr. G

APPENDIX A

PATTERNS AND EXAMPLES OF SEX ADDICTION

1. Fantasy sex: neglecting commitments because of fantasy life, masturbation.
2. Seductive role sex: extramarital affairs (heterosexual or homosexual), flirting and seductive behavior.
3. Anonymous sex: engaging in sex with anonymous partners, having one-night stands.
4. Paying for sex: paying prostitutes for sex, paying for sexually explicit phone calls.
5. Trading sex: receiving money or drugs for sex.
6. Voyeuristic sex: patronizing adult bookstores and strip shows, looking through windows of houses, having a collection of pornography at home or at work.
7. Exhibitionist sex: exposing oneself in public places or from the home or car, wearing clothes designed to expose.

8. Intrusive sex: touching others without permission, using position of power (e.g., professional, religious) to sexually exploit another person, rape.
9. Pain exchange: causing or receiving pain to enhance sexual pleasure.
10. Object sex: masturbating with objects, cross-dressing to add to sexual pleasure, using fetishes as part of sexual rituals, having sex with animals.
11. Sex with children: forcing sexual activity on a child, watching child pornography.[292]

BIBLIOGRAPHY

"1 Corinthians 7 (KJV)." *Blue Letter Bible.* Accessed November 16, 2016. http://blueletterbible.org/kjv/1co/7/9/p0/t_conc_1069009.

"5 Ways to Develop Emotional Intimacy in Your Relationship." *Power of Positivity*, Accessed July 27, 2020. https://www.powerofpositivity.com/emotional-intimacy-relationship.

Alexander, T. Desmond, Brian S. Rosner, D. A. Carson, Graeme Goldsworthy, and Steve Carter, eds. *New Dictionary of Biblical Theology*. Downers Grove, IL: InterVarsity Press, 2000.

Ambrosiater. *Ancient Christian Texts: Romans and 1-2 Corinthians.* Translated by Gerald Bray. Downers Grove, IL: IVP Academic, 2009.

American Psychiatric Association. *Diagnostic and Statistical Manual of Mental Disorders*. 5th ed. Washington, DC: American Psychiatric Association, 2013.

American Society of Addiction Medicine Board of Directors. "Definition of Addiction." American Society of Addiction Medicine, April 19, 2011. Accessed April 05, 2017. http://www.asam.org/quality-practice/definition-of-addiction.

Augustinus, Aurelius. *The Confessions of Saint Augustine*. Franklin, PA: The Franklin Library, 1982.

Balswick, Jack O., and Judith K. Balswick. *A Model for Marriage*. Downers Grove, IL: InterVarsity Press, 2006.

Barna Group. "American Lifestyles Mix Compassion and Self-Oriented Behavior." Barna Research Releases, February 5, 2007. Accessed March 17, 2017. https://www.barna.com/research/american-lifestyles-mix-compassion-and-self-oriented-behavior.

Behm, Johannes. "*Kardia*." In *Theological Dictionary of the New Testament*. Vol. 3., Translated by Geoffrey Bromiley. Edited by Gerhard Kittel, 605-614. Grand Rapids, MI: Eerdmans, 1964.

Bell, Caleb. "Americans Love the Bible but Don't Read It Much, Poll Shows." *Huffington Post*, April 4, 2013. Accessed June 09, 2016. http://www.huffingtonpost.com/2013/04/04/americans-love-the-bible-but-dont-read-it-much_n_3018425.html.

Blocher, Henri. *In the Beginning*. Downers Grove, IL: InterVarsity Press, 1984.

Boteach, Shmuley. *Kosher Sex*. New York: Broadway Books, 1999.

Breazeale, Kathlyn A. *Mutual Empowerment: A Theology of Marriage, Intimacy, and Redemption*. Minneapolis: Fortress, 2008.

Burns, J. Lanier. "The Biblical Use of Marriage to Illustrate Covenantal Relationships." *Bibliotheca Sacra* 173 (July-September 2016): 273-296.

Buttrick, George. "Adultery and Lust." In *The Interpreter's Bible*. Vol. 7, *New Testament Articles, Matthew, Mark*. Edited by Nolan Harmon, 297-298. Nashville: Abingdon-Cokesbury Press, 1951.

Calhoun, David. "Sin and Temptation." In *Fallen: A Theology of Sin*. Edited by Christopher Morgan and Robert Peterson, 243-265. Wheaton, IL: Crossway, 2013.

Calvin, John. *Calvin's New Testament Commentaries*. Vol. 1, *Genesis*. Edited by David and Thomas Torrance. Translated by A. W. Morrison. Grand Rapids, MI: Eerdmans, 1972.

Carnes, Patrick. *Don't Call It Love: Recovery from Sexual Addiction*. New York: Bantam, 1991.

──────. *Out of the Shadows: Understanding Sexual Addiction*. Center City, MN: Hazelden, 2001

Catechism of The Catholic Church. "The Love of Husband and Wife #2363." Part three, Life in Christ, Section Two. Accessed 11 December 2017. http://www.vatican.va/archive/ccc_css/archive/catechism/p3s2c2a6.htm.

Chappell, Clovis. "I'd Risk Something." In *20 Centuries of Great Preaching*. Vol. 9., Edited by Clyde E. Fant Jr. and William M. Pinson, Jr. Waco, TX: Word Books, 1971.

Collins, George, N. *Breaking the Cycle: Free Yourself from Sex Addiction, Porn Obsession, and Shame*. Oakland, CA: New Harbinger Publications, 2010.

Conte, Ronald, L., Jr. "Questions and Answers on Catholic Marital Sexual Ethics." Question 4. "Which types of acts are moral for a husband and wife to use as foreplay?" Accessed September 20, 2017, http://www.catechism.cc/articles/QA.htm#04.

Crenshaw, James. "Sirach." In *The New Interpreter's Bible*. Vol. 5, *Introduction to Wisdom Literature, Proverbs, Ecclesiastes, Song of Songs, Wisdom, Sirach*, edited by Leander Keck, 646-867. Nashville: Abingdon, 1997.

CWR Staff, "The Sacrament of Marriage Is the Icon of God's Love for Us." *Catholic World Report*, April 2, 2014. Accessed March 17, 2017. http://www.catholicworldreport.com/Blog/3045/pope_francis_the_sacrament_of_marriage_is_the_icon_of_gods_love_for_us.aspx.

Driscoll, Mark. *Porn-Again Christian*. Seattle: Mars Hill Church, 2009.

Dryden-Edwards, Roxanne. "What Is Sexual Addiction and What Are the Types of Sexual Addiction?" MedicineNet, last modified November 9, 2015. Accessed March 28, 2017. https://www.medicinenet.com/sexual_addiction/article.htm.

Durden-Smith, Jo, and Diane Desimone. *Sex and the Brain*. New York: Arbor House, 1983.

Ellason, Joan, W., and Ross, Colin A. "Childhood Trauma and Dissociation in Male Sex Offenders." *Sexual Addiction and Compulsivity: The Journal of Treatment and Prevention* 6, no. 2 (November 2007): 105-110.

Elwell, Water A., ed. *Evangelical Dictionary of Theology*. 2nd ed. Grand Rapids, MI: Baker Academic, 2001.

Entwistle, David N. *Integrative Approaches to Psychology and Christianity*. 2nd ed. Eugene, OR: Cascade Books, 2010.

Farrel, Bill, and Pam Farrel. *The Before-You-Marry Book of Questions*. Eugene, OR: Harvest House, 2013.

———. *Red-Hot Monogamy*. Eugene, OR: Harvest House, 2006.

Fletcher, Joseph. "Sex, Ethics Of." In *The New Schaff-Herzog Encyclopedia of Religious Knowledge*. Vol. 15, *Twentieth Century Encyclopedia of Religious Knowledge*. Edited by Lefferts A. Loetscher, 1023-1024. Grand Rapids, MI: Baker, 1977.

Fox, Matthew. *The Hidden Spirituality of Men: Ten Metaphors to Awaken the Sacred Masculine*. Navato, CA: New World Library, 2008.

Freedman, David, ed. *The Anchor Bible Dictionary*. Vol. 5, *O-SH*. New York: Doubleday, 1992.

Gallagher, Steve. *At the Altar of Sexual Idolatry*. Dry Ridge, KY: Pure Life Ministries, 2000.

Gardner, Tim Alan. *Sacred Sex*. Colorado Springs, CO: WaterBrook Press, 2008.

Geisler, Norman L. *Christian Ethics*. 2nd ed. Grand Rapids, MI: Baker, 2010.

Goodrick, Edward W. *Zondervan NIV Exhaustive Concordance*. 2nd ed. Grand Rapids, MI: Zondervan, 1999.

Grant, Jonathan. *Divine Sex*. Grand Rapids, MI: Baker, 2015.

Grenz, Stanley J. *Sexual Ethics*. Louisville, KY: Westminster John Knox, 1990.

Gundry, Robert H. *A Commentary on the New Testament*. Peabody, MA: Hendrickson, 2010.

Hamilton, Victor P. *Handbook on the Pentateuch*. Grand Rapids, MI: Baker, 1982.

Hastings, James, ed. *Encyclopedia of Religion and Ethics*. Vol. 11, *Sacrifice-Sudra*. New York: Morrison and Gibb, 1920.

———. ed. *The Greater Men and Woman of the Bible*. Vol. 4, *Hezekiah-Malachi*. New York: Morrison and Gibb, 1915.

Hastings, Kelly. "What is Emotional Intimacy?" *Marriage.com*, updated March 13, 2020. Accessed July 27, 2020. https://www.marriage.com/advice/emotional-intimacy/what-is-emotional-intimacy.

Heimbach, Daniel. *True Sexual Morality: Recovering Biblical Standards for a Culture in Crisis*. Wheaton, IL: Crossway, 2004.

Hill, Andrew. *Malachi*. New York: Doubleday, 1998.

Hollinger, Dennis. *The Meaning of Sex*. Grand Rapids, MI: Baker Academic, 2009.

Hunter, David G. "Sex, Sin and Salvation: What Augustine Really Said." Accessed March 13, 2017. http://www.jknirp.com/aug3.htm.

Hyde, Janet Shibley, and John D. DeLamater, *Understanding Human Sexuality*, 8th ed. New York: McGraw-Hill, 2003.

Jeremiah, David. *What the Bible Says about Love, Marriage and Sex: The Song of Solomon*. New York: Faith Words, 2012.

———. *Shelter in God: Your Refuge in Times of Trouble*. Nashville: W Publishing, 2020.

Jones, Lindsay, ed. *Encyclopedia of Religion*. 2nd ed. Farmington Hills, MI: Thomson and Gale, 2005.

Jungling, Laurie. "Passionate Order: Order and Sexuality in Augustine's Theology." *Word and World* 27, no. 3 (Summer 2007): 315-324.

Kantor, David. Quoted in Amy Hertz, "To Love, Honor, and Last Longer than a Year." *O, The Oprah Magazine*, March 2002.

Kaiser, Walter C., Jr. "Exodus." In *The Expositor's Bible Commentary*. Edited by Frank E. Gaebelein. Vol. 2. *Genesis, Exodus, Leviticus, Numbers*. Edited by John H. Sailhamer, Walter C. Kaiser Jr., R. Laird Harris, and Ronald B. Allen, 287-497. Grand Rapids, MI: Zondervan, 1990.

Keener, Craig. *The IVP Bible Background Commentary New Testament*. Downers Grove, IL: InterVarsity Press, 1993.

Keil, C. F., and F. Delitzsch. *Commentary on the Old Testament, The Minor Prophets*. Vol. 10, Peabody, MA: Hendrickson, 1996.

Kelley, Page. *Layman's Bible Book Commentary*. Vol. 14, Nashville: Broadman, 1984.

Koenig, Harold, Dana King, and Verna Carson. *Handbook of Religion and Health*. 2nd ed. New York: Oxford University Press, 2012.

Kolarcik, Michael. "The Book of Wisdom." In *The New Interpreter's Bible*. Vol. 5, *Introduction to Wisdom Literature, Proverbs, Ecclesiastes, Song of Songs, Wisdom, Sirach*, edited by Leander Keck, 437-600. Nashville: Abingdon, 1997.

Kuehne, Dale S. *Sex and the iWorld*. Grand Rapids, MI: Baker, 2009.

Lambert, Heath. *Finally Free: Fighting for Purity with the Power of Grace*. Grand Rapids, MI: Zondervan, 2013.

Laurin, Roy. *First Corinthians: Where Life Matures*. Findlay, OH: Dunham, 1957.

Lee, Chris. "The Sex Addiction Epidemic." *Newsweek*, November 25, 2011. Accessed February 26, 2014. http://www.newsweek.com/sex-addiction-epidemic-66289.

Loader, William. *The New Testament on Sexuality*. Grand Rapids, MI: Eerdmans, 2012.

Mahony, John. "A Theology of Sin for Today." In *Fallen: A Theology of Sin*, edited by Christopher Morgan and Robert Peterson, 187-217. Wheaton, IL: Crossway, 2013.

Mallard, Timothy. "The (Twin) Wounds of War." *Providence*, February 13, 2017. Accessed July 26, 2020, https://providencemag.com/2017/02/twin-wounds-war-spiritual-injury-moral-injury/#_ednref12

Mallory, D. James. *The Battle of the Sexes: How Both Sides Can Win with Honor*. Wheaton, IL: Crossway Books, 1996.

Manley, Ginger. "Treating Chronic Sexual Dysfunction in Couples Recovering from Sex Addiction and Sex Coaddiction." *Sexual Addiction and Compulsivity: The Journal of Treatment and Prevention* 6, no. 2 (November 2007): 111-124.

McIlhaney, Joe S., Jr., and Freda Bush. *Hooked: New Science on How Casual Sex Is Affecting Oour Children*. Chicago: Northfield, 2008.

McLeod, Saul. "Classical Conditioning." *Simply Psychology*, last modified 2014. Accessed March 24, 2017. https://www.simplypsychology.org/classical-conditioning.html.

Merrill, Eugene. "Malachi." In *The Expositor's Bible Commentary*. Rev. ed. Vol. 8, *Daniel-Malachi*. Edited by Tremper Longman III and David Garland, 837-863. Grand Rapids, MI: Zondervan, 2008.

Miles, Carrie A. *The Redemption of LOVE: Rescuing Marriage and Sexuality from the Economics of a Fallen World*. Grand Rapids, MI: Baker, 2006.

Milkman, Harvey B., and Stanley Sunderwirth. *Craving for Ecstasy: The Consciousness and Chemistry of Escape*. Lexington, MA: Lexington Books, 1986.

Mills, Stanford. *A Hebrew Christian Looks at Romans*. New York: American Board of Missions to the Jews, 1971.

Mish, Frederick. ed., *Merriam-Webster's Collegiate Dictionary*, 10th ed. Springfield, MA: Merriam-Webster, 1999. s.v., "conjugal rights."

Moo, Douglas. "Sin in Paul." In *Fallen: A Theology of Sin*, edited by Christopher Morgan and Robert Peterson, 107-130. Wheaton, IL: Crossway, 2013.

New Oxford American Dictionary, s.v. "meta." New York: Oxford University Press, 2010.

"Pawned." *The Free Dictionary*. Accessed October 26, 2018. https://www.thefreedictionary.com/pawned.

Pate, C. Marvin. *Romans*. Grand Rapids, MI: Baker, 2013.

Penner, Clifford, and Joyce Penner. *The Gift of Sex: A Guide to Sexual Fulfillment*. Nashville: Thomas Nelson, 2003.

Piper, John, and Justin Taylor, eds. *Sex and the Supremacy of Christ*. Wheaton, IL: Crossway, 2005.

Pope Paul VI. *Humanae Vitae, On Human Life*. Washington, DC: United States Catholic Conference, 1968.

"Rev Up a Low Libido." *WebMD*. Accessed July 27, 2020. https://www.webmd.com/men/features/revving-up-low-libido.

Roberts, Ted. *Pure Desire*. Minneapolis: Bethany House, 1999.

Rosberg, Gary, and Barbara Rosberg. *The 5 Sex Needs of Men and Women*. Carol Stream, IL: Tyndale House Publishers, 2006.

Rosenau, Douglas E. *A Celebration of Sex*. Nashville: Thomas Nelson, 2002.

Rosenau, Doug, and Michael Wilson. *Soul Virgins*. Atlanta: Sexual Wholeness Resources, 2006.

Roth, Cecil. *Encyclopaedia Judaica*. Vol. 14, *Red-Sl*. Jerusalem, Israel: Keter, 1973.

Rowland, Christopher C. "The Book of Revelation." In *The New Interpreter's Bible*, ed. Leander E. Keck. Vol. 12, *Hebrews-Revelation*. Edited by David L. Bartlett, C. Clifton Black, Fred B. Craddock

Luke Timothy Johnson, Christopher C. Rowland, and Duane F. Watson, 503-736. Nashville: Abingdon, 1998.

Sacks, Jonathan. *The Dignity of Difference: How to Avoid the Clash of Civilizations*. New York: Bloomsbury, 2014.

Sailhamer, John. "Genesis." In *The Expositor's Bible Commentary*. Edited by Frank E. Gaebelein. Vol. 2, *Genesis, Exodus, Leviticus, Numbers*. Edited by John H. Sailhamer, Walter C. Kaiser Jr., R. Laird Harris, and Ronald B. Allen, 3-284. Grand Rapids, MI: Zondervan, 1990.

Sakenfeld, Katharine Doob. *The New Interpreter's Dictionary of the Bible*. Nashville: Abingdon Press, 2006.

Schaumburg, Harry. *False Intimacy: Understanding the Struggle of Sexual Addiction*. Colorado Springs: NavPress, 1997.

Schneider, Jennifer. "How to Recognize the Signs of Sexual Addiction: Asking the Right Questions May Uncover Serious Problems." *Postgraduate Medicine* 90, no. 6 (November 1991): 171-182. Accessed April 05, 2017. http://www.jenniferschneider.com/index.php/articles.

Smedes, Lewis B. *Sex for Christians*. Grand Rapids, MI: Eerdmans, 1994.

Smith, Jerome, ed. *The New Treasury of Scripture Knowledge*. Nashville: Thomas Nelson, 1992.

Sonnenberg, Roger R. *Human Sexuality: A Christian Perspective*. St. Louis: Concordia Publishing House, 1998.

Sparks, Richard C. *Contemporary Christian Morality: Real Questions, Candid Responses*. New York: Crossroad Herder, 1996, 88.

Sproul, R. C. *The Consequences of Ideas*. Wheaton, IL: Crossway, 2000.

Stafford, Matthew S. *The Biology of Sin*. Downers Grove, IL: InterVarsity Press, 2010.

Strauch, Barbara. *The Primal Teen*. New York: Random House, 2003.

Strong, James. *The New Strong's Exhaustive Concordance of The Bible*. Nashville: Thomas Nelson, 1990.

Stott, John. *The Message of Romans*. Downers Grove, IL: IVP Academic, 1994.

Sun, An-Pyng, Larry Ashley, and Lesley Dickson. *Behavioral Addiction: Screening, Assessment, and Treatment*. Las Vegas, NV: Central Recovery Press, 2013.

Thayer, Joseph. *Thayer's Greek-English Lexicon of the New Testament*. Grand Rapids, MI: Zondervan, 1970.

Toll, David. "Spiritual Injury." *Healing the Storm*, August 16, 2017. Accessed July 26, 2020. https://healingthestorm.com/2017/08/16/spiritual-injury.

Tozer, A. W. *The Pursuit of God*. Minneapolis: Bethany House, 2013.

Turner, Yolanda, and William Stayton. "The Twenty-First Century Challenges to Sexuality and Religion." *Journal of Religion and Health* 53, no. 2 (2014): 483-497.

VanGemeren, Willem, ed. *New International Dictionary of Old Testament Theology and Exegesis*. Grand Rapids, MI: Zondervan, 1997.

Walvoord, John. *Revelation*. Chicago: Moody, 2011.

Walvoord, John, and Roy Zuck, eds. *The Bible Knowledge Commentary*. Colorado Springs: Chariot Victor, 1985.

Whalen, John. *New Catholic Encyclopedia*. Vol. 13, *Seq-the*. Washington, DC: McGraw-Hill, 1967.

Wier, Terry. *Holy Sex*. New Kensington, PA: Whitaker House, 1999.

Wilson, Dawn. "Trusting God to Heal the Scars of Sexual Abuse." *Revive Our Hearts*, February 16, 2017. Accessed July 25, 2020. https://www.reviveourhearts.com/true-woman/blog/sexual-abuse-trusting-god-with-my-past-hurts.

Winner, Lauren F. *Real Sex: The Naked Truth about Chastity*. Grand Rapids, MI: Baker, 2006.

Wright, Christopher. *The Mission of God: Unlocking the Bible's Grand Narrative*. Downers Grove, IL: InterVarsity Press, 2006.

Yarhouse, Mark. *Understanding Gender Dysphoria: Navigating Transgender Issues in a Changing Culture*. Downers Grove, IL: IVP Academic, 2015.

ABOUT THE AUTHOR

DR. GARY FOSHEE is a minister, speaker and author of *THE REDMADAFA*. An expert in biblical sex and sexuality, he speaks at conferences, churches, men's and women's groups, and addiction centers. His seminar, "The Heart of Sex," teaches God's design for sex and how to keep the body and marriage bed pure. He has served as a chaplain for over 20 years in the United States Navy and Marine Corps serving at air wings, ships, hospitals, and SEAL Team FOUR. Dr. Foshee is also a board-certified chaplain who specializes in mental health and emergency medicine. He has been married to his wife, Julie, since 1997 and they have four sons: Aspen, Gabe, Sport, and Summit.

ENDNOTES

[1] All Scripture quotations, unless otherwise noted, are from the English Standard Version.

[2] "A garden locked is my sister, my bride, a spring locked, a fountain sealed" (Song of Songs, 4:12). The words "garden, spring, and fountain" in this passage refer to a woman's vagina, and the words "locked and sealed," refer to her virginity.

[3] Dale S. Kuehne, *Sex and the iWorld* (Grand Rapids, MI: Baker, 2009), 73-74.

[4] "The heart of sex" refers to the implicit core and fundamental design for sex created by an omniscient and omnipotent God who alone manifests all hope, meaning, and purpose. The majority of material covered in this book is the culmination of my Doctor of Ministry project, entitled "The Heart of Sex: Exploring God's Design for Sexuality."

[5] "Pawned," The Free Dictionary, accessed October 26, 2018, https://www.thefreedictionary.com/pawned.

[6] The Presbyterian Church (USA), the Evangelical Lutheran Church of America, the Episcopal Church, and the United Church of Christ are just a few that allow same-sex marriages.

[7] Romans 1:27.

[8] I say "subconsciously" because people often don't realize sexual immorality distorts the meaning and purpose of sex, which directly affects their belief and practice of sex.

[9] "Marriage should be honored by all and the marriage bed kept pure, for God will judge the adulterer and all the sexually immoral" (Heb. 13:4, NIV).

[10] The husband should give to his wife her conjugal rights, and likewise the wife to her husband" (1 Cor. 7:3).

[11] "Catch the foxes for us, the little foxes that spoil the vineyard, for our vineyards are in blossom" (Song 2:15).

[12] Genesis 29:18-30.

[13] Gen. 2:24; Matt. 19:5; Mark 10:7-8; 1 Cor. 6:16; Eph. 5:31. (canonical order)

[14] "Marriage should be honored by all and the marriage bed kept pure" (Heb. 4:13, NIV).

[15] Dennis P. Hollinger, *The Meaning of Sex* (Grand Rapids, MI: Baker Academic, 2009), 13.

[16] Ibid., 135.

[17] I will explain the process of "classical conditioning" in chapter 3.

[18] A trespasser is anyone, other than the spouse, who eats and drinks or has any type of sexual experience in another person's private garden—in simple language, any sexual experience with a person other than a person's spouse is a trespass that dishonors marriage and defiles the marriage bed.

[19] "Marriage should be honored by all and the marriage bed kept pure, for God will judge the adulterer and all the sexual immoral" (Heb 13:4, NIV).

[20] The "One Flesh Covenants" are covered in detail in chapter 5.

[21] "Even as he chose us in him before the foundation of the world, that we should be holy and blameless before him" (Eph. 1:4). "Now the word of the LORD came to me, saying, 'Before I formed you in the womb I knew you and before you were born I consecrated you; I appointed you a prophet to the nations'" (Jer. 1:4-5).

[22] Hollinger, *The Meaning of Sex*, 130.

[23] Bill Farrel and Pam Farrel, *The Before-You-Marry Book of Questions* (Eugene, OR: Harvest House, 2013), 23.

[24] Yolanda Turner and William Stayton, "The Twenty-First Century Challenges to Sexuality and Religion," *Journal of Religion and Health* 53, no. 2 (2014): 485.

[25] Norman L. Geisler, *Christian Ethics*, 2nd ed. (Grand Rapids, MI: Baker, 2010), 260.

[26] "I guide you in the way of wisdom and lead you along straight paths. When you walk, your steps will not be hampered; when you run, you will not stumble" (Prov. 4:11-12).

[27] Turner and Stayton, "Twenty-First Century Challenges," 485.

[28] Terry Wier, *Holy Sex* (New Kensington, PA: Whitaker House, 1999), 24. The Old Testament speaks plainly about the sexual sins of the people of that day and the consequences they suffered, giving people the golden opportunity to learn from their mistakes so they do not repeat them.

[29] Joe S. McIlhaney Jr. and Freda Bush, *Hooked: New Science on How Casual Sex Is Affecting Our Children* (Chicago: Northfield, 2008), 16.

[30] "The spouses' union achieves the two-fold end of marriage: the good of the spouses themselves and the transmission of life. These two

meanings or values of marriage cannot be separated without altering the couple's spiritual life and compromising the goods of marriage and the future of the family. The conjugal love of man and woman thus stands under the twofold obligation of fidelity and fecundity." Catechism of The Catholic Church, "The Love of Husband and Wife #2363," Part three, Life in Christ, Section Two, The Vatican, accessed December 11, 2017, http://www.vatican.va/archive/ccc_css/archive/catechism/p3s2c2a6.htm.

[31] Pope Paul VI, *Humanae Vitae, On Human Life* (Washington, DC: United States Catholic Conference, 1968), 11.

[32] CWR Staff, "The Sacrament of Marriage Is the Icon of God's Love for Us," *Catholic World Report*, April 2, 2014, accessed March 17, 2017, http://www.catholicworldreport.com/Blog/3045/pope_francis_the_sacrament_of_marriage_is_the_icon_of_gods_love_for_us.aspx.

[33] Laurie Jungling, "Passionate Order: Order and Sexuality in Augustine's Theology," in *Word and World* 27, no. 3 (Summer 2007): 316-317.

[34] Aurelius Augustinus, *The Confessions of Saint Augustine*, trans. Edward Pusey (Franklin, PA: The Franklin Library, 1982), 25-34.

[35] Stanley J. Grenz, *Sexual Ethics* (Louisville, KY: Westminster John Knox, 1990), 5.

[36] David G. Hunter, "Sex, Sin and Salvation: What Augustine Really Said," The National Institute for the Renewal of the Priesthood, accessed March 13, 2017, http://www.jknirp.com/aug3.htm.

[37] Tim Alan Gardner, *Sacred Sex* (Colorado Springs: WaterBrook Press, 2008), 3-4.

[38] *New Oxford American Dictionary*, s.v. "meta" (New York: Oxford University Press, 2010).

[39] Kathlyn A. Breazeale, *Mutual Empowerment: A Theology of Marriage, Intimacy, and Redemption* (Minneapolis: Fortress, 2008), 139.

[40] Gardner, *Sacred Sex*, 76.

[41] Ibid., 75.

[42] Jonathan Grant, *Divine Sex* (Grand Rapids, MI: Baker, 2015), 24.

[43] Clovis Chappell, "I'd Risk Something," in *20 Centuries of Great Preaching*, vol. 9, eds. Clyde E. Fant Jr. and William M. Pinson, Jr. (Waco, TX: Word Books, 1971), 223.

[44] Kuehne, *Sex and the iWorld*, 73-74.

[45] Ibid.

[46] Gardner, *Sacred Sex*, 8.

[47] Bill Farrel and Pam Farrel, *Red-Hot Monogamy* (Eugene, OR: Harvest House, 2006), 9-10.

[48] Steve Gallagher, *At the Altar of Sexual Idolatry* (Dry Ridge, KY: Pure Life Ministries, 2000), 150.

[49] Hollinger, *The Meaning of Sex*, 72.

[50] Daniel Heimbach, *True Sexual Morality: Recovering Biblical Standards for a Culture in Crisis* (Wheaton, IL: Crossway, 2004), 144.

[51] Carrie A. Miles, *The Redemption of LOVE: Rescuing Marriage and Sexuality from the Economics of a Fallen World* (Grand Rapids, MI: Baker, 2006), 15.

[52] A self-idolatrous, narcissistic, sexual act performed in isolation for self-gratification that leaves individuals laden with shame and guilt and resides completely outside of the one-flesh covenant God designed for marriage.

53 Roger R. Sonnenberg, *Human Sexuality: A Christian Perspective* (St. Louis: Concordia Publishing House, 1998), 90.

54 Shmuley Boteach, *Kosher Sex* (New York: Broadway Books, 1999), 89.

55 "Classical conditioning theory involves learning a new behavior via the process of association. In simple terms two stimuli are linked together to produce a new learned response in a person or animal. There are three stages of classical conditioning. **Stage 1: Before Conditioning:** In this stage, the **unconditioned stimulus** produces an **unconditioned response** in an organism. In basic terms, this means that a stimulus in the environment has produced a behavior/response which is unlearned (i.e. unconditioned) and therefore is a natural response which has not been taught. **Stage 2: During Conditioning:** During this stage a stimulus which produces no response (i.e. neutral) is associated with the unconditioned stimulus at which point it now becomes known as the **conditioned stimulus**. **Stage 3: After Conditioning:** Now the conditioned stimulus has been associated with the unconditioned stimulus to create a new conditioned response." Saul McLeod, "Classical Condition," Simply Psychology, last modified 2014, accessed March 24, 2017, https://www.simplypsychology.org/classical-conditioning.html.

56 "The [sexual] drive is relatively constant [i.e., most often daily] for a male, while a female's drive is more periodic. This system becomes activated at puberty, when two structures in the brain, the hypothalamus and the anterior pituitary gland, cause the gonads to release steroid sex hormones. In males, these hormones are called androgens, of which testosterone is the most important. In females, the ovaries release estrogens. When androgens and estrogens become active in our bodies for the first time, they generate sexual desire—not a sinful desire, but a God-given drive to seek out and be near members of the opposite sex for the ultimate purpose of finding a mate. Steroid sex hormones are also responsible for sexual maturation, shaping our

bodies into adult men and women." Matthew S. Stafford, *The Biology of Sin* (Downers Grove, IL: InterVarsity Press, 2010), 49-50.

[57] Ted Roberts, *Pure Desire* (Minneapolis: Bethany House, 1999), 156-157.

[58] I counseled a married couple who were both sex addicts. They both were compulsive masturbators, and they used dildos and vibrators on each other. I challenged them to stop masturbating and using sex toys as part of their recovery plan. After several failed attempts, they both reported they had stopped masturbating and using sex toys on themselves and each other. In one of our counseling sessions the wife said, "I am much more sensitive to his touch now, and sex is better than ever. My sexual desire for my husband has increased, and I finally got my one-month coin." The couple attends a sexual addiction group and the group gives a coin to anyone who has stopped masturbating for more than a month.

[59] Hollinger, *The Meaning of Sex*, 140.

[60] In the course of my research for my doctoral research, I talked with three different males who reported that when they were young and before they masturbated, seminal build up passed through their urethra during urination, thus bringing sexual release and buildup of seminal fluid.

[61] Mark Driscoll, *Porn-Again Christian* (Seattle: Mars Hill Church, 2009), 21.

[62] Michael Kolarcik, "The Book of Wisdom," in *The New Interpreter's Bible*, vol. 5 (Nashville: Abingdon, 1997), 554.

[63] *New Oxford American Dictionary*, s.v. "self-control" (New York: Oxford University Press, 2010).

[64] "Masturbation is a form of monosexuality because it is sex that does not include another person. Since sex is given for such purposes

as oneness (Gen. 2:24), intimate knowledge (Gen. 4:1), and comfort (2 Sam.12:24), having sex with oneself seems to miss some of the significant biblical reasons for sexual intimacy." Driscoll, *Porn-Again Christian*, 21.

[65] James Crenshaw, "Sirach," in *The New Interpreter's Bible*, vol. 5 (Nashville: Abingdon, 1997), 737.

[66] A pseudonym used to protect the identity of the individual.

[67] The majority of individuals and couples I counsel for sexual issues identify as Christian. A large number of them either do not know God's instructions regarding sex and sexual behavior, or they simply refuse to follow biblical standards, opting to decide for themselves what is permissible or not. I often hear, "This is my body. I have the right to do with it as I choose." Numerous women say the same thing with regard to abortion. More and more denominations are also ordaining homosexual men and women and have fully embraced homosexuality as an alternative lifestyle. This is nothing more than hedonism.

[68] See Genesis 19:5; Leviticus 18:22; 20:13; Deuteronomy 23:17; Judges 19:22; 1 Kings 14:24; 15:12; 22:46; 2 Kings 23:7; Romans 1:24-27; 1 Corinthians 6:9-11; 1 Timothy 1:9-11; 2 Peter 2:4-10; Jude 7.

[69] James Hastings, ed., *Encyclopedia of Religion and Ethics*, vol. 11 (New York: Morrison and Gibb Limited, 1920), 672.

[70] Nocturnal emissions are natural and not sinful or depraved. They are the body's natural way of releasing built-up seminal fluid.

[71] "Some women report orgasm during anal intercourse, particularly when it is accompanied by hand stimulation of the clitoris. Men also report orgasms from anal intercourse, primarily due to stimulation of the prostate." Janet Shibley Hyde and John D. DeLamater, *Understanding Human Sexuality*, 8th ed. (New York: McGraw-Hill, 2003), 264.

[72] Not her real name but one made up to protect her anonymity.

[73] "And the Lord's servant must not be quarrelsome but kind to everyone, able to teach, patiently enduring evil, correcting his opponents with gentleness. God may perhaps grant them repentance leading to a knowledge of the truth, and they may come to their senses and escape from the snare of the devil, after being captured by him to do his will" (2 Tim. 2:24-26).

[74] The term "homosexuality" includes both male and females who practice same-sex relations.

[75] "The continual abandoning of oneself to immorality in general can be a slippery slope to more perverse sexual activities. And, for Paul, all of this starts with idolatry: to exchange worship of the Creator for worship of the creature is to invite the exchange of normal sexual relations for unnatural ones." C. Marvin Pate, *Romans* (Grand Rapids, MI: Baker, 2013), 37.

[76] John Stott, *The Message of Romans* (Downers Grove, IL: IVP Academic, 1994), 76.

[77] "To *hand over* means to permit, not to encourage or to force, so that they were helped by the devil to put into practice the things which they conceived in their lusts. They never thought of doing anything good, and so they were handed over to uncleanness and damaged each other's bodies with abuse. Even now there are still men of this type, who are said to dishonor each other's bodies. When the thought of the mind is wrong, the bodies are said to be dishonored. Is not a stain on the body a sign of sin in the soul? When the body is contaminated, nobody doubts that there is sin in the soul." Ambrosiater, *Ancient Christian Texts: Romans and 1-2 Corinthians*, trans. Gerald Bray (Downers Grove, IL: IVP Academic, 2009), 12.

[78] Stott, *The Message of Romans*, 77-78.

79 "The husband should give to his wife her conjugal rights, and likewise the wife to her husband. For the wife does not have authority over her own body, but the husband does. Likewise the husband does not have authority over his own body, but the wife does. Do not deprive one another, except perhaps by agreement for a limited time, that you may devote yourselves to prayer; but then come together again, so that Satan may not tempt you because of your lack of self-control." (1 Cor. 7:3-5).

80 Frederick Mish, ed., *Merriam-Webster's Collegiate Dictionary*, 10th ed. (Springfield, MA: Merriam-Webster, 1999), s.v. "conjugal rights."

81 Sexual drive or desire.

82 "Rev Up a Low Libido," *WebMD*, accessed July 27, 2020, https://www.webmd.com/men/features/revving-up-low-libido.

83 Kelli Hastings, "What is Emotional Intimacy?" *Marriage.com*, accessed July 27, 2020, https://www.marriage.com/advice/emotional-intimacy/what-is-emotional-intimacy.

84 David Kantor, quoted in Amy Hertz, "To Love, Honor, and Last Longer than a Year," *O, The Oprah Magazine* (March 2002): 205.

85 Gary Rosberg and Barbara Rosberg, *The 5 Sex Needs of Men and Women* (Carol Stream, IL: Tyndale House Publishers, 2006), 50-51.

86 "5 Ways to Develop Emotional Intimacy in Your Relationship," *Power of Positivity*, accessed July 27, 2020, https://www.powerofpositivity.com/emotional-intimacy-relationship.

87 "If a man lies with a woman during her menstrual period and uncovers her nakedness, he has made naked her fountain, and she has uncovered the fountain of her blood. Both of them shall be cut off from among their people. You shall not approach a woman to uncover her nakedness while she is in her menstrual uncleanness" (Lev. 20:18-19).

[88] Sonnenberg, *Human Sexuality*, 159.

[89] Ibid., 161.

[90] Ibid.

[91] Ibid., 160.

[92] Kuehne, *Sex and the iWorld*, 23. See Barna Group, "American Lifestyles Mix Compassion and Self-Oriented Behavior," *Barna Update*, February 5, 2007, accessed March 17, 2017, https://www.barna.com/research/american-lifestyles-mix-compassion-and-self-oriented-behavior.

[93] Heath Lambert, *Finally Free: Fighting for Purity with the Power of Grace* (Grand Rapids, MI: Zondervan, 2013), 142.

[94] Douglas E. Rosenau, *A Celebration of Sex* (Nashville: Thomas Nelson, 2002), 11.

[95] Ronald L. Conte Jr., "Questions and Answers on Catholic Marital Sexual Ethics," Question 4. "Which types of acts are moral for a husband and wife to use as foreplay?" accessed September 20, 2017, http://www.catechism.cc/articles/QA.htm#04.

[96] Lauren F. Winner, *Real Sex: The Naked Truth about Chastity* (Grand Rapids, MI: Baker, 2006), 106.

[97] David Jeremiah, *What the Bible Says about Love, Marriage and Sex: The Song of Solomon* (New York: FaithWorks, 2012), 156-157.

[98] Rosenau, *A Celebration of Sex*, 10.

[99] Ibid.

[100] "Bodily fluids and secretions are exchanged between partners during sexual contact. The exchange occurs not only during intercourse, but also during other activities such as oral sex. If a person has a sexually transmitted infection, some of the germs of that infection are in the

person's bodily fluids. Those germs can then infect their partner with herpes, gonorrhea, even HPV, or other diseases one of them might be infected with." McIlhaney and Bush, *Hooked*, 81.

[101] Sonnenberg, *Human Sexuality*, 142.

[102] Interviews by author, 2005-2017.

[103] Boteach, *Kosher Sex*, 10.

[104] Not his real name but made up to protect the anonymity of the couple.

[105] Sexual desire, lust, longing, a strong desire.

[106] "Do not deprive each other except perhaps by mutual consent and for a time, so that you may devote yourselves to prayer. Then come together again so that Satan will not tempt you because of your lack of self-control" (1 Cor. 7:5).

[107] "I am my beloved's, and his desire is for me" (Song 7:10).

[108] "Now to the unmarried and the widows I say: It is good for them to stay unmarried, as I am. But if they cannot control themselves, they should marry, for it is better to marry than to burn with passion" (1 Cor. 7:8-9).

[109] "Or do you not know that he who is joined to a prostitute becomes one body with her? For, as it is written, 'The two will become one flesh'" (1 Cor. 6:16).

[110] There are numerous other issues that affect sexual desire: health, guilt, anxiety, stress, previous sexual experiences, sexual abuse, lack of family sexual training or extreme religious teachings, masturbation, feelings about one's spouse and marriage, age of children, feeling about one's body/a poor self-image, energy levels, hormones. These issues and numerous other issues interact to enhance or diminish sexual desire.

[111] James Strong, *The New Strong's Exhaustive Concordance of The Bible* (Nashville: Thomas Nelson, 1990), 44.

[112] Ibid.

[113] Ibid.

[114] "The husband should give to his wife her conjugal rights, and likewise the wife to her husband" (1 Cor 7:3).

[115] The Shulamite was not Solomon's only sexual outlet as he had numerous wives and concubines. However, the polygamous practices of Solomon and other men in the Bible were never God's design for marriage nor the heart of sex. One man and one woman has always been God's divine plan for marriage, and within the marriage, they are to serve as each other's only sexual outlet.

[116] In the book of Song of Solomon, King Solomon rescues a peasant girl, who was forced by her brothers to work in a vineyard.

[117] I realize the serpent is Satan, and at this particular time in history, he did not have any "seed," for sin had not entered the world. God in his foreknowledge is making a divine proclamation and referring to the ultimate battle of Satan and Jesus—the providential "seed" of woman. The serpent in this scene is also a real creature that looked completely different than it does now.

[118] "And God said, Let us make man in our image, after our likeness: and let them have dominion over the fish of the sea, and over the fowl of the air, and over the cattle, and over all the earth, and over every creeping thing that creepeth upon the earth" (Gen. 1:26, KJV).

[119] Even though the Bible does not address childbirth until after the fall, I believe Eve already had numerous children, grandchildren and great grandchildren. This is evident when God curses Cain and Cain becomes afraid of people who will find and kill him.

[120] James D. Mallory, *The Battle of the Sexes: How Both Sides Can Win With Honor*. (Wheaton, IL: Crossway Books, 1996), 62.

[121] "Wives, submit to your own husbands, as to the Lord" (Eph. 5:22).

[122] God does give direct instructions to husbands and men outside of the admonishments that they are to be the head of their wives and women in 1 Corinthians 11:3 and Ephesians 5:23.

[123] Proverbs 10:12; 1 Peter 4:8.

[124] Mallory, 56.

[125] Education that indoctrinates people into destructive ideologies i.e. evolution, racism, discrimination, and terrorism, etc., significantly alters how men and women view themselves, others and their purpose in the world. These factors can lead people toward certain goals and ambitions, and can severally limit and influence their physical and mental abilities.

[126] "'For the LORD God of Israel says that He hates divorce, for it covers one's garment with violence,' Says the LORD of hosts. 'Therefore, take heed to your spirit, that you do not deal treacherously'" (Mal. 2:16, NKJV).

[127] A garden locked is my sister, my bride, a spring locked, a fountain sealed" (Song 4:12).

[128] "We destroy arguments and every lofty opinion raised against the knowledge of God and take every thought captive to obey Christ" (2 Cor. 10:5).

[129] "My son, be attentive to my wisdom; incline your ear to my understanding, that you may keep discretion, and your lips may guard knowledge. For the lips of a forbidden woman drip honey, and her speech is smoother than oil, but in the end she is bitter as wormwood, sharp as a two-edged sword. Her feet go down to death; her steps

follow the path to Sheol; she does not ponder the path of life; her ways wander, and she does not know it. And now, O sons, listen to me, and do not depart from the words of my mouth. Keep your way far from her, and do not go near the door of her house, lest you give your honor to others and your years to the merciless, lest strangers take their fill of your strength, and your labors go to the house of a foreigner, and at the end of your life you groan, when your flesh and body are consumed" (Prov. 5:1-11).

[130] "I am a rose of Sharon, a lily of the valleys." (Song 2:1).

[131] "And it shall come to pass that everyone who calls upon the name of the Lord shall be saved" (Acts 2:21).

[132] "Catch the foxes for us, the little foxes that spoil the vineyards, for our vineyards are in blossom" (Song 2:15).

[133] "Then I said about the one worn out by adultery, 'Now let them use her as a prostitute, for that is all she is.' And they slept with her. As men sleep with a prostitute, so they slept with those lewd women, Oholah and Oholibah" (Ezek 23:43-44, NIV). Men who watch porn, visit strip clubs, masturbate, engage in other acts of sexual immorality, and have other sexual outlets other than their spouse **approach their wives and sleep with her as with a prostitute**. This means that even when a man is having sex with his wife, his mind and heart are having sex with someone else, i.e., a prostitute, someone he saw while watching porn, or some woman he saw at work or in public. His wife is fully aware of this.

[134] Jeremiah, *What the Bible Says about Love, Marriage and Sex*, 8.

[135] Hollinger, *The Meaning of Sex*, 92.

[136] John Piper and Justin Taylor, eds., *Sex and the Supremacy of Christ* (Wheaton, IL: Crossway, 2005), 26.

[137] Boteach, *Kosher Sex*, 28.

[138] Ibid.

[139] Doug Rosenau and Michael Wilson, *Soul Virgins* (Atlanta, GA: Sexual Wholeness Resources, 2006), 16.

[140] Ibid.

[141] Jack O. Balswick and Judith K. Balswick, *A Model for Marriage* (Downers Grove, IL: InterVarsity Press, 2006), 164-165.

[142] Winner, *Real Sex*, 38.

[143] "As you saw iron mixed with ceramic clay, they shall mingle themselves with the seed of men; but they will not adhere to one another, just as iron does not mix with clay" (Dan. 2:43, NKJV). The "seed of men" referenced in this passage seems out of place. This may refer to Genesis 6:2. Although interpretations on this Scripture vary widely, this passage highlights the significance of the will of humans versus the will of God. Whether this Scripture references governments, fallen angels, or humans, the overarching theme is that their efforts will fail. As Psalm 127:1 says, "Unless the LORD builds the house, those who build it labor in vain."

[144] "Enmity" (*eybah*) means hostility, hatred, or a hostile mind. It is first mentioned in Genesis 3:15 concerning the seed of the woman and that of the serpent. Satan's attempt to distort cultural and societal views of sexuality, marriage, and coitus advances his quest to "bruise the heel" of the seed of woman. God's curse, and the sexual battle waging in society, renders casualties (a crushed head and bruised heel) on both sides. John Sailhamer suggests, "Though wounded in the struggle, the woman's 'seed' will be victorious. . . . As representatives the snake and the woman embody the fate of their seed, and that fate is their fate as well. . . . At first in v. 15 the 'enmity' is said

to have been put between the snake and the woman and between the 'seed' of the snake and the 'seed' of the woman. The second half of v. 15, however, says that the 'seed' of the woman ('he') will crush the head of the snake ('your head'). The woman's 'seed' is certainly intended to be understood as a group (or individual) that lies the same temporal distance from the woman as the 'seed' of the snake does from the snake itself. Yet in this verse it is the 'seed' of the woman who crushes the head of the snake. Though the 'enmity' may lie between the two 'seeds,' the goal of the final crushing blow is not the 'seed' of the snake but rather the snake itself; his head will be crushed." John Sailhamer, "Genesis," in *The Expositor's Bible Commentary*, ed. Frank E. Gaebelein, vol. 2, *Genesis, Exodus, Leviticus, Numbers*, by John H. Sailhamer et al. (Grand Rapids, MI: Zondervan, 1990), 55-56.

[145] Rosberg, *The 5 Sex Needs of Men and Women*, 265.

[146] Clifford Penner and Joyce Penner, *The Gift of Sex: A Guide to Sexual Fulfillment* (Nashville: Thomas Nelson, 2003), 100.

[147] Timothy Mallard, "The (Twin) Wounds of War," accessed July 26, 2020, https://providencemag.com/2017/02/twin-wounds-war-spiritual-injury-moral-injury/#_ednref12.

[148] David Toll, "Spiritual Injury," *Healing the Storm*, August 16, 2017, accessed July 26, 2020, https://healingthestorm.com/2017/08/16/spiritual-injury.

[149] Dawn Wilson, "Trusting God to Heal the Scars of Sexual Abuse," *Revive Our Hearts*, accessed July 25, 2020, https://www.reviveourhearts.com/true-woman/blog/sexual-abuse-trusting-god-with-my-past-hurts.

[150] Ibid. Emphasis added by author.

[151] Gardner, *Sacred Sex*, 75.

[152] A. W. Tozer, *The Pursuit of God* (Minneapolis: Bethany House, 2013), 94-95.

[153] David Jeremiah, *Shelter in God: Your Refuge in Times of Trouble* (Nashville: W Publishing, 2020), 113.

[154] "And it shall come to pass that everyone who calls on the name of the LORD shall be saved" (Joel 2:32a).

[155] Dawn Wilson, "Trusting God to Heal the Scars of Sexual Abuse," *Revive Our Hearts*, accessed July 25, 2020, https://www.reviveourhearts.com/true-woman/blog/sexual-abuse-trusting-god-with-my-past-hurts.

[156] "But whoever hates his brother is in the darkness and walks in the darkness. He does not know where he is going, because the darkness has blinded his eyes" (1 John 2:11).

[157] "My son, if you receive my words and treasure up my commandments with you, making your ear attentive to wisdom and inclining your heart to understanding; yes, if you call out for insight and raise your voice for understanding, if you seek it like silver and search for it as for hidden treasures, then you will understand the fear of the Lord and find the knowledge of God" (Prov. 2:1-5).

[158] Jonathan Sacks, *The Dignity of Difference: How to Avoid the Clash of Civilizations* (New York: Bloomsbury, 2014), 63-64. An old Jewish tradition about the creation of man reads, "When God was about to create Adam, the ministering angels split into contending groups. Some said, 'Let him be created.' Others said, 'Let him not be created.' That is why it is written: 'Mercy and truth collided, righteousness and peace clashed' (Psalm 85:11). Mercy said, 'Let him be created, because he will do merciful deeds.' Truth said, 'Let him not be created, for he will be full of falsehood.' Righteousness said, 'Let him be created, for he will do righteous deeds.' Peace said, 'Let him not be created, for he will never cease quarrelling.' What did the Holy One, blessed be He, do?

He took truth and threw it to the ground. The angels said, 'Sovereign of the universe, why do You do thus to Your own seal, truth? Let truth arise from the ground.' Thus it is written, 'Let truth spring up from the earth' (Psalm 85:12)."

[159] Tikva Frymer-Kensky, "Sex and Sexuality," in *The Anchor Bible Dictionary*, ed. David Freedman (New York: Doubleday, 1992), 1144.

[160] Deborah Sawyer, "Sex, Sexuality," in *The New Interpreter's Dictionary of the Bible*, ed. Katharine Sakenfeld (Nashville: Abingdon, 2006), 5:200.

[161] "Sex was meant for enjoyment, as the brief but joyful allegory of Prov. 5:15-21 demonstrates when it refers to enjoying the wife of one's youth. The emphatically positive outlook on the value of legitimate sexual enjoyment is expressed in the positive, affirmative attitude toward sex within marriage, its only legally and morally approved context. Man and woman were not only allowed, they were even commanded, to marry. They were not only permitted, they were actually supposed, to enjoy the sexual act in each other's legally sanctioned embrace. They were, by religious law as well as by social expectation, bound to procreate many children." Jackie A. Naude, "Sexual Ordinances," in *New International Dictionary of Old Testament Theology and Exegesis*, ed. Willem VanGemeren (Grand Rapids, MI: Zondervan, 1997), 4:1201.

[162] Hyde and DeLamater, *Understanding Human Sexuality*, 676.

[163] Matthew Fox, *The Hidden Spirituality of Men: Ten Metaphors to Awaken the Sacred Masculine* (Novato, CA: New World Library, 2008), 114-115.

[164] Ibid.

[165] Ibid., 114.

[166] "The point of the narrative is that there was no helper who corresponded to man among the animals. A special act of creation of the woman was necessary." John H. Sailhamer, "Genesis," in *The Expositor's Bible Commentary*, ed. Frank E. Gaebelein, vol. 2, *Genesis, Exodus, Leviticus, Numbers*, eds. John H. Sailhamer, Walter C. Kaiser Jr., R. Laird Harris, and Ronald B. Allen (Grand Rapids, MI: Zondervan, 1990), 46.

[167] "A homiletic midrash often quoted by commentators says that 'just as the rib is found at the side of the man and is attached to him, even so the good wife, the rib of her husband, stands at his side to be his helper-counterpart, and her soul is bound up with his.'" Ibid., 47.

[168] Raymond C. Ortlund Jr., "Man and Woman," in *New Dictionary of Biblical Theology*, eds. T. Desmond Alexander et al. (Downers Grove, IL: InterVarsity Press, 2000), 651.

[169] Edward W. Goodrick, *Zondervan NIV Exhaustive Concordance*, 2nd ed. (Grand Rapids, MI: Zondervan, 1999), 1463.

[170] Victor P. Hamilton, *Handbook on the Pentateuch* (Grand Rapids, MI: Baker, 1982), 29.

[171] "Obviously one does not need an extensive or even a superficial knowledge of mythology in order to understand the message of Genesis 1-2. And yet I am persuaded that the implications of the creation story of Genesis emerge most dramatically when it is compared with the creation literature of, for example, Mesopotamia (be that literature Sumerian, Assyrian, or Babylonian). For it is in the comparison of literature of identical general theme that the distinctiveness of biblical faith and message appear." Ibid., 35.

[172] Lindsay Jones, *Encyclopedia of Religion*, 2nd ed. (Farmington Hills, MI: Thomson and Gale, 2005), 8248.

[173] "In sex man gives himself. The conjugal act involves so deep and radical a self-donation that it itself actualizes the indissoluble union to which spousal love aspires. The becoming 'one flesh,' of the very nature of this reciprocal gift, clearly presupposes not only love, but consensus, i.e., the solemn will of the spouses to bind themselves forever." John Whalen, *New Catholic Encyclopedia*, ed. Catholic University of America (Washington, DC: McGraw-Hill, 1967), 13:148.

[174] Deuteronomy 22:17 protects women from false accusations of sexual immorality before marriage.

[175] Whalen, *New Catholic Encyclopedia*, 149.

[176] Joseph Fletcher, "Sex, Ethics of," in *The New Schaff-Herzog Encyclopedia of Religious Knowledge*, vol. 15, *Twentieth Century Encyclopedia of Religious Knowledge*, ed. Lefferts A. Loetscher (Grand Rapids, MI: Baker, 1977), 1023.

[177] Lewis B. Smedes, *Sex for Christians* (Grand Rapids, MI: Eerdmans, 1994), 14.

[178] "As a result of the first sin, man lost his liberty but not his free will. He was plunged, as a divine punishment, into a corrupt state known as original sin, losing the ability to incline himself to the things of God. . . . Fallen man is in bondage to sin. He still has the faculty of choosing, a will free from coercion, but he now is free only to sin, because his desires are inclined only toward sin and away from God." R. C. Sproul, *The Consequences of Ideas* (Wheaton, IL: Crossway, 2000), 63.

[179] A similar story about social ethics and sexual immorality is found in Judges 19:22-30.

[180] "According to the most probable reading, in Job 36:14 it is said of the wicked: 'They die in their youth and perish like sodomites.' This parallelism implies that the life of sodomites was proverbially short, possibly from the fact that they contracted venereal disease." George

A. Barton, "Sodomy," in *Encyclopedia of Religion and Ethics*, ed. James Hastings (New York: Morrison and Gibb Limited, 1920), 11:672.

[181] Other biblical accounts include Rom. 1:27; 1 Cor. 6:9; 1 Tim. 1:10; Heb. 13:4; Jude 7; Rev. 21:8; 22:15.

[182] "Dogs return to eat their vomit, just as fools repeat their foolishness" (Prov. 26:11).

[183] Walter C. Kaiser Jr., "Exodus," in *The Expositor's Bible Commentary*, ed. Frank E. Gaebelein, vol. 2, *Genesis, Exodus, Leviticus, Deuteronomy*, eds. John H. Sailhamer, Walter C. Kaiser Jr., R. Laird Harris, and Ronald B. Allen (Grand Rapids, MI: Zondervan, 1990), 420. The purpose of the Law of God was to show (1) humanity's awful sinfulness in their moral distance from God, (2) humanity's need for a mediator if they ever were to approach God, and (3) how to live more abundantly by using the unchangeable perfections of the nature of God as revealed in the moral law as humanity's guide.

[184] "The ANE cult of sex continuously posed a threat to the integrity of Israel's life. Indeed, Israelites up to the return from Babylon were often involved in this cult. Orgies of a sexual nature were the consequence whenever Israel threw off, for a short while, the yoke of the law, as witness the incidents of the golden calf (Ex. 32:6, 19) and the whoring with the Moabite women in honor of Baal Peor (Num. 25:1)." Jackie A. Naude, *Sexual Ordinances*, 1203.

[185] "Judaism regards moderation and self-control in sex as the essence of 'holiness' (Lev. 19:2, and commentaries), condemning unchaste conduct as among the most heinous offences against God and Society, and branding as capital crimes such perversions as sodomy and pederasty as well as adultery and incest. On the other hand, it rejects the notion of considering the sex instinct as intrinsically sinful or shameful. The sex drive should be sublimated rather than suppressed, for 'were it not for the evil inclination, no man would build a home

and marry.' Indeed, to the Rabbis, who frowned on celibacy, it was this instinct which completed the creation of the world and caused God to pronounce His work as 'very good.'" Immanuel Jakobovits, "Sex," in *Encyclopedia Judaica*, ed. Cecil Roth (Jerusalem, Israel: Keter, 1973), 14:1206.

[186] "Aberrant sexuality could pollute the land and endanger the very survival of Israel. Israel felt that its right of occupation was contingent upon its preserving the purity of the land: if Israel indulged in the same behavior as the people before it, the defiled land would spew them out as it spewed out the nations before Israel (Lev. 18:28)." Tikva Frymer-Kensky, "Sex and Sexuality, 1146.

[187] Hamilton, *Handbook on the Pentateuch*, 302.

[188] John Hannah, "Exodus," in *The Bible Knowledge Commentary*, ed. by John Walvoord and Roy Zuck (Colorado Springs: Chariot Victor, 1985), 140.

[189] "Marriage is the most profound bond that exists between two individuals and nothing should be withheld thus making all other relational claims subordinate to marriage. The bond of marriage is a barrier surrounding the husband and wife and it completely destroys any other barrier between them allowing them to fully belong to each other and no other." Ortlund, "Man and Woman," 655.

[190] Ibid., 656.

[191] Christopher J. H. Wright, *The Mission of God: Unlocking the Bible's Grand Narrative* (Downers Grove, IL: InterVarsity Press, 2006), 429.

[192] Ibid.

[193] Ibid.

[194] "You shall not fall in with the many to do evil, nor shall you bear witness in a lawsuit, siding with the many, so as to pervert justice" (Exod 23:2).

[195] "Then desire when it has conceived gives birth to sin, and sin when it is fully grown brings forth death" (Jas 1:15).

[196] "Gender dysphoria refers to the experience of having a psychological and emotional identity as either male or female, and that your psychological and emotional identity does not correspond to your biological sex—this perceived incongruity can be the source of deep and ongoing discomfort." Mark Yarhouse, *Understanding Gender Dysphoria: Navigating Transgender Issues in a Changing Culture* (Downers Grove, IL: IVP Academic, 2015), 19.

[197] Eugene Merrill, "Malachi," in *The Expositor's Bible Commentary Revised*, vol. 8, *Daniel-Malachi*, eds. Tremper Longman III and David Garland (Grand Rapids, MI: Zondervan, 2008), 855.

[198] "It was resolved in David's mind that Uriah must die—that innocent, valiant, and gallant man, who was ready to sacrifice his life for the honor of his prince. . . . This was the greatest treachery and villainy on the part of David." Jerome Smith, ed., *The New Treasury of Scripture Knowledge* (Nashville: Thomas Nelson, 1992), 343.

[199] "Temptation plays with the facets of things that are good, and highlights the attractions of the beauties in creation. Sin then perverts the excitement which these objects quite rightly cause within us. Thus, to revert to John's words, 'the lust of the flesh' perverts and corrupts the excitement which drives us towards what is good and beneficial. The 'lust of the eyes' likewise corrupts the drive towards what is beautiful and true." Henri Blocher, *In the Beginning* (Downers Grove, IL: InterVarsity Press, 1984), 140-141.

[200] Jeremiah, *What the Bible Says about Love, Marriage and Sex*, 163. David Jeremiah says the Song of Solomon is so beautifully written that no poet except God himself could have constructed it: "The Song is all about beauty and passion, and there's a unique beauty and passion in its perfect construction. This is one of the countless signatures of

our Creator that turns up repeatedly in Scripture. No man or woman could have written this Book of Books."

[201] "1 Corinthians 7 (KJV)," Blue Letter Bible, accessed November 16, 2016, http://blueletterbible.org/kjv/1co/7/9/p0/t_conc_1069009.

[202] William Loader, *The New Testament on Sexuality* (Grand Rapids, MI: Eerdmans, 2012), 220.

[203] Jeremiah, *What the Bible Says about Love, Marriage and Sex*, 162.

[204] James Hastings, ed., *The Greater Men and Women of the Bible*, vol. 4, *Hezekiah-Malachi* (New York: Morrison and Gibb, 1915), 558. Across the land of Judah there remained a remnant of scattered Jews left over by Nebuchadnezzar. These Jews began to intermarry with the local Samaritans who themselves possessed a rich and fertile land. By intermarrying with the Samaritans, the Jewish men were able to form alliances and become wealthy, but their lust for land, wealth, and power degraded their commitments to God and their wives. The Samaritans required the Jewish men to first divorce their Jewish wives before they could marry Samaritan women. An eagerness for gain and a blatant disregard concerning God's laws for marriage resulted in great suffering for Jewish women and a strong rebuke by Malachi.

[205] "Among the prevalent sins of social life there was one which the prophet lays particular stress. Those who professed a great regard for God's covenant violated the covenant when it pleased them, putting away their wives, not (as the Pharisees of our Lord's time said) 'for every cause,' but for no cause at all, simply because they had contracted a passion for some strange woman, the daughter of one of the heathen races with whom the children of the covenant were forbidden to intermarry." Ibid., 565.

[206] A similar message about women is found in Proverbs 2:17.

[207] C. F. Keil and F. Delitzsch, *Commentary on the Old Testament*, vol. 10, *The Minor Prophets* (Peabody, MA: Hendrickson, 1996), 652.

[208] "Do not be unequally yoked with unbelievers. For what partnership has righteousness with lawlessness? Or what fellowship has light with darkness? What accord has Christ with Belial? Or what portion does a believer share with an unbeliever? What agreement has the temple of God with idols? For we are the temple of the living God; as God said, 'I will make my dwelling among them and walk among them, and I will be their God, and they shall be my people. Therefore go out from their midst, and be separate from them, says the Lord, and touch no unclean thing; then I will welcome you, and I will be a father to you, and you shall be sons and daughters to me,' says the Lord Almighty" (2 Cor. 6:14-18).

[209] *Evangelical Dictionary of Theology*, 2nd ed., ed. Walter A. Elwell (Grand Rapids, MI: Baker Academic, 2001), 346.

[210] "The polemic against divorce had a sociological function then, serving to augment the ongoing stabilization of traditional Hebrew society in postexilic Yehud (cf. Wells [1987:51-52] on the role marriage plays in socializing the members of a culture). However, Malachi's diatribe against the treachery of divorce is more than simply an exhortation to fidelity in marriage. Rather, the prophet seeks to 'ensure the continuity of traditional religious practice' in Yehud— the maintenance of covenant relationship with Yahweh (Ogden and Deutsch [1987:97]). The divorce customs of Yehud contributed both to the dehumanization of women in Hebrew society (cf. Wells [1987:51]) and the depersonalization and desacralization of covenant relationship with Yahweh because he is the loving Father of all Israel (Mal 1:2-3; 2:10, 15). Yahweh hates divorce 'because it violates the covenant relationship both with God and with the wife, because it is a cruel act of violence, and because it negatively affects the rearing

of godly offspring' (Garland [1987:421]; cf. Hugenberger [1994: 166-67]). How can Yahweh 'return' to his people (cf. Mal 3:7) when they cannot even 'return' to each other as husband and wife bonded together in covenant relationship? How can the community of Yehud 'return' to Yahweh (cf. Mal 3:6) when crimes of marital faithlessness only compound the charges of social injustice against restoring Israel?" Andrew Hill, *Malachi* (New York: Doubleday, 1998), 258-259.

[211] Page Kelley, *Layman's Bible Book Commentary*, vol. 14, *Micah, Nahum, Habakkuk, Zephaniah, Haggai, Zechariah, Malachi* (Nashville: Broadman Press, 1984), 149. Divorce brings harm and decrease to marriage, which stands opposed to God's providential charge to "be fruitful and multiply and fill the earth" (Gen. 1:28). When Jewish men divorced their wives and intermarried with heathen women, they experienced rapid declines in moral and ethical standards, causing them to embrace pagan practices of nearby cultures. After being ravished by sin and pagan immorality, Jewish men often found themselves bankrupt and in debt. Pagan money lenders would then seize Jewish children from all who defaulted on their loans.

[212] Harold Koenig, Dana King, and Verna Carson, *Handbook of Religion and Health*, 2nd ed. (New York: Oxford University Press, 2012), 534. A study on risky sexual practices showed having sexual activity outside of a monogamous relationship (typically marriage) increases the risk of HIV infection and other sexually transmitted diseases such as gonorrhea, chlamydia, trichomoniasis, bacterial vaginosis, lymphogranuloma venereum, human papillomavirus, genital herpes, and syphilis. Sexual activity here includes vaginal, anal, or oral intercourse.

[213] J. Lanier Burns, "The Biblical Use of Marriage to Illustrate Covenantal Relationships," in *Bibliotheca Sacra* 173, no. 691 (July-September 2016): 287.

214 "'Every [man]' leaves no exceptions—even, or especially, of professing disciples. On the one hand, Jesus isn't condemning the natural desire of a man for a woman. On the other hand, Jesus does escalate the Mosaic prohibition by condemning the leering look. In the Bible, adultery means having sex with somebody else's spouse. Like irreconciliation with your fellow disciple and like adultery in the flesh, adultery in the heart will land you in hell." Robert Gundry, *A Commentary on The New Testament* (Peabody, MA: Hendrickson, 2010), 19.

215 "Like many wisdom sayings of ancient Jewish teachers, this saying is a general rule; (Matt. 5:32 and 1 Cor. 7:15) give exceptions (on behalf of the innocent party divorced against his or her will). The saying is *hyperbolic—that is, it has exaggerated, intensified force: because God does not accept divorce as valid, any man who divorces his wife is not really divorced, and if he marries someone else, he commits adultery. No one else in antiquity spoke of divorce in such strong terms. (Because most Jewish teachers allowed polygamy, they would not have seen marrying a second wife as adultery, even if they had agreed that the man was still married to the first wife. But Jesus eliminates the double standard; a man consorting with two women is as adulterous as a woman consorting with two men. Jesus' point is to advocate fidelity to one's first wife, not to break up existing polygamous unions.)" Craig Keener, *The IVP Bible Background Commentary New Testament* (Downers Grove, IL: InterVarsity Press, 1993), 161.

216 Johannes Behm, "Kardia," in *Theological Dictionary of the New Testament*, ed. Gerhard Kittel, trans. Geoffrey Bromiley (Grand Rapids, MI: Eerdmans, 1964), 3:611.

217 Ibid., 612.

218 "And he said to them, 'You are those who justify yourselves before men, but God knows your hearts. For what is exalted among men is an abomination in the sight of God'" (Luke 16:15).

[219] "Whoever conceals his transgression will not prosper, but he who confesses and forsakes them will obtain mercy" (Prov. 28:13).

[220] "Christ's purpose is in general to condemn the lust of the flesh. So He says that they are adulterers in God's sight who not only have intercourse with others' wives, but who have stained their eyes with unchaste glances. It is an expression by synecdoche, for it is not only the eyes which convict men of adultery, but also the unseeing passions of the heart. So Paul places chastity (1 Cor. 7:34) both in body and in spirit. But Christ was content to refer to the current foolish interpretation, for they thought that only outward adultery was to be guarded against. Since it is the eyes which most solicit souls by their panderings, and lust reaches through their portals, Christ used this form of speech in His will to condemn concupiscence: the word lust after shows this clearly." John Calvin, *A Harmony of the Gospels: Matthew, Mark and Luke*, Calvin's Commentaries 1, ed. David Torrance and Thomas Torrance, trans. A. W. Morrison (Grand Rapids, MI: Eerdmans, 1972), 188.

[221] George Buttrick, "Adultery and Lust," in *The Interpreter's Bible*, vol. 7, *New Testament Articles, Matthew, Mark*, ed. Nolan Harmon (Nashville: Abingdon-Cokesbury Press, 1951), 297.

[222] "Marriage, the very matrix of continuity in traditional societies, is rapidly being eroded by serial relationships, cohabitation and divorce. Fewer people are marrying. Fewer marriages last a lifetime. In Britain, four in every ten children are born outside marriage. Four in every ten marriages end in divorce. The very concept of belonging to a place, a neighborhood, a locality—somewhere we belong and call home—has all but disappeared." Sacks, *The Dignity of Difference*, 71.

[223] "The continual abandoning of oneself to immorality in general can be a slippery slope to more perverse sexual activities. And, for Paul, all of this starts with idolatry: to exchange worship of the Creator

for worship of the creature is to invite the exchange of normal sexual relations for unnatural ones." C. Marvin Pate, *Romans* (Grand Rapids, MI: Baker, 2013), 37.

[224] John Stott, *The Message of Romans* (Downers Grove, IL: IVP Academic, 1994), 76.

[225] "To *hand over* means to permit, not to encourage or to force, so that they were helped by the devil to put into practice the things which they conceived in their lusts. They never thought of doing anything good, and so they were handed over to uncleanness and damaged each other's bodies with abuse. Even now there are still men of this type, who are said to dishonor each other's bodies. When the thought of the mind is wrong, the bodies are said to be dishonored. Is not a stain on the body a sign of sin in the soul? When the body is contaminated, nobody doubts that there is sin in the soul." Ambrosiater, *Ancient Christian Texts: Romans and 1-2 Corinthians*, trans. Gerald Bray (Downers Grove, IL: IVP Academic, 2009), 12.

[226] Jo Durden-Smith and Diane Desimone, *Sex and the Brain* (New York: Arbor House 1983), 58.

[227] Barbara Strauch, *The Primal Teen* (New York: Random House, 2003), 142.

[228] Durden-Smith and Desimone, *Sex and the Brain*, 58-59.

[229] An-Pyng Sun, Larry Ashley, and Lesley Dickson, *Behavioral Addiction: Screening, Assessment, and Treatment* (Las Vegas, NV: Central Recovery Press, 2013), 12.

[230] Stanford Mills, *A Hebrew Christian Looks at Romans* (New York: American Board of Missions to the Jews, 1971), 46.

[231] "Verses 26-27 are a crucial text in the contemporary debate about homosexuality. The traditional interpretation, that they describe and

condemn all homosexual behavior, is being challenged by the gay lobby. Three arguments are advanced. First, it is claimed that the passage is irrelevant, on the ground that its purpose is neither to teach sexual ethics, nor to expose vice, but rather to portray the outworking of God's wrath. This is true. But if a certain sexual conduct is to be seen as the consequence of God's wrath, it must be displeasing to him. Second, 'the likelihood is that Paul is thinking only about pederasty' since 'there was no other form of male homosexuality in the Greco-Roman world,' and that he is opposing it because of the humiliation and exploitation experienced by the youths involved. All one can say in response to this suggestion is that the text itself contains no hint of it. Third, there is the question what Paul meant by 'nature.' Some homosexual people are urging that their relationships cannot be described as 'unnatural,' since they are perfectly natural to them. John Boswell has written, for example, that 'the persons Paul condemns are manifestly not homosexual: what he derogates are homosexual acts committed by apparently heterosexual people.' Hence Paul's statement that they 'abandoned' natural relations, and 'exchanged' them for unnatural. Richard Hays has written a thorough exegetical rebuttal of this interpretation of Romans 1, however. He provides ample contemporary evidence that the opposition of 'natural' (*kata physin*) and 'unnatural' (*para physin*) was 'very frequently used . . . as a way of distinguishing between heterosexual and homosexual behavior.' Besides, differentiating between sexual orientation and sexual practice is a modern concept; 'to suggest that Paul intends to condemn homosexual acts only when they are committed by persons who are constitutionally heterosexual is to introduce a distinction entirely foreign to Paul's thought-world,' in fact a complete anachronism." Stott, *The Message of Romans*, 77-78.

[232] Joseph Thayer, "Haptomai," in *Thayer's Greek-English Lexicon of the New Testament* (Grand Rapids, MI: Zondervan, 1970), 70.

[233] "I praise you because I am fearfully and wonderfully made; your works are wonderful, I know that full well" (Ps. 139:14, NIV).

[234] Roy Laurin, *First Corinthians: Where Life Matures* (Findlay, OH: Dunham, 1957), 123.

[235] Frederick Mish, ed., *Merriam-Webster's Collegiate Dictionary*, 10th ed. (Springfield, MA: Merriam-Webster, 1999), s.v. "conjugal rights."

[236] John Walvoord, *Revelation* (Chicago: Moody, 2011), 66.

[237] "Oh, let the evil of the wicked come to an end, and may you establish the righteous—you who test the minds and hearts, O righteous God!" (Ps. 7:9).

[238] "But as for the cowardly, the faithless, the detestable, as for murders, the sexually immoral, sorcerers, idolaters, and all liars, their portion will be in the lake that burns with fire and sulfur, which is the second death" (Rev. 21:8).

[239] "Not many of you should become teachers, my brothers, for you know that we who teach will be judged with greater strictness" (Jas. 3:1).

[240] Christopher C. Rowland, "The Book of Revelation," in *The New Interpreter's Bible*, ed. Leander E. Keck, vol. 12, *Hebrews-Revelation*, David L. Bartlett et al. (Nashville: Abingdon, 1998), 632.

[241] Richard C. Sparks, *Contemporary Christian Morality: Real Questions, Candid Responses* (New York: Crossroad Herder Book, 1996), 88. Human sexuality is a wonderful gift of God and, therefore, an awesome responsibility. Some might suggest, yes, it's a "wonderful gift" but with "lots of potential for sin." While there is surely the potential for sexual misuse and abuse of ourselves and others, Christianity for too long has accentuated the negative rather than the positive. Learning to live morally as sexual beings is a lifelong process. The more and

better we can integrate our sexuality into our lives, the greater will be the blessing and the lesser the potential for moral harm.

[242] "Answer me, O LORD, answer me, that this people may know that you, O LORD, are God and that you have turned their hearts back" (1 Kgs. 18:37).

[243] "So I gave them over to their stubborn hearts, to follow their own counsels" (Ps. 81:12).

[244] John Mahony, "A Theology of Sin for Today," in *Fallen: A Theology of Sin*, eds. Christopher Morgan and Robert Peterson (Wheaton, IL: Crossway, 2013), 202-203.

[245] "Communal sins are particularly hard to notice because one's peers comfortably practice them. . . . Things such as racism, prejudice, materialism, discrimination, loosening of sexual standards and many other sins are hard to see when they are embedded within one's culture." David N. Entwistle, *Integrative Approaches to Psychology and Christianity*, 2nd ed. (Eugene, OR: Cascade, 2010), 130.

[246] "Christian ethics, pastoral care, and public policy are not the same. Societies must accord basic rights to all humans; the church and individual Christians must grant empathy and love to all sinners; but the Christian ethic of sex cannot capitulate to our fallen impulses. God designed from creation that this good gift be experienced only in the covenant relationship of a man and a woman, for only there can the meaning of sex be found." Hollinger, *The Meaning of Sex*, 197.

[247] Most of this section on unhealthy sexuality was first researched and written for a final project in Clinical Pastoral Education Residency program at the Veterans Affairs San Diego Healthcare System, submitted July 2014.

[248] Roxanne Dryden-Edwards, "What Is Sexual Addiction and What Are the Types of Sexual Addiction," accessed March 28, 2017, https://www.medicinenet.com/sexual_addiction/article.htm.

[249] American Society of Addiction Medicine, "Definition of Addiction," accessed April 5, 2017, http://www.asam.org/quality-practice/definition-of-addiction.

[250] Ibid.

[251] An-Pyng Sun, Larry Ashley, and Lesley Dickson, *Behavioral Addiction: Screening, Assessment, and Treatment* (Las Vegas, NV: Central Recovery Press, 2013), 12.

[252] Dryden-Edwards, "What Is Sexual Addiction?"

[253] Ibid.

[254] McIlhaney and Bush, *Hooked*, 113.

[255] Dryden-Edwards, "What Is Sexual Addiction?"

[256] Patrick Carnes, *Out of the Shadows: Understanding Sexual Addiction* (Center City, MN: Hazelden, 2001), 3.

[257] McIlhaney and Bush, *Hooked*, 18.

[258] George Collins, *Breaking the Cycle: Free Yourself from Sex Addiction, Porn Obsession, and Shame* (Oakland, CA: New Harbinger Publications, 2010), 10.

[259] Harvey B. Milkman and Stanley Sunderwirth, *Craving for Ecstasy: The Consciousness and Chemistry of Escape* (Lexington, MA: Lexington Books, 1986), 45. "Modern neuroscience research has uncovered startling new information about how sex affects our brains. The effect of sex on our brains can have all sorts of consequences, including many that scientists are still working to understand. But we do know

that sex can literally change a person's brain, influencing the thought process and affecting future decisions. And therein lies both the benefit and the risk. When sex is experienced in healthy ways it adds great value and satisfaction to life, but when experienced in unhealthy ways, at the wrong time, it can damage vital aspects of who we are as human beings." McIlhaney and Bush, *Hooked*, 7-8.

[260] Milkman and Sunderwirth, *Craving for Ecstasy*, 45.

[261] Patrick Carnes, *Don't Call It Love: Recovery from Sexual Addiction* (New York: Bantam, 1991), 11-12.

[262] American Psychiatric Association, *Diagnostic and Statistical Manual of Mental Disorders*, 5th ed. (Washington, DC: American Psychiatric Association, 2013), 685-686.

[263] Ibid., 685. Paraphilic disorders include eight conditions: exhibitionistic disorder, fetishistic disorder, frotteuristic disorder, pedophilic disorder, sexual masochism disorder, sexual sadism disorder, transvestic disorder, and voyeuristic disorder.

[264] Sun, Ashley, and Dickson, *Behavioral Addiction*, 76.

[265] "Idolatry is manifested in an infinite variety of ways: pursuing money, power or sex." Douglas Moo, "Sin in Paul," in *Fallen: A Theology of Sin*, eds. Christopher Morgan and Robert Peterson (Wheaton, IL: Crossway, 2013), 115.

[266] David Calhoun, "Sin and Temptation," in *Fallen: A Theology of Sin*, eds. Christopher Morgan and Robert Peterson (Wheaton, IL: Crossway, 2013), 244.

[267] Ibid.

[268] "Flee from sexual immorality. Every other sin a person commits is outside the body, but the sexually immoral person sins against his own body" (1 Cor. 6:18).

[269] See Appendix A, "Eleven Examples of a Sex Addict."

[270] Chris Lee, "The Sex Addiction Epidemic," *Newsweek*, November 25, 2011, accessed February 26, 2014, http://www.newsweek.com/sex-addiction-epidemic-66289.

[271] Carnes, *Out of the Shadows*, 69.

[272] Ibid.

[273] Sun, Ashley, and Dickson, *Behavioral Addiction*, 76-77.

[274] Ginger Manley, "Treating Chronic Sexual Dysfunction in Couples Recovering from Sex Addiction and Sex Coaddiction," *Sexual Addiction and Compulsivity: The Journal of Treatment and Prevention* 6, no. 2 (November 2007): 120.

[275] See Appendix B, "Patterns and Examples of Sex Addiction."

[276] Carnes, *Out of the Shadows*, 20.

[277] Ibid., 19-20.

[278] Carnes, *Don't Call It Love*, 16-17.

[279] Carnes, *Out of the Shadows*, 63-64.

[280] See, for example, Exodus 20:14; Leviticus 18; 1 Corinthians 6:9-10; and Revelation 21:8.

[281] Jennifer Schneider, "How to Recognize the Signs of Sexual Addiction: Asking the Right Questions May Uncover Serious Problems," *Postgraduate Medicine* 90, no. 6 (November 1991): 182, accessed April 05, 2017, http://www.jenniferschneider.com/articles/recognize.html.

[282] An-Pyng Sun, Larry Ashley, and Lesley Dickson, *Behavioral Addiction: Screening, Assessment, and Treatment* (Las Vegas, NV: Central Recovery Press, 2013), 93.

[283] George N. Collins, *Breaking the Cycle: Free Yourself from Sex Addiction, Porn Obsession, and Shame* (Oakland, CA: New Harbinger Publications, 2010), 167-169.

[284] Ibid., 13-18.

[285] Ibid., 34-35.

[286] Ibid., 171-173.

[287] Sun, Ashley, and Dickson, 94.

[288] Harry Schaumburg, *False Intimacy: Understanding the Struggle of Sexual Addiction* (Colorado Springs: NavPress, 1997), 237-238.

[289] Ibid., 237-238.

[290] Joan Ellason and Colin Ross, "Childhood Trauma and Dissociation in Male Sex Offenders," *Sexual Addiction and Compulsivity: The Journal of Treatment and Prevention* 6, no. 2 (November 2007): 109.

[291] See Appendix C, "Treatment."

[292] Jennifer Schneider, "How to Recognize the Signs of Sexual Addiction: Asking the Right Questions May Uncover Serious Problems," *Postgraduate Medicine* 90, no. 6 (November 1991), accessed April 5, 2017, http://www.jenniferschneider.com/articles/recognize.html.

Printed in the United States
by Baker & Taylor Publisher Services